The God of
Statism

And The History of Jewish Defiance

By Tim Orum

Table of Contents

First Woe—Attack of The Fierce Hippy

In The Beginning There Were Radicals

An eccentric individual living on the river was beginning to gain a large following. The river guy was different from most people but was friendly and enjoyed talking to anyone that would spend time with him. The eccentric, whose name was John, would explain how he looked forward to life every day. He wore clothing he made himself and ate food he gathered from nature. Being self-sufficient was a source of pride for John, but his message of self-reliance went far beyond his own personal lifestyle. Many of the people who approached John at the river spoke of the unhappiness in their own lives, and he had a reputation for offering sage advice. He would explain to them why they might be better off plunging themselves into a whole new cultural existence of mental and moral self-sufficiency, and if successful, how it would greatly improve their attitude about life as well. His ideas were beginning to appeal to a lot of people.

As his reputation spread among the people, an unemployed construction worker met and got to know John, and both agreed they had much in common in their attitudes regarding independence and self-reliance. They realized there were many others that would benefit from their ideas and decided to go public with a plan to create an entirely new cultural system. From their interactions with the multitudes, they knew any social improvement would need to focus on the relationship people had with each other, instead of the relationship they had with their leadership, which seemed to be the source of most unhappiness. They both knew from personal experience that elitist government and religious leaders had a strong tendency to be corrupt, and often engineered the culture of the people in ways that benefited themselves. This in turn often led to oppression of the citizens. Their idea of escaping this cycle of manipulation by becoming culturally less dependent, and less subject to the whims of the "Powers That Be" was considered a radical idea, so they were viewed with suspicion by the authorities.

And so begins the story of Jesus the carpenter, John the Baptist, and the gang that would help to spread their idea among the people.

Unfortunately for them, the "radical" nature of their message would mean most of them would be murdered by elitists within the government and religious institutions of the time. This was not a new story. Others had made the same attempt in the past and has been repeated many times since. They were among a long history of stiff-necked Jewish rebels that had been punished for a message of resistance against "The Powers That Be".

"The Powers That Be" is the closest English translation of the Hebraic word "Elohim" {1}. For some reason, this phrase was then later translated into the word "God" {2}. God is a Germanic or Celtic word that should never have found its way into the bible because it detracts from the true meaning of the stories. The word "God" {3} {4} was not used in the bible until sometime around the fourth century and seems to be a catch-all for centralized power, but no one seems to know for sure. As we go through the tribulations of the Jewish ancestors in their rebellious relationship with God, "The Powers That Be" will refer to politics, and not to any deity. As we will see, that changes the entire meaning of the books put together to form the bible, and in a way that makes the bible understandable and sensible to anyone. In the process, we will come to understand why the Jewish ancestors were relentlessly punished and Jesus and John were "sacrificed".

Far from being stories of a loving and benevolent God worshiped by loyal followers as most of us are taught, the bible stories are a testament to the valiant resistance against an oppressive God (The Powers That Be) that actually represents the Power of The State by the Jewish people and their ancestors. The endless revolutionary war against God by their ancestors, or more

---

[1] https://www.phrases.org.uk/meanings/the-powers-that-be.html

[2] https://wahiduddin.net/words/name_god.htm

[3] http://www.avesta.org/kerr/The_advent_of_the_word_GOD.pdf

[4] https://en.wikipedia.org/wiki/God_(word)

specifically a subset of the Jewish people referred to as Yahwists {[5]}, did not take place over a few years but over thousands of years, and the war continues today, not just for the Jewish descendants but for all humanity. The "Powers That Be" of the Old Testament continues the manipulation and persecution of the Jewish people and all other independent thinkers around the world by methods described in the bible. As we go through the books, we will see the true message as the writers use graphic parables to portray their history of resistance.

Most of the Old Testament is devoted to stories of social division, endless laws, invasion and retaliation, threats, intrigue, the slaughter of warfare, famine, nepotism, corruption, purging, persecution, and of course taxes and more taxes—mostly at the direction of the omnipotent "Powers That Be" used by the authors to make their point. If any of these plagues sound familiar it is because everything the god in the Old Testament does is exactly what Statism does to We The People. The writers make it clear that the god that so persecuted the Jews and their ancestors for their lack of loyalty is not a god that served their best interests. In fact, it did the opposite. That is because the "Powers That Be" in the Old Testament is what we now refer to as "Statism", which is still the most common form of social organization.

To understand the importance of Statist influence in the lives of those who wrote the bible we should take a closer look at Statism. Of course, they didn't use the same words as today, but the phenomenon of Statism, not to be confused with Satanism, (or can it?) has plagued mankind almost since the beginning of civilization and that is the main theme of the bible. A search for a definition of Statism in WordReference.com says it is:

"the principle or policy of concentrating extensive economic, political, and related controls in the state at the cost of individual liberty"

This a remarkably simple definition of a system that included all the centralized governments of the time the bible was written

---

[5] https://www.britannica.com/topic/Yahwist-source

and is still true today. In their time it would have included the Warlords, Kings, Pharaoh monarchies, and the Caesars of Rome—all of which persecuted the Jewish ancestors for their resistance. Statism has since grown to include many other versions of cultural manipulation, and now includes Communism, Fascism, Socialism, Radical Islamism, and many other "isms". Statism would today also include Totalitarianism of all sorts such as Dictatorships and contrary to what many think—even most Democracies.

They called this oppressive phenomenon "The Powers That Be". In their language the word was often "Elohim", or simply "El". The oddly misplaced word in more recent anglicized versions of the bible is the word "God" and is still presented as the force which watches over and judges and either punishes or rewards the citizens according to their loyalty or lack thereof. To the ancient Hebrews the "Powers That Be" would have been understood as being the elitists who used persecution and manipulation to assure their "chosen" status. The Old Testament "God" was always portrayed as a fearsome, oppressive, and divisive force manipulating the population.

Written in the form of a warning, it is my contention that the Bible was meant to be similar to the first Declaration of Independence, Constitution, and Bill of Rights rolled into one collection of books. The Old Testament points out in virtually every book the dangers of coexisting with the Powers That Be that centralize power and authority. The later stories of Jesus and John were simply a continuation of ancient stories of persecution. In the New Testament, the story of the crucifixion openly exposes the authoritarians in politics and religion by emphasizing who is doing the crucifying. The purpose of the bible was to warn of the many tools of Statism, and crucifixion was just one tool of terror and oppression in their arsenal.

Under any name, one thing all Statist cultural systems have in common is they often come to power through the promise of salvation for the people by leading them to a utopian "promised land" that never materializes. This and other deceptions from The Powers That Be is something the writers already recognized and point out in the bible. Their knowledge and wisdom were derived from many sources and included ideas from surrounding cultures that experienced similar difficulties. During the time the bible was still under construction, the ancient Greeks even had a place specifically used to discuss the myriad political problems of the time concerning The Powers That Be. It was called an *ecclesia*, which was mistranslated to *church* {⁶}.

The story of Jesus and John is the age-old story of Statist persecution. The story may be convoluted in some ways, but it is not a murder mystery. That the writers depict these Jewish "radicals" as being sacrificed as they were strongly suggest salvation would be in refuting a cultural system that allows authorities to put people to death despite their innocence and good intentions. They were put to death not because of any threat to other citizens, but for their perceived threat to a culture of Statism by both the Roman authorities and the oppressive Jewish clergy of the time. Unfortunately, we appear to have learned very little because persecution and crucifixion is still taking place thousands of years later to anyone representing a threat to The Powers that Be (God). Twisting the meaning of the bible to deprive us of the true message is just one more method of crucifixion.

As we go through the books of the Old Testament, we will see this god has great powers of defense against nonbelievers. Modern forms of crucifixion still occur through slander in the media, economic manipulation, social engineering, corrupt judges, censorship, the division of identity politics, and cultural degradation just as in the Old Testament. Murder also still takes place but currently, except in the most backward of Statist societies, public assassination through beheading or hanging people from poles, as happened to Jesus and John is embarrassingly primitive.

Due to the distortion of the meaning of the books, many unknowing but well-meaning people seeking enlightenment and joy by reading the bible for the first time become so repulsed and

---

⁶ https://www.merriam-webster.com/dictionary/ecclesia

confused and discouraged by what they read they put the book down and never pick it up again. Although they may go to a church or a synagogue regularly, they secretly think there must be something wrong with themselves for not feeling good about reading the "Good Book". They feel very uncomfortable about how the god in the Old Testament could be a part of so much evil, all the while being taught the narrative God represents only good and that receiving punishment from him was a blessing for the ancient Hebrews, and still is for us. That response is because the real message and purpose has been buried in deceitful political correctness, which discourages debate and open discussion. If you violate the rules by objecting or asking the wrong questions you will be subjected to persecution and isolation, which most of us fear and want to avoid. Political correctness and persecution are both powerful tools of Statism and are used extensively by the God (The Powers That Be) in the Old Testament.

Don't confuse Statism with government. Government is something done by and for the people, is necessarily more decentralized, and is at least partially responsive to public needs. Statism, on the other hand, is something done by elitists to remove social and cultural control from the people to and to place that power in the hands of the State to assure the perpetuation of their own power and authority. Statists replace government with one of the "isms" to rule for their own benefit over the people.

Despite the obvious evil effects of Statism, there is no sense of "us against them" mentality by the authors of the bible. They point out it is cultural weakness that allows the God of Statism to exist. In the bible there are no perpetrators—only victims. They saw corrupt leaders as being given an evil spirit, as portrayed by king Saul.

> **I Samuel 18:10 And it came to pass on the morrow, that the evil spirit from God came upon Saul, and he prophesied in the midst of the house: and David played with his hand, as at other times: and there was a javelin in Saul's hand. 11. And Saul cast the javelin;**

9

**for he said, I will smite David even to the wall with it.
And David avoided out of his presence twice.**

God's evil spirit represents the temptation to use violence and social manipulation to achieve and maintain control over the people. Saul knew David was a threat to his power and privilege. The writers recognized the only effective deterrent against the evil spirit of Statism would be through the creation of a culture that would resist the temptations Statism offers. To them, the enemy was not those given God's evil spirit because those given this spirit were victims. In the end, they knew that when it comes to Statism everyone is a victim and the evil spirit of Statism is created through the culture we choose for ourselves. The evil spirit exists within any culture that allows the creation of the God of Statism.

Their observations are still relevant today, and many modern comparisons can be made. For example, both king Saul in the bible and another stereotypical Statist called Hitler began as simple people with humble beginnings. Because of God's evil spirit, which is the desire to rule rather than to serve, they both became extreme victims that would in turn victimize others. As pointed out in the bible, this is the most dangerous aspect of the God of Statism. The only solution for Yahwists was cultural resistance to the source of this God, and they learned that without a culture of virtue and wisdom there would always be those who would rise to power with God's evil spirit. Their mission was to create a more successful culture that refuted the temptations of the Powers That Be and to warn the people to recognize when it was happening. Through their parables, combined with historical examples of Statism as they witnessed it, they were sending a message. The bible could be rewritten today using modern examples to replace their parables because culturally speaking, there are still only a few exceptions to Statism geopolitically.

Through the expert use of parables that can be horrible, ironic, or even humorous but always incredibly insightful, they warn us of the pitfalls of a culture determined by the God of Statism. Just as today, Statism was already the most dominant influence on culture when and where the bible was written. The Yahwists who wrote the books devote a great deal of effort into demonstrating not just resistance, but also to the possibility of a better way of life for everyone. One way they attempt to reach a solution in the books of the bible is by demonstrating the terrible experiences of their ancestors as they resist the Powers That Be, and through pointing out the many ways Statism can manipulate culture and why it should be avoided.

Most of us don't consider the bible to be blasphemous, but one reason they used parables rather than simple documents or accurate historical accounts is because at the time the early books were written they would have been considered quite blasphemous. Jesus and his followers would later use similar methods in the New Testament when speaking publicly, because their message was also seen as blasphemous by The Powers That Be.

Their message was considered blasphemous because it was commonly taught and accepted at the time that the Caesars of Rome, the Pharaohs of Egypt, and even other lesser kings and warlords were all chosen and installed by deities that made the decision to "anoint" them to rule over the people. They sometimes even claimed to be deities themselves. The bible goes against this concept by pointing out the true nature of the gods that were "anointing" the leadership. Those gods were always the same God of Statism, which is probably why they were the first to recognize there is only one god. They realized that no matter when or where it occurred, or what name it used, it was always the same monotheistic god. Once the stories are understood I don't think there is any mystery as to why the Jewish ancestors kept straying from this god. Since they continue to do so, the Jewish people continue be persecuted, threatened, and punished by the God of Statism. Just as in the ancient books, they fall firmly into the category of the "'unchosen", and not the "chosen", in the world of Statist politics and have been persecuted relentlessly. If the Jewish ancestors were "chosen" it was to be victims, and not the receivers of any benefit.

Once it is understood that the God in the Old Testament is a metaphor for cultural Statism, and the books were written in the form of a warning, every story in the bible that you may have thought confusing or depressing suddenly makes sense. They now become a clear lesson in how Statism controls culture. Contrary to popular dogma and propaganda, worshiping a centralized authority figure is the opposite of what the stories in the bible are trying to teach us.

If the bible wasn't making the point that we can create our own Eden {7} (which means a cultural state of delight) through the creation of a culture designed by and for the people, the bible would be pointless. Anyone can wait to be saved by someone or something else and requires nothing beyond faith those benefits will eventually be obtained, and no knowledge would be required. You would simply be expected to believe whatever narrative The Powers That Be tell you to believe, and to wait for salvation to arrive. The hope is to be found acceptable when the time of judgment comes, which is usually after death. In this scenario there is no use for books such as the bible that educate. In fact, The Powers That Be often assume a "burn the books" mentality to impose their own ideology because they fear knowledge and understanding. Separating people from knowledge and wisdom is one of the first methods of crucifixion pointed out in Genesis. More on that later.

At no point in the bible are the Jewish ancestors held up as prime examples of faith and loyalty towards The Powers That Be, and for good reason. They have always resisted characters such as the Pharaohs of Egypt, the Caesars of Rome, and countless others like them. They used parables such as the story of Moses to demonstrate how these people come to power. They recognized the falsehood of following those that acquire loyalty by promising utopian salvation, and deliverance to a "promised land". They knew from experience that none of this ilk ever encourage a culture of self-reliance, independence, self-determination, and the critical thinking and self-accountability that most of us call common sense,

---

[7] https://www.hebrewversity.com/deeper-hebrew-meaning-garden-eden/

and which would provide the people with the highest likelihood of success in the pursuit of happiness and a cultural state of Eden.

Despite their teachings, the concept of being saved by a powerful State or Messiah is still being taught and encouraged in both our State subsidized educational systems and in our religious institutions because loyalty and faith is something easily subject to manipulation. The bible stories point out this manipulation has been the bane of mankind almost since the very beginning. The bible is a record of Jewish defiance, not loyal worship.

What the bible teaches instead of mindless faith and subservience is the incredible force of our own capabilities to save ourselves, and to create our own Eden through a virtuous and cooperative culture which resists the God of Statism through Yahwist wisdom. This is a wisdom which includes truth in education, and the message of wise and peaceful resistance is the real story of the bible. Their stories should be seen through the eyes of the writers, rather than the spin and altered narrative that is so commonly taught instead by those who benefit from the false idol of Statism, whether it be political or religious. Either way, the Yahwists realized their true cultural adversary was always the monotheistic Powers That Be.

The stories in the Old Testament are not pleasant to read because the authors are demonstrating the resistance of the Jewish people to the Elohim, (The Powers That Be) for which they were being constantly punished. The stories leading up to the rebelliousness of Jesus and John make Steven King horror novels look like childhood bedtime stories. The nightmare continues into the New Testament with murders and martyrdom. Don't think you will learn joy and what is referred to as righteousness simply through reading the books in the bible unless you get the real message.

Thanks to their age-old contrarian instincts, Israel is still a shining light in the resistance to the God of Statism. Here's a little mental exercise you can use to prove the point. Give yourself ten seconds to think about it, then name the currently most famous Grand Poohbah, Charismatic Socialist Leader, Pope, Ayatollah,

King, Supreme Leader, Dictator, Most Wanted Terrorist of the Jewish religion or the country of Israel. Give up? That's right, there isn't one. To be sure, they have a few elders and politicians that are respected and revered (or despised, because the people get to choose) but none of them have fame outside their own culture. You will never see an iconic Jewish religious leader washing the feet of people he doesn't know for the benefit of carefully placed cameras broadcasting worldwide to show false humility. I am not criticizing, only sympathizing, with the victims of Statism and their propaganda.

All religious and political institutions have the potential to fall victim to Statism, including Judaism, as is demonstrated in the bible. We can see their vulnerability through their history with groups such as the Pharisees, that often became tools for the Roman State when they weren't manipulating or oppressing their own population. Despite setbacks, the Jewish culture overall still rejects Statism, even though many within the orthodox clergy still may not, just as in the time of Jesus.

Just as with the U.S. Constitution, written by relatively modern rebels against Statism, whether there is a happy ending to the bible is left open, and will be determined by We The People. Success depends on the strength of our desire for freedom, and our ability to create a virtuous culture free of Statism to make a happy ending possible. The writers of the bible are telling us We the People can create our own resurrection of freedom and a return to Eden, but the end of the story has not yet been written and there are two paths we can follow. For now, with few exceptions, the God of Statism is still winning because the real message of the bible is still being ignored or buried in a controlled narrative that has contributed to the stagnation or even degradation of culture. Partially because of this degradation, freedom loving cultures created only recently, such as in the U.S. and other modern Western countries, are already at risk of once again succumbing to the God of Statism. Modern religions have been a dismal failure at preventing this degradation because of their own bias towards a centralized authority figure of their own.

It is hard to learn the lessons of the bible when we are taught to believe the evil doers in the bible are a testament against man, who are acting against the wishes of a benevolent God, when in fact most of the evil acts are being done either directly or on orders from God. The bible makes no attempt to disguise this fact. The bible is not a testament against the iniquities of mankind as we are often told—it is a testament against the God of Statism that manipulates We The People. That the message of the bible is still being twisted to distort the message is shown by methods such as turning the characters of the bible into fairy tale heroes or making colorful illustrations of figures such as Noah and Moses in children's books and movies. This is ironic because many of the characters in the Old Testament were murderers of children, and often at the direction of God. This is clearly pointed out in the stories, and the accuracy and relevancy are indisputable, because this practice is still seen in many war-torn societies today by Statists who desire to obtain control over a population.

The effectiveness of cultural control through spin, political correctness, narrative control, terrorism, and propaganda are demonstrated by their continued ability to blind the minds of the people, even if the truth is right in front of them, and this happens in both politics and religion. Their effectiveness is especially true with young children, the effects of which then continues into adulthood. This is how the god in the Old Testament can punish throughout generations. The use of lovable caricatures of bible characters in children's books are the "Joe Camels" {8} of Statist religion and are used to indoctrinate young people into accepting the false narrative of a benevolent central figure that picks out and rewards the chosen, while wreaking havoc on the rest of society. Young minds are taught they must seek favor from that false idol to assure they are among the "chosen".

---

8 https://en.wikipedia.org/wiki/Joe_Camel

The Creation of the God of Statism

As one of the main points in the bible, the problem with having a centralized power structure is that the "The Powers that Be" invariably become the God of Statism, and once created has a natural tendency towards self-preservation through oppression. Their main lesson being that the "Power" should remain in the hands of We The People because we are able to evolve in ways that best allow an adaptable and successful culture. They show why we should never underestimate our own power. It is always the people in the bible that negotiate with God to force change. God never alters a course of action voluntarily except to punish. It is important to understand, God in the bible is never represented as inherently good or evil but represents a cultural status which is subject to change depending on the actions of the people, and that is how God was seen by the original writers. God is often seen negotiating with determined individuals.

If God were static and unchangeable the cumbersome concept of Trinity would be pointless, as would the entire bible, which itself points out the changing nature of God. This is pointed out many times in the Old Testament and emphasized again in the New Testament. The Old Testament God was meant by the writers to be our Teacher through example, and as a warning against our own tendency to allow the creation of an unbending Statist culture. They then show that through resistance we can negotiate for a better existence. We make God who he is, and that is why we are created in his image. Whenever we feel the need to see the face of God, we need only to hold our own collective culture up to the mirror.

If the bible were used properly it would be the main curriculum in all schools around the world, because all purposeful human interaction relies on an inquisitive and virtuous culture, which the bible encourages. The books also go a long way to point out mistakes in the past which serve as teachable lessons. But rather than encourage wisdom, religion must be corralled as a threat to public education in freedom loving societies because of the Statism being taught in religious institutions of a central authority figure that demands faith and loyalty. This is in opposition to the teachings of the bible, because they believed the cultural system we now refer to as Statism was a very fearful and vengeful God and was a clear and present danger to most people and should be avoided.

However, they were not allowed to write or speak openly of such issues, so they used parables.

> **Mark 5:33 And with many such parables spake he the word unto them** (the public)**, as they were able to hear it. 34: But without a parable spake he not unto them: and when they were alone, he expounded all things to his disciples.**

All things considered, I think it is time to allow the authors to go around the charlatans of religion and politics and allow the authors of the bible to speak directly to We The People. Let's see how they made their point. Every story in the Old Testament serves as a warning, and we will come back and follow them from the beginning, but let's pick one out right away and start with my favorite, which is the parable of Moses. This story is particularly astute because the writers describe in intimate detail the cycles of Statism.

As before with Jesus and John, I will use extreme paraphrasing for the sake of brevity, but to those of you who are familiar with the story you will know I am sticking to the main story line as it is laid out, but in a way that makes the message clear to anyone interested in asking all the questions, instead of accepting the Statist narrative. We can use one form of the King James Version which, despite some translation problems, still sticks fairly close to the original story, so we will make frequent references to that source. If you haven't already, I suggest you read the original for verification. Don't worry, the bible isn't boring, especially now that you will never again have to feel guilty or fearful or confused when reading the "Good Book". You will instead discover the optimistic and incredible capabilities of We The People and why Statists fear us.

The Parable of Moses

How Statism Begets More Statism

The story of Moses begins in Egypt and demonstrates how Statism spreads and becomes self-perpetuating through predictable cycles. It is appropriate that many of the stories of the bible warn of Egypt. The ancient Egyptians are known for their pyramids, built by the lower classes for elitists who wanted not only to consolidate wealth and power during their lifetimes, but even to take it with them after death. The Pharaohs of Egypt invented a Statist political and religious pyramid scheme in a quite literal sense. Their great wealth was made possible because of their ability to nationalize the resources of the Nile River, which allowed the concentration of most of that wealth within the nobility. The people had many gods to appeal to, but sadly their gods would only speak through their "exalted leaders", whose interests were heavily favored by the gods. Often the exalted leaders in Egypt would even promote themselves as being gods, just as would the Caesars in Rome. Word on the street is that the Jewish ancestors didn't fare well in either case, and in fact those cultures would serve as examples for some of their hard-earned Yahwist wisdom regarding Statism.

As an aside, kudos to the tomb robbers that took most of the wealth back and reintroduced it into the general population, but how much better would it be had they been allowed to do the same with wisdom and virtue and the concept of liberty, instead of just the material treasures? The pyramids are monuments to the God of Statism and represent the conditions under which the Yahwists were working as they wrote their books. This is the story of Moses.

This isn't how they teach it in Sunday school, but the real story of Moses goes like this:

A high-ranking official named Moses was on the run for murder, and left Egypt to escape punishment from the Pharaoh by fleeing to Midian. While he was there, he married the daughter of a rich and powerful priest, who provided him with employment. As he was working for his wealthy father-in-law, an idea began to take

19

shape. As a child, Moses had been adopted by one of Pharaohs' daughters and had grown up inside the Egyptian palace with the royals. Since he knew the inner workings of the palace, he knew the Pharaoh desperately wanted to rid his land of the Israelites, who were of Moses' own tribe, but were foreigners living in Egypt that had never truly assimilated.

An earlier Pharaoh had originally taken in the Israelites long before during a famine. Joseph, another Israelite who also had become an insider of the Egyptian high court, had welcomed them. They had initially been forced to come to Egypt for food because they were not able to feed themselves. Once their money ran out, they had nothing more to offer so they had taken jobs as servants to earn their way. The problem was that after a time there were so many Israelites they eventually became a threat to Egypt because they multiplied so fast. The Pharaoh of that time figured if war broke out with another nation the Israelites would turn against the Egyptians to rid themselves of debt and servitude. He was no doubt correct in this assumption.

The Pharaoh had tried to encourage the Israelites to leave by increasing their work-load and having them do work the Egyptians wouldn't do, but they still wouldn't leave. He then came up with a planned parenthood idea by ordering his Egyptian midwives to kill all male children born to the Israelites, but most of them didn't use Egyptian midwives. Besides, most of the midwives weren't down with that idea anyway, so that plan wasn't working well enough either. Desperate to save his own country, and of course his own position of authority, the Pharaoh issued an executive order that all male Israelite newborns were to be cast into the river. As an Israelite himself, Moses had barely escaped this fate by being found floating in the river in a basket as an infant, and was adopted by, of all people, the Pharaohs' daughter. As a result, Moses grew up appreciating all the perks of power and wealth but would eventually become a fugitive by committing a murder against an Egyptian. Since he was apparently defending a fellow tribesman, he knew it was unlikely the Egyptians would appreciate his side of the story, so he fled Egypt.

Fortunately for Moses, the Egyptians didn't have picture ID's and computer records in those days, and the Pharaoh and other witnesses knowing of his crime died off eventually, making it safe to return to pursue his plan. His plan would require a lot of charisma to convince enough followers, and he knew he wasn't a good enough speaker to pull it off. However, he still had a large family inside Egypt, so after illegally returning to Egypt he recruited his brother Aaron to be his spokesman and convinced other friends and family members to help.

To initiate their plan, which was to create a new nation by separating the Israelites from their current host, the first clever thing Moses and Aaron did was to demand more benefits. Moses asked the Pharaoh for time off so the Israelite workers could go into the desert to worship. He knew that wouldn't happen because the Pharaoh had no intention of making life easier for the Israelites. If life was made more pleasant, they would be even less likely to leave. This goading had the expected effect and created even more resentment and enmity. The Pharaoh increased the workload of the Israelites in response. This created even more hardship for the Israelites and set the stage for some community disorganization that would eventually convince the Israelites to turn against Egypt and form a new nation with Moses and Aaron leading them. We know the goading was intentional because the bible speaks of God "hardening the heart" of the Pharaoh so he wouldn't allow them to leave, even though he wanted to get rid of them.

> **Exodus 12:9 And the Lord said unto Moses, Pharaoh shall not hearken unto you; that my wonders may be multiplied in the land of Egypt. 10. And Moses and Aaron did all these wonders before Pharaoh: and the Lord hardened Pharaohs' heart, so that he would not let the children of Israel go out of his land.**

There followed many other plagues that would also help Moses with his plan, all initiated by God. Whether God's wonders and plagues were sabotage, natural phenomenon, or even if they happened at all as described is irrelevant, because that is not the point of the story. The writers of the bible were making the point that someone wanting to become a powerful leader never wastes a crisis, and will many times even create them when it serves his purpose. To gain followers for a new Statist society, you must first create division among the people. Moses and Aaron needed to assure the division would be permanent, because even with all the extra resentment in Egypt created unnecessarily between the Israelites and the Pharaoh, there were times the Israelites would tell Moses they would rather return than wander aimlessly in the wilderness where there were hardships not faced in Egypt. At least in Egypt they had something to eat, they just had to work for it. As their new leader, this is a temptation Moses wanted to avoid, so it was a good tactic to use plagues to "harden the heart" of the Pharaoh against those following Moses to prevent them from returning.

Presumably a God that can harden the heart can also soften the heart, but that isn't how the God of Statism works. Moses would be able to take credit for "rescuing" the Israelites from the now vilified Egyptians. The purpose of the plagues wasn't to convince the Pharaoh to let them leave. If the Pharaoh had his way, he would have helped pack their fanny packs and waved goodbye before the first plague. The purpose of the plagues was to prevent the Israelites from returning to work and abandoning Moses. The social division was necessary for another reason. It was necessary to vilify the Egyptians, because all Statist societies require some other group to vilify as the enemy, from which they are "protecting and saving" their loyal followers. Despite the oppressive culture in Egypt, turning the people against each other required many plagues to be effective.

The final straw for the Pharaoh was when Moses' God killed all the first-born children of Egypt. "But first God requested that blood be smeared on the doors of the Israelites, so their houses would be "Passed Over", and their own children not killed. This concept was also not new among the ancestors of the Israelites. They originated from those called Hebrews {⁹}, which literally

---

9 http://www.abarim-publications.com/Meaning/Hebrew.html#.

means "Passed Over", and is how they depict themselves as being culturally resistant to the temptations of this god from the very beginning.

> **Exodus 12:12 For I will pass through the land of Egypt this night and will smite all the firstborn in the land of Egypt, both man and beast; and against all the gods of Egypt I will execute judgment: I am the Lord. 13. And the blood shall be to you for a token upon the houses where ye are: and when I see the blood I will pass over you, and the plague shall not be upon you to destroy you, when I smite the land of Egypt.**

The stage was now set for an exodus of the Israelites from Egypt. As their new leader, Moses would promise the Israelites great things in return for following him to form a new nation. He promised to lead them to a wonderful "promised land" of milk and honey, where they would no longer have to work as servants. But first, there was yet another plague that was to come in addition to the terrorism against the firstborn children and animals. Moses would need financing, so he suggested to his people it might be a good idea to steal gold, silver, jewelry and other riches from the Egyptians and hide it among the tribesmen. God was happy to help.

> **Exodus 12:35 And the children of Israel did according to the word of Moses; and they borrowed of the Egyptians jewels of silver, and jewels of gold, and raiment: 36. And the Lord gave the people favour in the sight of the Egyptians, so that they lent unto them such things as they required. And they spoiled the Egyptians.**

These stolen riches would come in handy for Moses later. In return for benefits, Moses would eventually demand taxes to be paid from the stolen wealth taken from the Egyptians. In short, he made many of the same deceptive promises many political leaders still use today to gain enough loyalty and resources to put themselves in power. It usually begins with victimizing those not

W0vSw9JKhpl

"chosen" who become vilified, but the taxes will eventually become a burden even on the "chosen", and always involves the transfer of wealth into the hands of the centralized structure of the Powers That Be.

"Passover"—The Jewish Declaration of Independence

The God of Statism did a lot of plaguing and smiting on behalf of Moses. The plagues in Egypt by the Powers That Be continues to this day. The Jews, however, still celebrate Passover, so that "the plague shall not be upon you to destroy you". This story is the heart and soul of the bible, but even many Jewish people probably no longer understand why. The writers are making the point that the God of Statism has "passed over" the Israelites and their future generations, and they would never succumb completely to Statism, as would the hapless children of Egypt. That prophecy is still true, so for the Hebrew descendants Passover is a holiday well worth celebrating. Passover is their declaration of independence. U.S. citizens also celebrate Passover. It is called Independence Day and happens on the Fourth of July. Meanwhile, the God of Statism still continues to inflict many plagues upon the people of Egypt and other nations in the Middle East and, although still presenting a great risk, has fortunately been much less active in Israel because of their resistance, represented by being "passed over".

Although future generations of the Israelites would eventually reject Statism, the purpose of the bible is to demonstrate how the Statists manipulated them and their continuing stories still serve as a timeless warning to the rest of us. The death of the Egyptians' children, which even included the Pharaoh's own son, finally convinced him the Israelites had become terrorists, so the Pharaoh let them leave despite his heart being hardened by God.

Then the Israelites, under instruction from Moses, stole as much as they could and left Egypt. In addition to the thievery, this parable is just one of many examples where the God of Statism is depicted by the writers as causing the death of innocent children (which always represent future generations), and to the degradation of culture by promoting criminality. The Egyptians decided to chase after them, presumably to recoup some of their losses and to punish the Israelites for their murdered children but were washed away and died in another plague in the form of a flood created by The Powers That Be, and the Israelites escaped with the goods to follow Moses and Aaron to seek the "promised land" of milk and honey.

The progression of Statism will now continue. The people no longer work, but they still eat, so they panic until they discover they have only to complain sufficiently and their needs will be met, at least to the extent necessary to retain their loyalty. Promising free stuff is a common tactic in the formation of virtually every Statist culture in the beginning stages. The writers emphasize the free stuff in turn is always plundered from others. When the tribesmen complain about thirst, water is provided for them, albeit not until they were nearly dead. When they complain about the lack of food, they are fed with magical "manna" from heaven for free to sustain loyalty to the God of Statism.

> **Exodus 16:14 And when the dew that lay was gone up, behold, upon the face of the wilderness there lay a small round thing, as small as the hoar frost on the ground. 15. And when the children of Israel saw it, they said one to another, It is manna: for they wist not what it was. And Moses said unto them, This is the bread which the Lord hath given you to eat. 16. This is the thing which the Lord hath commanded, Gather of it every man according to his eating, an omer for every man, according to his eating, an omer for every man, according to the number of your persons; take ye every man for them which are in his tents. 17. And the children of Israel did so, and gathered, some more, some less. 18. And when they did mete it with an omer, he that gathered much had nothing over, and he that gathered little had no lack; they gathered every man according to his eating.**

Something similar would be repeated much later by another famous Statist called Karl Marx, who himself also offered a "promised land", and who said "From each according to his abilities, to each according to his needs" {[10]}. The point being everyone gets an equal share according to their needs regardless of their efforts, which became the basis for a Statist plague we would eventually come to call Communism. This type of cultural manipulation was apparently already nothing new long before Comrade Karl came along. If the people had been familiar with the lessons in the bible, this is a plague that could have been avoided.

The small round thing called manna represents the introduction of money into society and is almost always created and distributed by the God of Statism. The dependency that is created through a centralized banking system in collusion with the State is one of the worst things that can happen to any society. This is especially true when that money becomes simply paper (or digital) which makes it even more easily subject to manipulation. The people can usually depend on having enough manna so long as they remain loyal. If they try to save to achieve security and independence, the State can render it worthless and wormy through inflation, recessions, or other methods. The people must remain dependent, but loyalty will be rewarded by a steady, predictable, and dependable supply of manna from the "benevolent" God. This process of dependency on manna is still being used very effectively to keep Statists in power. The fiat money we use today is, once again, literally created out of nothing. That magical manna from The Powers That Be, along with propaganda suggesting there is still a utopian "promised land" in the future for the "chosen", is still the most effective method of maintaining a loyal following. The threat created by the State through dependence on the magical "manna" was recognized early on by the Yahwists.

The usefulness of magical manna is still being demonstrated today through Statist methods such as ensuring the loyalty of government employees and their labor unions, the many welfare recipients (which can be enlarged through immigration if necessary), and for all others who receive entitlements and government contracts, which assure the loyalty of even more

---

[10] https://en.wikipedia.org/wiki/From_each_according_to_his_ ability,_to_each_according_to_his_needs

citizens. These and other groups who are dependent on manna from God still comprise the loyal core of all Statist regimes, therefore the goal is to enlarge these groups to the greatest extent possible.

On the other hand, uncontrolled prosperity and the resultant independent thinking is of little use to a Statist culture. That the steady and dependable supply of manna may have something to do with impoverishing and oppressing those not as "chosen" is rarely mentioned. We now know this type of manipulation is very dangerous, but nevertheless is still popular among Statists, so deficit spending, inflation, credit supply manipulation, market bubbles, and other forms of economic social engineering are common signs of Statist oppression {11}.

Once back in Midian, Moses heeded the advice from his wealthy high priest father-in-law who congratulated him on his success at gaining so many followers. Being a powerful man himself, he used his experience to encourage Moses to create a bureaucratic hierarchy to help distance himself from the people, and to achieve a position of superior authority. The people are taught to use assigned bureaucratic judges and other officials to settle their differences, rather than doing it among themselves as they had before.

Exodus 18:20 And thou shalt teach them ordinances and laws, and shalt shew them the way wherein they must walk, and the work that they must do. 21. Moreover thou shalt provide out of all the people able men, such as fear God, men of truth, hating covetousness; and place such over them, to be rulers of thousands, and rulers of of hundreds, rulers of fifties, and rulers of tens: 22. And let them judge the people at all seasons: and it shall be, that every great matter they shall bring unto thee, but every small matter they shall judge: so shall it be easier for thyself, and they shall bear the burden with thee.

---

[11] https://en.wikipedia.org/wiki/Statism#Economic_statism

As the people soon discover, the bureaucrats now in place often have far more fear of "The Powers That Be" than for the people they are meant to serve, especially when they are accountable only to those who gave them the job to begin with. Nevertheless, the important thing to impress upon the people is that they must always turn to the bureaucracy to solve their problems. There is no mention of representation or self-rule in the process as a hierarchy is created, and the people are no longer able to judge for themselves or work together for solutions, and the creation of a new Statist society continues. The bureaucrats would now claim a higher moral authority for being more "chosen" than the rest of the population.

The writers continue to make their point that Statism, as always, continues to grow and increase its grip over the population. The next step for Moses has become a ritual so common that it has become infinitely predictable. Now that a system of judges and lawmakers and tax collectors are in place, a select few of the "chosen" insiders decide to have a meeting with God. All others are restricted and threatened with death if they interfere or violate God's personal space.

> **Exodus 19:12. And thou shalt set bounds unto the people round about, saying Take heed to yourselves, that ye go not up into the mount, or touch the border of it: whosoever toucheth the mount shall be surely put to death: 13. There shall not an hand touch it, but he shall surely be stoned, or shot through; whether it be beast or man, it shall not live:**

The people are then shown a place of fire and fumes, probably because of oil and gas abundance, which would have been very frightening. God then gave Moses instructions for the people.

> **Exodus 19:24 And the Lord said unto him, Away get thee down, and thou shalt come up, thou, and Aaron with thee: but let not the priests and the people break through to come up unto the Lord, lest he break forth upon them.**

Moses and Aaron have a private visit with God (the "Powers that Be" the Yahwists are warning us about) and lo and behold. Upon their return, they inform the congregation that God now requires sacrifices to be made from each member of the group. The creator of all material in the universe now needs to be provided with a percentage of the gold, silver, jewels, and other riches they were instructed to steal from their neighbors in Egypt, which are to be given directly to Moses' tax collectors. The collection of wealth will in turn be redistributed to his inner circle made up mostly of friends and relatives. The purpose of the taxes is to maintain a court dedicated to the worship of God, who only speaks through them. The writers again go out of their way to make the point that taxes represent stolen wealth. Moses learned his lessons well, first in Egypt and now from his father-in-law. The taxes, they explain, are for serving the people by pleasing God, and it is strictly for the benefit of the people they are doing this. These private and exclusive meetings with God have persisted throughout the ages and are still common.

One of the most epic stories written about Moses is the Ten Commandments story. This is the story of how the imposition of most Statist laws come about. They describe how once again only Moses can climb the mountain for another conversation with God. As the bible says, the commandments come from a very special high place where the people, as usual, are restricted from access. Therefore, there is no input from the people and the laws are chosen solely at the discretion of those at the top, and the collection of laws are made in secret. Strangely, most of the laws resemble normal customs of the people. If the people were so primitive it had not yet occurred to them that murdering might be wrong, and must be placed as one of the commandments, then why did Moses flee to Midian? Anyway, those cultural norms are now abducted by the God of Statism and are made permanent and protected from the people who might otherwise alter or disagree with them. However, along with the existing cultural laws already accepted by the people, some of the laws will now deal with loyalty to the State, which are added in as earmarks and are now "carved into stone" with the rest of the laws. Not surprisingly, these new laws are figured prominently in the beginning of the list.

Exodus 20:3 Thou shalt have no other gods before me. 4. Thou shalt not make unto thee any graven image, or any likeness of anything that is in heaven above, or that is in the earth beneath, or that is in the water under the earth: 5. Thou shalt not bow down thyself to them, nor serve them: for I the Lord thy God am a jealous God, visiting the iniquity of the fathers upon the children unto the third and fourth generation of them that hate me; 6. And shewing mercy unto thousands of them that love, and keep my commandments.

The jealous god requires that people love and keep his commandments. The laws and statutes will eventually extend far beyond the original commandments, especially those involving the payment of taxes, and are voluminous and complicated under Moses. He eventually creates a group dedicated solely to tax collection. The unwashed masses are only allowed to approach close enough to drop off their mandatory sacrifices and offerings. God apparently loves the smell of barbecue so killing animals and spilling the blood upon the altar is quite popular, but the usual money, gold, silver, brass, and jewelry are even more desirable.

There are many taxes in the form of offerings—sin offerings, atonement offerings, trespass offerings, peace offerings, wave offerings, and so on. My favorite is the wave offering, in which you take choice cuts of meat, raise it into the air, wave it around at God and then eat it. This is the equivalent of throwing money into the air and letting God keep what he wants and keeping what falls back onto the ground. It is important that you use someone else's contributions.

There are elaborate rituals created for offerings that only the priests can perform, which is why Aaron and other insiders must remain in charge. The tax laws become so complicated that specialists become crucial. At this point in history, many taxes are paid in food, given directly to the priests. Grilling is common for meat, but God apparently prefers honey, bread ingredients, oil, and fruit in their natural state. The Powers That Be have finicky eating habits that seem to closely coincide with the preferences of those in charge of collecting the offerings.

There are additional offerings if a person is sick and must be tended by a priest. There is no talk of healing, other than that which takes place naturally, but nevertheless diseases must be diagnosed by a priest to determine whether the person is "unclean", and additional offerings must be made for this service. Oddly, this is not an equal opportunity God. As God says to Moses...

> **Leviticus 21:17 Speak unto Aaron, saying Whosoever he be of thy seed in their generations that hath any blemish, let him not approach to offer the bread of his God. For whatsoever man he be that hath any blemish, he shall not approach: a blind man, or a lame, or he that hath a flat nose, or anything superfluous, or a man that is broken footed, broken handed or crook backed, or a dwarf, or that hath a blemish in his eye, or be scurvy, or scabbed, or hath his stones broken.**

If you were ugly, scarred, sickly, deformed, or injured you were just too profane to participate directly in the bureaucracy and were not as "chosen". God is selective and wants to be represented by only attractive people, so if you were physically ill or objectionable in appearance you were not allowed into the inner circle. But if you were acceptable in appearance and health, and made and collected regular sacrifices and offerings, God offered the usual saving, serving, and protecting that Statists always claim to offer in return for loyalty, which usually includes the covenant that the people will be led to that elusive and utopian "promised land".

Those in power will continue to claim an ever higher moral authority and declare that thou shalt not be a traitor or heretic that disagrees with God. More laws continue to be created. Many of these were ill thought out but were always based roughly on cultural norms of the times and will now be strictly enforced by Moses and Aaron and used to judge the people at the discretion of themselves and the assigned law givers. The laws are complicated, so some of them would lead to some tragic consequences. It reads...

> **Exodus 22:29 "Thou shalt not delay to offer the first of thy ripe fruits and of thy liquors: the firstborn of thy sons shalt thou give unto me."**

It is thought some religious sects would eventually come to believe that not only must they give their ripe fruits and liquors to God, but they must also offer their own children in sacrificial rites. Like many of the laws, it wasn't spelled out well enough to be clear because obscure and complicated laws are a tool of Statism. The original intent was probably to have a constant supply of warriors to fight their wars.

At any rate, a Statist culture now replaces a culture of the people. That the writers of the bible would devote such importance to a very long list of laws and statutes and taxes, even right down to the pricing of a slave given in shekels, is a good indication of what the bible was actually teaching us to fear. Meanwhile, once a State has the control dictated by dependency on bureaucracy and manna, those who still show little loyalty can now be purged through persecution laws encouraged by The Powers That Be.

> **Leviticus 24:15 And thou shalt speak unto the children of Israel, saying, Whosoever curseth his God shall bear his sin. 16. And he that blasphemeth the name of the Lord, he shall surely be put to death, and all the congregation shall certainly stone him: as well the stranger, as he that is born in the land, when he blasphemeth the name of the Lord, shall be put to death.**

There must always be a threat of punishment for a lack of loyalty, and the political correctness and persecution must have communal participation. Anyone not participating in the persecution could run the risk of suffering the same consequences. The gang or mob mentality, so long as it is deflected away from themselves, is always beneficial for the Powers That Be. The consequences of not being loyal can often be severe.

> **Leviticus 26:15 And if ye shall despise my statutes, or if your soul abhor my judgments, so that ye will not do all my commandments, but ye break my covenant: 16. I also will do this unto you; I will even appoint over you terror, consumption, and the burning ague, that shall consume the eyes, and cause sorrow of the heart: and ye shall sow your seed in vain, for your enemies shall eat it. 17. And I will set my face against you, and ye shall be slain before your enemies: they that hate you shall reign over you; and ye shall flee when none pursueth you. 18. And if ye will not yet for all this hearken unto me, then I will punish you seven times more for your sins. 19. And I will break the pride of your power; and I will make your heaven as iron, and your earth as brass: 20. And your strength shall be spent in vain: for your land shall not yield her increase, neither shall the trees of the land yield their fruits. 21. And if ye walk contrary unto me, I will bring seven times more plagues upon you according to your sins. 22. And I will also send wild beasts among you, which shall rob you of your children, and destroy your cattle, and make you few in number; and your high ways shall be desolate.**

So, the list of threats of all the different ways Statism has at its disposal to punish the people who lack loyalty continues...

> **Leviticus 26:29 And ye shall eat the flesh of your sons, and the flesh of your daughters shall ye eat.**

...and so on and so forth. The writers show there is no lack of imagination when it comes to God's oppression. History has borne out their observations and prophecies. This is a very fearful God indeed.

That Moses was not meant to be a hero or a savior, but rather an example of how Statism comes about becomes even more obvious as the story continues. The materials provided through taxes are necessary for the making of beautiful robes and ribbons to clothe Moses, his brother Aaron, and the rest of their family to set them apart from the rest of the population. An expensive closed off tabernacle made from confiscated wealth is built where only the inner circle of the most "chosen" has access. God has decided to give Aaron permanent job security in the organization which will pass down through nepotism and are called the Levites (who levy taxes). The Levites do not produce anything, own no land or animals unless given to them in the form of taxes, and do not work the land nor act as herdsmen. Their purpose is not to create or produce. Their job security is maintained by the necessity of the collection of taxes. The taxes in turn are made necessary because of the existence of the tax collectors and other bureaucrats. These groups need to be supported because they can't support themselves. After they take their cut, some of the wealth is redistributed to assure loyalty. This is how all Statist systems still work today.

The story of Moses continues with ever more laws, regulations, statutes, precepts, and commandments that never stop flowing. This is a continuation of the process of the people gradually replacing their own culture with Statist laws and bureaucracy. There are rules about where to sleep, what to eat and what not to eat, how the food should be prepared, where to put up your tent, price controls on everything including slaves, and the list goes on. This is more and more a micromanagement God. As they knew even then, replacing culture with Statist laws results in an ever growing and expensive bureaucracy, and they make that message very clear.

A great deal of emphasis in the bible deals with all the horrible and oppressive things God will do to the people if their loyalty wavers in the slightest, especially once the bureaucracy is in place. They continue with long descriptions of adversities and plagues that will befall the people, especially if they become involved with other people's inferior gods (other governments or different cultures that are a threat to the status quo).

Leviticus 26:15 And if ye shall despise my statutes, or if your soul abhor my judgments, so that ye will not do all my commandments, but that ye break my covenant: 16. I also will do this unto you; I will even appoint over you terror, consumption, and the burning ague, that shall consume the eyes, and cause sorrow of heart: and ye shall sow your seed in vain, for your enemies shall eat it.

A lack of input from the people has predictable consequences, and show this God only has mercy for those that love and obey his laws and bureaucrats. As Moses is busy creating and recording laws for judging the people, he knows they are likely to stray, so he gives an order to his surrogates.

Deuteronomy 31:26 Take this book of the law and put it in the side of the ark of the covenant of the Lord your God, that it may be there for a witness against thee. 27. For I know thy rebellion, and thy stiff neck: behold, while I am yet alive with you this day, ye have been rebellious against the Lord; and how much more after my death?

The defiance of the Jewish ancestors started very early, and long before Moses they had already gained a reputation of resistance. Sure enough, some of the congregation had decided maybe there might be a better way, including Aaron. Left to their own devices, people are sometimes prone to try to find something better, especially the stiff-necked Israelites. They decided maybe a god of fertility might be a better route, because the survival of men, animals, and plants depend on fertility to survive. A god of fertility did not require communal obedience or loyalty, and instead connected the people with nature.

Although no doubt far from perfect, they could at least participate as a group without the necessity of having to stone their neighbors, there were no priests constantly demanding tribute to atone for their supposed sinfulness and may even have involved dancing and having a good time. This made Moses' God feel threatened because of his own admission of jealousy and wanted to destroy the lot of them on the spot. Luckily for the congregation, Moses stepped in, negotiated with God, and took credit for talking God out of destroying them all. God then killed a bunch of them anyway to serve as an example for those not adequately loyal. Those darned Israelites have always been a stiff-necked bunch, and let's hope they stay that way as an example to us all.

Also, it turns out all that manna isn't free after all. If you aren't producing anything, it must be stolen from someone else—and then taxed. The manna, even though free to the "chosen", at one point became something of a problem. The Israelites discovered that despite the free manna there was still something missing in their lives, and eventually arranged protests.

> **Numbers 11. 4 And the mixed multitude that was among them fell a-lusting: and the children of Israel also wept again, and said, Who shall give us flesh to eat? 5. We remember the fish, which we did eat in Egypt freely; the cucumbers, and the melons, and the leeks, and the onions, and the garlick: 6. But now our soul is dried away: there is nothing at all, beside this manna before our eyes.**

This is what Moses had feared. That's the trouble with people who are made dependent. Just as you think giving them free stuff to be loyal is working, they become ever needier and even more dependent. Or even worse, they start wanting something more out of life. This is the sort of thing that really annoys a Statist God, so he got even.

> **Numbers 11:19 Ye shall not eat one day, nor two days, nor five days, neither ten days, nor twenty days; 20. But even a whole month, until it come out your nostrils, and it be loathsome unto you: because that ye have despised the Lord which is among you, and have wept before him, saying, Why came we forth out of Egypt?**

God buried the people in quail two cubits high—but it was not to be enjoyed.

Numbers 11:33 And while the flesh was yet between their teeth, ere it was chewed, the wrath of the Lord was kindled against the people, and the Lord smote the people with a very great plague.

The lesson is if you allow yourself to become dependent by accepting free stuff, then unless you want to be smited with a plague, you keep your mouth shut and be loyal to the God of Statism that's feeding you. Instead, you will be allowed to vent your frustrations through smiting and oppressing those less chosen. In democracies today, smiting is usually done through the voting process to determine who is the most "chosen", and to allow those who are favored to oppress those not as chosen. Russia, China, and North Korea are all democracies where they have ballots for voting—not to determine who will do the representing, but who will do the oppressing and smiting, and demonstrate the difference between a democracy and a republic. In republics such as the United States, those not as chosen still retain rights reserved for them in the Constitution. This also angers the God of Statism, which is why our constitution is always under siege.

Meanwhile, there were continuous wars against the people living in the lands where the Israelites passed in their search for the "promised land". To obtain enough provisions to maintain the loyalty of his followers, Moses had now become a successful warlord. The genocide, burning, and pillaging would continue throughout their journeys. There was an encounter with the plague that was blamed on the inequities of the people (never waste a crisis), and a demand from God to slaughter the people of Midian for not letting them pass through their land. Despite the fact they were Moses' in-laws, God took this as a very personal insult. Instructions were given to slaughter even the women and children. One exception was they would be allowed to keep the girl virgins for themselves. There were of thousands of them, so God wasn't totally without compassion towards survivors of other tribes after the slaughter. Speaking of the Midianite captives God said:

Numbers 31:17. Now therefore kill every male among the little ones, and kill every woman that hath known

man by lying with him. 18. But all the women children, that have not known man by lying with him, keep alive for yourselves.

The God of Statism is always very adept at using stolen wealth and resources to keep loyal followers happy. After the successful slaughter, the warriors were promptly taxed for the booty they had stolen before the wealth and virgins were redistributed, because God and his priests needed a percentage.

Numbers 31:27. And the Lord spake unto Moses, saying, 26. Take the sum of the prey that was taken, both of man and of beast, thou, and Eleazar the priest, and the chief fathers of the congregation: And divide the prey into two parts; between them that took the war upon them, who went out to battle, and between all the congregation: 28. And levy a tribute unto the Lord of the men of war which went out to battle: one soul of five hundred, both of the persons, and of the beeves, and of the asses, and of the sheep: 29. Take it of their half, and give it unto Eleazar the priest, for an heave offering of the Lord.

As Moses became old after leading his people into a cultural wilderness for forty years while plundering and slaughtering, he began to worry about his legacy of "saving" his followers. He installed a surrogate called Joshua to enforce all the laws, statutes, executive orders, and commandments, and to tend to the tax collection. It becomes apparent the reason one generation had been allowed to wander aimlessly through the cultural desert for a full generation while getting free manna was because God had plans.

He really wasn't all that confident in the first generation after all, because they weren't worthy of the "promised land". However, he did have great plans for future generations. The original group of Israelites were stubborn, and had refused to attack the Canaanites, which God had told them lived on their "inheritance" land. This is how God knew his people weren't adequately loyal. The people loved all that manna and plunder and not working, but they still weren't totally obedient.

The people could see the Canaanites living and working on their "inheritance" land were much stronger and lived in walled cities, so had refused God's orders to attack. That they would question the logic in slaughtering and being slaughtered by a strong opponent must have been annoying to God, so God increased their tax burden, enlarged the bureaucracy, put many of the most disloyal to death, and informed them this generation would now die wandering in the wilderness. Instead, it would be the next generation that would receive the promised "inheritance". It would be up to his surrogate Joshua to lead the next generation to the land of "milk and honey", where other people already lived and had built towns and cities.

So now the truth comes out. The utopian "promised land" of milk and honey never existed. Their "inheritance" was to be taken by force from others who had created it. And since an entire new generation had been taught to accept dependency on manna, they had now become mindless followers buried in confusing and often contradictory laws which discouraged independent or critical thinking. Through accepting dependency, the first generation had led a meaningless life and had degraded the culture of the next generation. The new generation had seen how God could turn on them in a moment's notice, so fear of God was part of everyday reality. There was now a whole new generation of people that had known no other way. This made it easy for Joshua to lead his people to the Jordan river and point to the other side and say in effect, "see all those towns and cities? They didn't do that. See all those farms and shops and businesses? Well, they didn't do that. God *allowed* them to do that, so we could murder and subjugate them and steal it for ourselves because this is your "inheritance".

The chosen people of this new generation would be much more compliant, so war would now begin, and they could now claim their inheritance. Canaanite {12} means *merchant or trader*, and the invasion and destruction continues today, because Statists still

---

12 https://www.biblestudytools.com/dictionary/canaanites/

consider the productivity of free market merchants to be their "inheritance", to be taken or taxed at will.

So now we see the message the writers were sending. The Yahwists were telling us how Statism comes about almost inevitably. First the people are made huge promises of free and wonderful stuff and had won the lottery by being "chosen". If the situation the people are living under isn't bad enough to convince them to follow, then it can always be made worse through plagues such as propaganda, economic manipulation, cultural degradation, and community disorganization to create division. Once the people have been sufficiently divided from those not "chosen" through identity politics then it may take a generation or two of dependency and suppression to create a culture of submission, but once they do it is easy to convince them that only the Statist God can guide and provide for them, provided they bend to "his" will.

Other Gods and the people who follow them are depicted as inferior and dangerous and must be vilified. The people become convinced it is normal to replace their own culture with Statist laws handed down by God, locked in a box where they cannot be touched, and where there is no debate or input from the people. The judges and other bureaucrats are chosen and controlled by The Powers That Be, to whom they are beholden. The State will eventually also convince the people that war and plunder is acceptable, because God wants them to take from others to support themselves and their "benevolent" bureaucracy, which is justified because they are the elite "chosen", and others are lesser beings.

Also, once dependency on manna from heaven is firmly established, no one wants it to stop. The new generation descended from the willingly dependent and oppressed are now the oppressors and the conquerors through indoctrination. Hitler used this method very effectively with his Hitler Youth program. The same is true of Mao Tse Tung with the Red Guard, Stalin with the Bolsheviks, and so on. The opponents, who are usually innocent victims, are vilified and dehumanized so the point that attacks are not only acceptable, it is necessary to rid the world of those who are inferior or to impose your Statist God upon them for their own good. The writers emphasize how easy it is for dependency to create a new generation of followers, who then become willing tools of The Powers That Be.

The authors of the bible had seen how Statism happens. They lived with it every day of their lives, just as most people still do today to various degrees, and they knew how leaders and their surrogates always claim to be saving, serving, and protecting, when they are simply creating dependency and control over the people for their own benefit. This is one of the most important "hidden" messages within the bible. They wanted to warn future generations to try and imagine a better way, and that the solution was within the people themselves. They first identify and illustrate the problem with parables in the Old Testament. They emphasize that in many ways the people can become part of the problem because of propaganda and dependency generated by Statism in only a few generations.

The lesson here is that if we are to maintain a successful and free society then part of our culture must be that we train each new generation to avoid Statism and dependency and teach them to avoid becoming part of the problem. The purpose of the writers is to point out the God of Statism is created by allowing ourselves to be manipulated by being offered temporary benefits, and by being taught we must always attempt to be among the "chosen". I believe avoiding this phenomenon is one of the main lessons of the Good Book. If we used the bible appropriately, the first curriculum in every educational institution would be How to Prevent Statism from Becoming Your Religion 101. Unfortunately, the opposite is happening because public schools and universities have become State-controlled institutions that dispense indoctrination, and often help degrade any hint of culture based on self-reliance and critical thinking. As Stalin once said:

"Education is a weapon, whose effect depends on who holds it in his hand and at whom it is aimed" {[13]}.

---

[13] https://www.goodreads.com/quotes/80201-education-is-a-weapon-whose-effect-depends-on-who-holds

The story of Moses shows how Statism begets more Statism. It shows the juxtaposition of a society that has achieved the pinnacle of a Statist cultural pyramid system as in Egypt, and the very beginnings of a new Statist society with a "charismatic" leadership, who leads the people away to create yet another Statist society. Living under an oppressive regime allows new "leaders" to take advantage of the situation to perpetuate the process of creating new Statist societies by promising better benefits to those already indoctrinated into Statism. If the people had been taught to understand the strength of their own culture, then neither the Pharaoh nor Moses could have come to power. The bible was written specifically to rectify this cultural flaw and educate the people. Considering how harmful this information is to the God of Statism, it is no wonder the bible was illegal for ordinary citizens to own for so many centuries, even into modern times {14}. Once the bible did become public, which resulted in the Protestant movement, it became necessary to twist the meaning.

Can we think of any other times in history where a "leader" appears from within a degraded society where this same story has taken place? I can think of one other time that the actions of a previous administration created poverty and servitude for their people. As a result, a charismatic figure would step forward to take advantage of their plight and tell the people of a "promised land" in exchange for loyalty. Once in power, he would encourage the people to expand their territory into other areas through warfare because it was their rightful "inheritance". He would degrade culture through hate propaganda and laws that justified theft and mass murder through elitism. He would enlist a younger generation to achieve his goals. He would use that younger generation to attack the "unchosen" people that had been participating in free market capitalism as had the Canaanites. Those people attacked would ironically be mostly Jewish merchants, who had integrated with the Canaanites much earlier in history despite protests from God. If you want to know this story turned out, you should study the history of World War II. Not surprisingly, just about all Statist

---

14 http://www.greatsite.com/timeline-english-bible-history/

societies have very similar characteristics, and there are thousands of similar examples.

The Old Testament is a Public Warning

Announcement

Now that we understand the real message, we can go back to the beginning and work our way through Genesis back up to the Moses story. Every story in the Old Testament is a parable of the God of Statism, and always serves as a warning. One thing is certain, and that is the Powers That Be in the Old Testament were deliberately portrayed as cruel, vengeful, and fearful, because the purpose of their parables is to teach us how to avoid this god through the same heroic defiance shown by the Jewish ancestors as they demonstrate the pitfalls of following this God.

Beginning with the very first story of creation, God has created the ultimate paradise in Eden. The people can live in perfect luxury where no one ever works or gets too hot or too cold, so they are free to run around naked, eating abundant food that grows everywhere for free, and the animals look up to you instead of eating you. Life in paradise is good so long as you obey God's orders and are mindful of his rules. However, paradise is short lived because the most important rule of all is that you must never eat of the "tree of knowledge" that allows you to know the difference between good and evil. You must remain ignorant of these things and live happily obeying God. Unfortunately, any paradise created by the God of Statism is only temporary.

As you might know if you are familiar with the story of Adam and Eve, the people writing the bible tell of them being tempted into eating from the "tree of knowledge" anyway and are sorely punished by being unceremoniously ejected from Eden. It's a bad thing for the God of Statism if the people can discern the difference between good and evil, so they need to be purged and ostracized. This would have been particularly true for the Yahwists who wrote the bible. They make their point in the very first bible stories the extent to which they have been persecuted by The Powers That Be.

Genesis 3:22 And the Lord God said, Behold, the man is become as one of us, to know good and evil: and

45

**now, lest he put forth his hand, and take also of the
tree of life, and eat, and live forever: 23. Therefore the
Lord God sent him forth from the garden of Eden, to
till the ground from whence he was taken. 24. So he
drove out the man; and he placed at the east of the
garden of Eden cherubims, and a flaming sword which
turned every way, to keep the way of the tree of life.**

They are told they will no longer be favored because of their
bad behavior in eating of "the tree of knowledge" and because of
the threat they may also eat "of the tree of life", so they will now
be subjected to punishment. God will be there to remind them of
their iniquities, but they must now be economic producers, part of
which must be given to God. They would not be allowed to remain
in Eden because of the sin of disloyalty. They are removed, and
must now be judged, punished, and then taxed—for their own
good.

But just in case they think they can willy nilly find their way
back into paradise, the first weapon of mass destruction is invented
by God in the form of a flaming sword and is placed at the entrance
to Eden to block them. Accurately depicted by the Yahwists as
Gods tool, the sword will go on to result in the slaughter of
countless thousands and unimaginable suffering and would in fact
serve the Powers That Be very well to prevent man from ever
recreating Eden. The sword would almost always be used at God's
direction, just as are modern weapons.

Just for good measure, the sword is accompanied by Cherubim,
which is an interesting clue the writers have included. Cherubim,{15}
(which means mighty, or approachers), are very unlike the concept
made up later by propagandists which show a cute little fat baby
with wings, and are horrible creatures. A Cherubim is a threatening
creature which always has too many heads, too many faces, too
many eyes, large claws, and almost always presents an obstacle or
brings bad news.

---

15 http://www.jewishencyclopedia.com/articles/4311-cherub

Ezekiel 1:10 As for the likeness of their faces, they four had the face of a man, and the face of a lion, on the right side: and they four had the face of an ox on the left side; they four also had the face of an eagle.

Walk into any bureaucratic government office and you will find yourself face to face with Cherubim. In Russia the people who run these bureaucratic offices even have their own name and are called Apparatchik {[16]}. These are God's visible agents of the State and, depending on circumstances, they must either present themselves as human, hence the human face; fierce and threatening, the lion; dumb and unknowing, as the ox; or noble and above you in their status, represented by the eagle. They have never been rare in any country, continue to serve the will of the State far more often than the people, and are almost always a threatening obstacle. We have all faced the guardian cherubim and yes, they are usually still very ominous obstacles ostracizing us from a cultural Eden. Think of the thousands of bureaus, agencies, and departments that now represent the Powers That Be to control our lives. Even the God of Statism no longer knows how many Cherubim there are preventing us from reentering Eden. As the writers point out, any paradise created by the God of Statism is only temporary and requires the rejection of true knowledge and understanding.

A Statist God will always remove man from Eden for the sin of eating of "the tree of knowledge of good and evil" and wanting to eat from "the tree of life". In the very beginning, the writers emphasize that the "Original Sin" of man is in the creation of the God of Statism, which in turn resulted in us being removed from Eden. So long as we continue to allow this God to banish us from entering an Eden created by and for We The People, we will always serve as little more than economic producers for The Powers That Be.

---

[16] https://www.collinsdictionary.com/dictionary/english/apparatchik

Adam and Eve are now forced to become producers and act as a tax base as punishment for being imperfect. Adam and Eve have children. Two of them are boys called Cain and Abel, and as they take to their new lifestyle their children mature and get their own careers. Cain becomes a farmer and Abel a rancher. Along with their parents, they are the first to have to pay taxes to God who, after tossing them out of Eden, continues to keep an eye on everything. In return for his services he now needs to be supported by the people through the first mandatory sacrificial offerings. Still today, unless you are among the most chosen, the producers are forced by law to support The Powers That Be.

God was apparently not a vegan because he wasn't at all impressed with the taxes Cain offered from his land, over the fattened animals offered by Abel.

Genesis 4:3 And in the process of time it came to pass, that Cain brought of the fruit of the ground an offering unto the Lord. 4. And Abel, he also brought of the firstlings of his flock and of the fat thereof. And the Lord had respect unto Abel and to his offering: 5. But unto Cain and to his offering he had not respect. And Cain was very wroth, and his countenance fell.

Abel's sacrifice allowed him favor in Gods eyes. God's favor apparently led to benefits not open to Cain, otherwise the jealousy and resentment Cain then felt would have been pointless. The distraught Cain killed Abel during a discussion about God's favoritism out in the field. What form of favoritism was offered to Abel we can only speculate, but what we do know is that more favorable offerings paid to a Statist God generally results in better treatment, and often is to the detriment of those who have less to offer.

Those who pay less taxes are generally left on their own except at voting time. That is, if you are fortunate enough to be allowed to vote, in which case the candidate will generally be chosen for you. If voting is allowed, then the promotion of some version of utopia or promised land will once again become popular at election time. To the writers, taxation is a major issue in the Old Testament because it was an important aspect of their lives, as it is in all Statist societies. For killing Abel, God curses Cain because he killed the source of "the fat thereof".

> **Genesis 4:11 And now art thou cursed from the earth, which hath opened her mouth to receive thy brothers' blood from thy hand;**

There is some speculation there may have been some societal changes taking place when this part of the bible was written in that agriculture was becoming more important than herding animals. The writers may have been predicting that taxes on agriculture would eventually "kill" the concept of sacrificing animals for taxes as the people became less nomadic herdsmen and more dependent on farming {[17]}. We only know for sure the story centered around the payment of taxes and because of favoritism from God, Cain killed Abel and was punished for this act by being separated from his land by God.

The necessity of owning land for agricultural purposes would leave the people susceptible to a new taxation in the form of property taxes and is one of the most unfortunate aspects of Statism. With this type of tax there is no such thing as land ownership and the independence ownership would allow. Everyone is simply renting from the State and if the rent is not paid sufficiently in the eyes of God, your land will be taken from you, which is exactly what happened to Cain. No doubt this is one of the reasons taxation was given such emphasis in the Old Testament. The intent of this story isn't to emphasize the murderous inclination of Cain, as we are taught. That is a diversion from the true lesson which is the conflict, division, and favoritism created by taxation from The Powers That Be.

You must appreciate the nature of the stories of Genesis because of their ability to hit the nail squarely on the head when pointing out the nature of Statism as they knew it. One of the recurring themes in the Bible is how the God of Statism chooses

---

[17] http://thetorah.com/the-evolution-of-civilization-the-biblical-story/

49

who wins and who loses, which is still happening today. Favoritism for the "chosen" occurs repeatedly.

The story of Noah is a case in point. We all know the story of Noah. This is the story of God collecting all the resources available into the hands of a few chosen insiders, while committing utter destruction on those not chosen, and is a common theme in the bible. God notified Noah that all creatures be gathered on an ark with the rest of the "chosen" so they can rise to the top of the flood waters. Everyone else is destroyed, along with all the other things on earth they could not keep for themselves. Only the most loyal to God would survive and prosper. Dictators understand this mindset perfectly, and this phenomenon was also already recognized in ancient times by the Yahwists. The desire to concentrate resources into the hands of a few while wreaking havoc on others is a trademark of the God of Statism, and there would continue to be many purges against the disloyal throughout the bible.

Once the flood of destruction against those not chosen subsides, and after a lot of begetting from the Noah clan with tribes that mysteriously reappeared despite the flood, the people began to create a new civilization. Noah would have three sons, all of which represent a different cultural condition. The sons would be Shem, Ham, and Japheth. The name Shem {[18]} in ancient Hebrew means "name", or self-awareness, or self-identity. From this cultural condition would be derived the Semites. They would eventually come to be known for their own recognition of their differences from other cultures.

The name Ham {[19]} denotes a hotness, or passion, or noisy, but emphasis seems to be mostly placed in his child Canaan (merchant), who will be forever cursed to be a servant to Statist cultures that would arise from the other sons. The punishment was because his father Ham had seen Noah drunk and naked.

---

[18] http://www.abarim-publications.com/Meaning/Shem.html#.XaH7BEZKjIU
[19] http://www.abarim-publications.com/Meaning/Ham.html#.XaH8hUZKjIU

Genesis 9:20 And Noah began to be an husbandman, and he planted a vineyard: 21. And he drank of the wine, and was drunken; and he was uncovered in his tent. 22. And Ham, the father of Canaan, saw the nakedness of his father, and told his two brethren without. 23. And Shem and Japheth took a garment, and laid it upon both their shoulders, and went backward, and covered the nakedness of their father; and their faces were backward, and they saw not their fathers' nakedness. 24. And Noah awoke from his wine, and knew what his younger son had done to him. 25. And he said, Cursed be Canaan; a servant of servants shall be be unto his brethren. 26. And he said, Blessed be the Lord God of Shem; and Canaan shall be his servant. 27. God shall enlarge Japheth, and he shall dwell in the tents of Shem; and Canaan shall be his servant.

For seeing him naked and drunk, which is bible talk for recognizing what he represented and making noise about it, Ham's descendants would be cursed by Noah. They would become servants forever to the Statist societies that would come to dominate culture. They would be called the Canaanites, which you will recall from the Moses story means merchantmen or traders. The Canaanites represent free market capitalism and would go on to be attacked and subjugated relentlessly. They would be made to be servants by the other cultures victimized by the God of Statism. As we know, this is still true. Statists cannot survive without the oppressed servants in the open markets who create an actual economy, even though they have tried on some occasions because of their fear of trade not controlled by the State. His other sons would choose not to see the truth and turn their backs and cover up for him in return for benefits. None of this is unusual in politics.

The name Japheth [20] would be associated with the act of enlargement or spreading of society in general. The word Japheth

---

[20] https://www.behindthename.com/name/japheth

means to enlarge, and as growth would continue there would eventually become many nation states ruled by Statism.

Before the people were divided into nation states, God must have made himself scarce for a while, because the people began to have confidence in themselves and realized that by working together, they could accomplish great things on their own. As the authors of the bible point out, this is exactly what God feared would happen in Eden. They had created a common culture and a common language and were inspired to work together to build a great city with a tower. At this point—God returned.

> **Genesis 11:1 And the whole earth was of one language, and of one speech. 2. And it came to pass, as they journeyed from the east, that they found a plain in the land of Shinar; and they dwelt there. 3. And they said to one another, Go to let us make brick, and burn them thoroughly. And they had brick for stone, and slime had they for mortar. And they said, Go to, let us build us a city and a tower, whose top may reach unto heaven; and let us make us a name, lest we be scattered abroad upon the face of the whole earth. 5. And the Lord came down to see the city and the tower, which the children of men builded. 6. And the Lord said, Behold, the people is one, and they have all one language; and this they begin to do: and now nothing will be restrained from them, which they have imagined to do. 7. Go to, let us go down, and there confound their language, that they may not understand one anothers speech. 8. So the Lord scattered them abroad from thence upon the face of all the earth: and they left off to build the city.**

Once again it became necessary to destroy an Eden the people had created among themselves. The city came to be called Babel, which is where the term "babbling" comes from and means talking nonsense. As in all biblical stories, there is a lesson here the writers of the bible wanted to convey. The enemy of Statism is self-reliance, self-determination and a common culture and language allowing cooperation among the people. You cannot allow this because if they do, they soon realize they do not need the God of Statism.

To protect the authority of God, you can always flood a city or nation with immigrants to break down the culture and language, because division is a necessary part of Statist control. If you cannot arrange warfare and division with some other nation then it must be within the community itself. Statism thrives best whenever there is a breakdown of culture and the division of identity politics.

Wholesale division can only be achieved on a grand scale through nation building, which will be the next strategy of The Powers That Be. Once there is a division of nations, the next step will be to turn them against each to create the cultural disharmony necessary for one of God's greatest tools, which is warfare. This is a tactic often used by the God in the Old Testament, so this method of introducing Statism is nothing new. Statism thrives on chaos and divisiveness until they achieve full power over the people's culture. Once control has been achieved, freedom for all concerned is a thing of the past, and social engineering can be used more effectively to benefit those more "chosen".

Abraham—The Divider in Chief

Whenever you see the deliberate dividing of the people, you will see the God of Statism rising to power. We continue with the stories of Abraham {[21]}, (whose name means "Father of many nations") who, with his relative Lot had some interesting adventures. Abraham is used by the writers to again demonstrate how Statism begins by dividing the people. Division is their primary strength and protection, so nations will now be separated politically and culturally. After having to confound the language and divide the people of Babel, The Powers That Be realize it will be necessary to find a more permanent way to divide the people to create the conflict necessary for Statism to thrive.

To avoid having the people once again create a common culture and language so that "nothing is restrained from them that they have imagined to do" God has chosen Abraham and his progeny to be the beginning of separate nation states, which will in turn lead to an endless process of warfare which continues to this day. It is this disastrous trend which makes up most of the stories of warfare and genocide in the Old Testament. Abraham, whom the writers depict as an example of the Ultimate Divider-in-Chief, comes forward and God tells him he needs to separate from his relatives. Division through destruction of family cohesiveness is also common among Statists, and God informs him...

> **Genesis 12:1 Now the Lord had said unto Abram, Get thee out of thy country, and from thy kindred, and from thy father's house, unto a land that I will shew thee. 2. And I will make of thee a great nation, and I will bless thee, and make thy name great; and thou shalt be a blessing: 3. And I will bless them that bless thee, and curse him that curse thee: and in thee shall all families of the earth be blessed.**

21

https://hermeneutics.stackexchange.com/questions/19868/whatis-the-meaning-of-abrahams-name

You can't successfully promote the concept of Statism long term without separate Nation States to turn against each other, so God begins the process through Abraham. That the nation states were created for the express purpose of facilitating strife and warfare between various groups is emphasized by the writers. Statism was already nothing new in Egypt, so a trip to Egypt is almost always a precursor to the processes of division through Statism. That will be the first destination for Abraham.

Egypt was originally seen as the core of Statism but as power shifted, the Powers That Be would later be centered in Babylon. Babylon may have also been the former Babel, which had been set up for failure earlier by God through confounding their common language and culture {22}. Babylon would fail again, and for much the same reason. Later, the center of Statism would be focused in Rome, which would also fail many times. In the meantime, Egypt was the University of Statism, and was the perfect place to perfect the art.

Once in Egypt, Abraham decided to introduce his wife Sarah as his sister because, well, she was apparently pretty hot and was afraid he would be killed if they knew he was her husband. The Egyptians must have been known for doing that sort of thing. He wasn't lying mind you, because she was in fact also his half-sister. This deception worked out well for a while, but after getting a pretty good payoff from the Pharaoh, who was trying to impress Sarah...

> **Genesis 12:16 And he entreated Abram** (Abraham's alias) **well for her sake: and he had sheep, and oxen and he asses, and menservants, and maidservants, and she asses, and camels.**

But the Pharaoh ran him off when he discovered he had been misled by Abraham, who had essentially been pimping out his sister/wife. In their parables the writers always seem to enjoy sticking it to Egypt. Being a lot richer now, and responding to the fact that the Pharaoh had invited them to leave...

---

22 https://en.wikipedia.org/wiki/Tower_of_Babel

Genesis 13:1 And Abram went up out of Egypt, he, and his wife, and all that he had, and Lot with him, into the south. 2. And Abram was very rich in cattle, in silver, and in gold. 3. And he went on his journeys from the south even to Beth-el, unto the place where his tent had been at the beginning, between Beth-el and Hai: 4. Unto the place of the altar, which he had made there at the first: and there Abram called on the name of the Lord.

Just as Moses would much later, Abraham had learned there was a lot of wealth and power involved in the Statism business after spending some time in Egypt. Abraham and Lot booked it back to where they started before their sojourn in Egypt, but soon realized that with their larger herds of livestock the land wouldn't support them both, so they separated. Abraham went his way and waged war with various groups who were less "chosen" for plunder, and once even pursued and slaughtered a group that had apparently abducted Lot, who had a habit of being in the wrong place at the wrong time. At some point Lot had gotten too close to one of the wars and was hauled away as a prisoner.

Leading up to Lot being taken captive there were two cities, one of which was called Sodom, where Lot and his family were living, and another city called Gomorrah. Both been invaded and looted repeatedly by larger armies. After being subjected to oppression for twelve years, Sodom and Gomorrah and three other cities had grown tired of being subservient to four other more powerful kingdoms and rebelled but were soon defeated by superior numbers.

Genesis 14:11 And they took all the goods of Sodom and Gomorrah, and all their victuals, and went their way. 12. And they took Lot, Abrams' brothers' son, who dwelt in Sodom, and his goods, and departed.

Seeing an opportunity to take advantage of what he had learned in Egypt, Abram pursued the offenders and did some smiting and rescued Lot and acquired the possessions that had been stolen from Sodom and Gomorrah. Upon his return, rather than returning the loot to Sodom, Abraham gave a percentage instead to a high priest of Salem (Jerusalem) who had shown up with wine and bread, which is bible talk for bribe. Apparently concerned Abraham would also not return the captives, the newly appointed king of Sodom agreed to forego all the remaining loot stolen from them in exchange for his captured citizens. Instead, Abraham accepted only recompense for his warriors, and whatever food they had consumed along the way. Since he did not agree to the deal, we can assume Abraham kept the captives and the remaining spoils to incorporate into his own tribe.

This would lead to a hue and cry from both Sodom and Gomorrah, which would make God very angry towards them. However, God was greatly pleased with Abraham. He had succeeded in both the slaughter of other tribes and growing the size and wealth of his own tribe through the abduction of the Sodom citizens. In congratulations, God promised again that from Abraham would be created many kings and nations. The hue and cry from Sodom and Gomorrah would be dealt with later.

Meanwhile, Abraham's tribe would continue to grow. First, he had progeny by way of his wife's maid-servant Hagar, at his wife's suggestion. His wife Sarai at this point was unable to have children. When Hagar did in fact become pregnant, Sarai then became jealous and decided to get rid of Hagar and mistreated her until she left. Before her child was born, Hagar ran away because of the abuse, but an angel {23} (messenger) told her to return...

> **Genesis 16:9 And the angel of the Lord said unto her, Return to thy mistress, and submit thyself under her hands. 10. And the angel of the Lord said unto her, I will multiply thy seed exceedingly, that it shall not be numbered for multitude. 11. And the angel of the Lord said unto her, Behold, thou art with child, and shalt bear a son, and shalt call his name Ishmael {24}** (which means listens to God); **because the Lord hath heard thy**

---

[23] https://en.wikipedia.org/wiki/Angels_in_Judaism
[24] https://en.wikipedia.org/wiki/Ishmael#Etymology

affliction. 12. And he will be a wild man; his hand will be against every man, and every man's hand against him; and he shall dwell in the presence of all his brethren.

God would not allow Hagar to leave because the purpose for her child was to create disharmony and division among "all his brethren". As a result, those who "listens" to the God of Statism are still living among us and will always be "a wild man" and "against every man" that prefers peace and freedom instead of division and conflict.

Genesis 17:5 Neither shall thy name any more be called Abram, but thy name shall be Abraham; for a father of many nations have I made thee. 6. And I will make thee exceeding fruitful, and I will make nations of thee, and kings shall come out of thee.

Because of Abraham's successes, God would be willing to create a covenant with Abraham to create kings and nations. But before he could receive the benefits of Statism, painful sacrifices would have to be made, beginning with circumcision, to prove submission and loyalty.

Genesis 17:10 This is my covenant, which ye shall keep, between me and you and thy seed after thee; Every man child among you shall be circumcised. 11. And ye shall circumcise the flesh of your foreskin; and it shall be a token of the covenant betwixt me and you.

Accepting a covenant from the Powers That Be is usually a painful and emasculating experience. The story of the creation of Statism continues. To achieve a loyal following, and regardless of the fact the land belonged to someone else, the Powers That Be promised to give Abraham the land wherever he pitched his tent and to use his progeny to divide the people into nations. These nations would be built on the division of identity politics and would result in a great deal of warfare.

A huge enticement for cooperating with nation building is that a Statist God loves giving, or at least promising, property and prosperity for the "chosen", no matter who it officially belongs to. This method is very effective. As we learned, the covenant of a "promised land" is the same method that would be used in the future by Moses. This temptation is how God brings to power those "whose hand will be against every man, and every man's hand against him".

The artificial creation of political borders often doesn't represent more natural cultural variations, and the desire to expand those political borders to increase their "inheritance" has historically resulted in most excuses for warfare by Statists. Borders are incredibly important, but they should be based upon a common culture and language, and not politically imposed to create division and warfare, or to claim more resources for the State. Once a culture has been established and shown to be successful, then the borders that mark that culture must be protected to prevent further division by The Powers That Be as in Babel. If there can be any chance of creating a successful culture that allows the people to pursue the liberty and happiness of Eden, rather than wars initiated by the God of Statism through political nation building, then cultural borders must exist. There will be more on this subject in the New Testament.

Meanwhile, God has decided the hue and cry coming out of Sodom and Gomorrah because of their subjugation and the refusal of Abraham to return the stolen captives and wealth causes these two cities to be of such evil they must be destroyed.

> **Genesis 18:20 And the Lord said, Because the cry of Sodom and Gomorrah is great, and because their sin is very grievous; 21. I will go down now, and see whether they have done altogether according to the cry of it, which is come unto me; and if not, I will know.**

After inspection, it is determined that sure enough, God sees the necessity of sending angels (who usually weren't very angelic) to wipe them out. You must wonder how these two cities were singled out as being particularly evil and are always mentioned together. There may be a clue in their names, which are Secret (Sodom) {25}, and Rebellious People {Gomorrah) {26}. At any rate, in the end they were both subjected to utter destruction for participating in behavior somehow threatening to the God of Statism.

Before the destruction would take place, Abraham would realize that in addition to the circumcision, there would be another painful sacrifice to make, and that would be with his own conscience. Knowing what is about to happen to the two cities, he urged God to consider there may be innocents involved and negotiated on what number would be acceptable as collateral damage. God and Abraham agreed on the arbitrary number of less than ten by the end of the conversation. The point being, there is always collateral damage when rebellion is on the rise against The Powers That Be. Also, God is often willing to negotiate when someone has the courage to question their own conscience.

Genesis 18:32 And he said, Oh let not the Lord be angry, and I will speak yet but this once: Peradventure ten shall be found there (righteous people)**. And he said, I will not destroy it for ten's sake. 33. And the Lord went his way, as soon as he had left communing with Abraham: and Abraham returned to his place.**

Lot's (which means covering or hidden) {[27]} part in the story was to meet and take in the messengers (again, the definition of angel in Hebrew) who are on the way to mete out the destruction and provide covering for them. The townspeople heard of their arrival and wanted to meet the interlopers lodging with Lot to determine their intentions. Trust of outsiders had understandably become a rare commodity in those towns because of the raiding and betrayals that had taken place.

Lot claimed the innocence of the messengers, but the townspeople said they wanted to judge for themselves. As a bribe, Lot offered up his virgin daughters, but the villagers would have none of it and insisted on meeting the newcomers. However, the

---

[25] http://www.ccel.org/ccel/hitchcock/bible_names.html?term=Sodom

[26] http://www.ccel.org/ccel/hitchcock/bible_names.html?term=Gomorrah

[27] http://www.ccel.org/ccel/hitchcock/bible_names.html?term=Lot

angels blinded the towns people, so they couldn't find the door. This was easy to do, because blinding the people as to their intentions is something the messengers of Statism are particularly good at. So, the angels and Lot and his wife and daughters were able to wait until morning before escaping the city, while the blinded townspeople searched in vain to discover their intentions.

Lot and his two virgin daughters escaped to a small insignificant town called Zoar {[28]} (we know because that's what Zoar means), but his wife looked back and turned into a pillar of salt. The significance of the salt has probably been lost in translation but having second thoughts or turning back from following God's instructions can sometimes have consequences.

Genesis 19:24 Then the Lord rained upon Sodom and Gomorrah brimstone and fire from the Lord out of heaven; 25. And he overthrew those cities, and all the plain, and all the inhabitants of the cities, and that which grew upon the ground. 26. But his wife looked back from behind him, and she became a pillar of salt.

The complaints from those cities were numerous and understandable. That they were at one point very prosperous cities suggests their greatest sin was probably participation in openly free markets and rejecting The God of Statism as represented by Abraham. The inhabitants were related to the Canaanites, so we know they were merchants who believed in free trade. Contrary to popular teachings, the only indication of sexual immorality was with Lot offering up his virgin daughters to protect God's angels.

We know the cries from the city dwellers must have been very vexing to a Statist God because of their secret rebelliousness, which in turn led to their destruction, and is another very common theme throughout the Bible. Whether their secret was their rebelliousness, or the fact all their walls had been made and glued together with flammable bitumen from their tar fields is not known {[29]}.

---

[28] https://www.biblestudytools.com/dictionary/zoar/
[29] http://biblehub.com/topical/b/bitumen-pits.htm

Now it was only Lot and his two daughters left surviving those cities as refugees, but it turns out he didn't need his wife anyway, so he didn't waste any time mourning. The three soon left Zoar to go live in a cave in the mountains. While there, Lot got drunk and slept with both his daughters and they both became pregnant. It must have seemed to the writers that God's chosen spent a lot of time getting "drunk", which to an ancient Hebrew would have been code for wealthy and corrupt. But as for Lot, he would explain it was the girls' fault because they had taken advantage of him and raped him while he was helpless in his drunken stupor.

The little virgin hussies had taken advantage of their drunken father. This atrocity has no doubt been committed against many well-meaning drunks who attempt to sell their children, yet no one ever seems to come to their defense except The Powers That Be. Their progeny would go on to create the Moabites and the Ammonites. These tribes would create new nations and prove useful to God by making war many times with the Israelites.

Do you still think the Jewish ancestors meant the characters in these stories to be heroes or loveable cartoon characters? I think they knew exactly how to make their point through parables demonstrating how what we now refer to as Statism works. This is just one of many examples of the incestuous and warlike nature of Statism.

Meanwhile, God has done lots of favors for Abraham from whom he has chosen to divide the people into separate nation states. In return, God now wanted another show of loyalty, so eventually Abraham was given yet another test to prove himself. He told Abraham to sacrifice Isaac, his only legitimate son at the time, in one of their burnt offering rituals. Abraham gathered up some wood, picked out a good knife, and rode three days to find the appropriate site at God's direction.

Genesis 22:3 And he said, Take now thy son, thine only son Isaac, whom thou lovest, and get thee into the land of Moriah; and offer him there for a burnt offering upon one of the mountains which I will tell thee of.

Abraham dutifully obeyed, but just as Abraham was about to kill Isaac, God stopped his hand because he had proven himself. Abraham had passed the test of Statism for God, because one of the most import aspects of Statism is to have the willingness to sacrifice the next generations to the Statist God in return for favoritism and benefits today. A similar theme would later be expressed in the story of Moses, when he sacrificed a whole generation wandering in a cultural wilderness looking for the "promised land" while turning the next generation into loyal and obedient warriors, many of which would be sacrificed for conquest.

We still sacrifice our children but sacrificing the future of our children is now most commonly achieved through allowing indoctrination into their education, encouraging dependency of all kinds such as through Statist employment and welfare, allowing deficit spending by the State to increase indebtedness which is passed on to later generations, and of course we continue to send them into unnecessary wars. As the writers point out, the willingness to sacrifice our children is necessary for the perpetuation of Statism.

Abraham's son Isaac lived, and went on to have many of the same traits of his father, including introducing his wife as his sister. Again, there was a famine just as in his father's time. Famine always seemed to follow these people. But this time God told him maybe it would be better not to go back to Egypt. After all, Isaac was already well trained in the art of Statism with help from his father.

Genesis 26:2 And the Lord appeared unto him, and said, Go not down into Egypt; dwell in the land which I shall tell thee of: 3. Sojourn in this land, and I will be with thee, and unto thy seed, I will give all these countries, and I will perform the oath which I sware unto Abraham thy father; And I will make thy seed to multiply as the stars of heaven, and will give unto thy seed all these countries; and in thy seed shall all the nations of the earth be blessed;

Again, the usual promise to help in the creation of new Nation States, which would result in more warfare. You would think a benevolent God would instead encourage tribes to come together in cultural cooperation but, as we know, that isn't how Statism works. Like his father, Isaac knows a good opportunity when he sees it, so he did as he was told and went instead to visit Abimelech, the king of the Philistines.

Just as the Egyptians would later with the Israelites, Abimelech decided Isaac's tribe was just a little too prolific for his liking, because their numbers grew enough to present a threat to his own kingdom. Besides, just as the Pharaoh had with Abraham, Abimelech discovered Isaac's sister was really his wife.

> **Genesis 26:8 And it came to pass, when he (Isaac) had been there a long time, that Abimelech king of the Philistines looked out the window, and saw, behold Isaac was sporting with Rebekah his wife. 9. And Abimelech called Isaac, and said, Behold, of a surety she is thy wife: and how saidst thou, She is my sister? And Isaac said unto him, Because I said, Lest I die for her.**

To help understand the stories of Abraham and Isaac and other characters it is helpful to know the authors often used male character names to represent nations, and wives often represent cities, and marriage often denotes possession or ownership of a city by a nation. The political significance of presenting a city as being owned or "married" by the nation as opposed to the availability of a sister city would have meant a sister city could trade openly with other nations, as opposed to a city owned by a nation, which would mean trade would be, at the very least, carefully controlled and taxed through trade tariffs, or maybe even forbidden through sanctions.

A city being presented as available was very profitable and safer in the short term. There were benefits in accepting gifts and bribes to encourage trade, so deceit was preferable. However, trade with a city/wife within a nation could be denied at any point. The deceitful denial or misrepresentation of relationships are still

64

common today among Statists. The whole issue here centers around who gets to control the trade, collect taxes, and subjugate the people.

As a beneficial aside in understanding the meaning of stories of the Old Testament, there are hints of how to be healthy enough to live for a very long time. In addition to eating plenty of fruits and vegetables, you need simply to transform yourself into a political entity. These may include tribes, cities, or whole nations. Once this is achieved, then you too may live hundreds of years just as many of the characters in the bible.

Isaac is important because he had two sons, one of whom would be vital to the main point in their books. Specifically, that would be their defiance against the culture of a Statist God. His two sons were twins named Esau and Jacob, who would represent the birth of two more nations that would, of course, participate in even more warfare. The one born first was Esau {[30]}, whose name in Hebrew means one who lives their lives doing things concerned with daily activities and more mundane practical affairs. Jacob {[31]} means "heeler", as in one who "trips up" others, or a trickster. He was so named because he was born last and was grabbing Esaus' heel at birth. The writers used these characters to further demonstrate their message. There were distinct differences between the two sons.

Genesis 25:27 And the boys grew: and Esau was a cunning hunter, a man of the field; and Jacob was a plain man, dwelling in tents.

Esau was the hardened and practical provider. As the firstborn of the twins, Esau had claim to the birthright of inheritance from his father. However, one day as Esau came in from an unsuccessful hunting trip he was on the verge of starving to death while Jacob had stayed home in the tent cooking the food Esau had already provided. The first trick Jacob played on Esau was to trick him into selling him his birthright for some of the food.

---

[30] https://www.etymonline.com/word/esau
[31] https://www.etymonline.com/word/jacob

Genesis 25:30 And Jacob sod pottage: and Esau came from the field, and he was faint: 30. And Esau said to Jacob, Feed me, I pray thee, with that same red pottage; for I am faint: therefore was his name called Edom. 31: And Jacob said, Sell me this day thy birthright. 32. And Esau said, Behold, I am at the point to die: and what profit shall this birthright do of me? 33. And Jacob said, Swear to me this day; and he sware unto him: and he sold his birthright unto Jacob.

If people are starving, it is easy to take advantage of the situation by stealing their birthright of individuality and freedom. Famine inflicted through economic policies is a very effective tool for Statists and has often been used to deprive the birthright of freedom from citizens.

Jacob's next trick is even more conniving. Their father Isaac, who eventually becomes blind and believes he will soon die, calls for Esau, as the provider of the family, to bring some food to celebrate the blessing (congratulation and praise) of the new status he will pass on to him. However, his mother Rebekah favors Esau's brother Jacob (maybe because he stays home and does the cooking). Together they conspired to steal the blessing by disguising Jacob as Esau. They covered his arms with goat skin so that he would feel like his brother, since Jacob was comparatively soft and smooth. They also put him in Esau's clothing, so he will smell more like his brother. The trick worked. While Esau was still out hunting, Jacob tricked his father into giving him the blessing instead of Esau. Because their ploy had been successful, their mother Rebekah now suspects Esau will try to kill Jacob, so she convinces Isaac to go away to where her brother Laban is living.

The point of their story is twofold. The first being that the God of Statism always favors the schemers and manipulators and those who trip up others as does Jacob. The second point is that it is easy to manipulate those that are overly concerned with day-to-day activities such as feeding oneself and their family as does Esau, with no thought as to the big picture as one goes through life. Eventually, there will be a weak moment where you will be willing to sell your birthright of freedom in return for security from a temporary threat, or because of an isolated tragedy such as a famine or natural disaster. The temporary assistance now becomes a permanent fixture, and there is an accompanying increase in the size and power of the State. Esau had surrendered his birthrights in return for temporary benefits. The Powers That Be are always waiting for an opportunity to gain control at any sign of temporary weakness or need, and even more often through outright trickery and manipulation. It is unfortunate the wisdom of the bible is so often ignored or misunderstood.

The trickery would continue. At his mother's suggestion, Jacob would go to his uncle's house where he would marry two of his cousins. One of them would be married by accident when his mother's brother Laban (his uncle) sneaked his older daughter into the marriage ceremony under a veil. But Jacob still wanted the younger cousin so he ended up with an extra wife. He would have many children with his wives, in addition to his wives' maidservants, so there was a lot of begetting taking place.

Jacob would work for Laban for seven years for each daughter, but there would be ulterior motives and more trickery. Jacob became the herdsman over the livestock owned by Laban and made a deal to keep all the speckled and spotted livestock for himself, and those not so marked would belong to Laban. The ones with the markings made up a percentage that was acceptable to Laban, so he agreed. Knowing a little something about begetting by now, and despite Laban taking away most of the livestock that were already marked, through more trickery Jacob arranged that virtually all livestock would now have the markings through selective breeding, and he soon became wealthy with livestock.

Laban's sons, predictably upset they had lost their inheritance through Jacob's clever breeding program, began to resent Jacob, so God suggested he move back to where his brother lived and take his new wealth and family with him. Jacob left without telling Laban, and so Laban gave chase. However, God would warn Laban not to mess with Jacob, just as God would do with those pursuing Moses, so when he caught up with him he basically had to admit that Jacob had gotten the best of him and returned home. This God always protects the tricksters if they are loyal and will threaten or destroy those who seek recompense. Laban and his sons were left impoverished, and Jacob went on his way with great wealth. His success earned God's approval, so on the way home Jacob has a dream given to him by The Powers That Be.

Genesis 28:12. And he dreamed, and behold a ladder set up on the earth, and the top of it reached to heaven: and behold the angels of God ascending and descending on it. 13. And, behold, the Lord stood above it, and said, I am the Lord God of Abraham thy father, and the God of Isaac: the land whereon thou liest, to thee will I give it, and to thy seed;

And God essentially goes on to make the same Statist promises as always. Then Jacob wakes up.

Genesis 28:16. And Jacob awaked out of his sleep, and he said, Surely the Lord is in this place; and I knew it not. 17. And he was afraid, and said, How dreadful is this place! This is none other but the house of God, and this is the gate of heaven.

But despite his fears and a feeling of dread, he would proclaim his loyalty because he knows the ladder of success offered by a Statist God when he sees it. He was sure the proverbial "promised land" was at the top of the ladder, and at first, he was prepared to accept the benefits.

Genesis 28:20. And Jacob vowed a vow, saying, If God will be with me, and will keep me in this way that I go, and will give me bread to eat, and raiment to put on, 21. So that I come again to my father's house in peace; then shall the Lord be my God:

Just as many still do today, Jacob decided it might be better to depend on the God of Statism to provide him with his basic needs and the security of a steady income. In return, he promised to give a percentage of whatever God gave him. It is very hard to resist

Statist employment where ones' needs are steadily, profitably, and dependably met, while returning only a small percentage.

> **Genesis 28:22 And this stone, which I have set for a pillar, shall be Gods' house: and of all that thou shalt give me I will surely give the tenth unto thee.**

It always pleases the God of Statism to get a percentage on his investment in the form of more political loyalty and more taxes.

The ancients now insert a new lesson to be learned in the next story that could be their most important, which is successful resistance to the God of Statism. As Jacob was returning to the home of his original family, he got into a wrestling match with God. After wrestling all night, they came to a draw, and God let Jacob go after agreeing to bless him.

> **Genesis 32:25 And when he saw that he prevailed not against him, he touched the hollow of his thigh; and the hollow of Jacobs' thigh was out of joint, as he wrestled with him. 26. And he said, Let me go, for the day breaketh. And he said, I will not let thee go, except thou bless me. 27. And he said unto him, What is thy name? And he said Jacob. 28. And he said, Thy name shall be called no more Jacob, but Israel: for as a prince has thou power with God and with men, and has prevailed. 29. And Jacob asked him, and said, Tell me, I pray thee, thy name. And he said, Wherefore is it that thou dost ask after my name? And he blessed him there. 30. And Jacob called the name of the place Peniel {[32]} (which means face of God): for I have seen God face to face, and my life is preserved.**

Jacob would be one of the first to "see the light".

---

[32] https://en.wikipedia.org/wiki/Penuel

Jacob Sees The True Face of God— and Israel is Born

Jacob's name is changed to Israel {33} which means "upright or forthright" in the struggle with God (The Powers that Be). Through wrestling with his conscience, Jacob had now seen the actual face of God and has a great revelation. Jacob had now recognized the God of Statism for who he was, just as Ham before him had seen the truth when he discovered Noah naked and drunk. Obeying his own conscience, Jacob had struggled against God and survived. He had decided not to accept the ladder of success with its many benefits offered by the God of Statism. That lesson has not been lost on the Jewish people even today. Israel is one of the few countries in the world that has still been "passed over" by Statism, and instead has continued to hold its own in the struggle.

That we all struggle with culture is a part of life, and a large part of the struggle historically is with those who want to rule over us. Just as with Jacob, whose wrestling match represents the struggle of the Israelites with the God of Statism, we know from history this struggle has at many times left the Jewish people limping with permanent wounds. Their cultural history will always include memories of the Holocaust because of their ongoing struggles with The Powers That Be. We also know from history there is virtually no society that has not struggled with this God. Most of the population of the world are continuing that battle, and the Israelites in the very beginning were the leader in that struggle, so they have rightfully earned the name "Israel" for their country.

After recognizing God and struggling against him, Jacob/Israel returns home with gifts instead of more trickery and reconciles with his family. Through this incredible parable, this is the first sign that if we struggle with enough determination, the people can at least win equal footing with the Powers That Be in our need for self-determination. Thanks to his ability to hold his own, Jacob would no longer engage in trickery and would now become a

---

33 https://en.wikipedia.org/wiki/Jacob_wrestling_with_the_angel

changed person. However, there would be many more struggles in the future.

Jacob/Israel has reason to believe that when he returns to the home of his family that he will not exactly be welcome. After all, he had deceived his father by pretending to be his brother Esau and had tricked Esau into giving him his birthright of inheritance as he was starving. But since he isn't welcome where he also deceived his father-in-law/uncle, he has a new plan. He has accumulated great wealth and has also begun to create his own tribe with a very large family with his two cousin wives and their maid servants. He sent ahead some of his sons with gifts, which he could now easily afford. As it turns out, Esau had forgiven him anyway, even without the gifts, and for now peace would prevail within the family. The first direct struggle against this God had paid off with a new attitude of reconciliation and generosity by Jacob, which reunited his family. Credit should also be given to his brother Esau's practical and understanding nature. Amazingly, some Statist religious leaders mistakenly teach that we should despise Esau, who was a forgiving victim.

Jacob/Israel would eventually end up in Canaan (which as we know represented merchants operating in free markets) where he would buy some land. As we will see, those struggling with the God of Statism often end up living with the Canaanites. On the other hand, those who cooperate with God were generally at war with the Canaanites.

Jacob/Israel bought some land, instead of stealing it through trickery or plunder, and settled near the city of Shalem, but there would soon be trouble with the natives. One of the princes of king Hamor seduced Dinah, one of the daughters of Jacob. We don't know if it was consensual, or if it might have taken place in the kitchen... (Sorry, I was referring to the song about someone being in the kitchen with....never mind.) The prince, Shechem {34} (which means shoulder, or sense of responsibility), really liked Dinah and

---

34 http://www.abarim-publications.com/Meaning/Shechem.html#.XaIelUZKjIU

71

wanted to marry her. We don't know if the feeling was mutual because in those days what women felt rarely mattered, and still doesn't in many cultures that continue to be culturally Statist.

The king and the prince even agreed to be circumcised and would let Jacob and his family live together with them in their land. They would allow marriages between the sons and daughters of their own tribe with the sons and daughters of Jacob and all would be well. However, two of Jacob's sons, who had taken offense to the fact their sister had relations with Shechem, sneaked into the city as the Canaanites were still healing from the circumcision and killed all the males. This included the king and the groom-to-be prince. This probably threw something of a wet blanket on the relationship between the tribes and says something about accepting painful subjugation from God.

One significant development from this story is that now he has a different attitude that allows him to see the true face of God, Jacob/Israel is genuinely disappointed in the two sons for the murders of the townspeople, so he denies them their birthright. One other son has already lost his birthright because he got caught sporting with one of his dad's concubines. That left the birthright going to the fourth son in line whose name was Judah, from which tribe the Israelites would eventually come to be called Judahites, and then eventually Jews. Credit should be given to these people for never exalting themselves or being given to pretentiousness. They never make excuses or exclude themselves from the lessons of the bible.

At this point, God stepped in and suggested they go to a place called Bethel {35} (which means house of God). The writers have Jacob being reminded his name was now Israel because of his valiant struggle against God, who in turn is still making all the usual tempting promises of free land, fertility, and the division of the people into nations and kingdoms.

In addition to Judah, another of Jacob's sons was Joseph. Joseph had the habit of telling his brothers about his dreams of

35 https://en.wikipedia.org/wiki/Bethel

someday ruling over the other sons who had all lost their birthright, so they conspired to murder him as they were sick of hearing of it. But in the end, at the suggestion of Judah, the brothers decided it would be even better to sell Joseph into slavery in Egypt. The son whose life was saved by Judah participating in a little free market capitalism by selling his brother into slavery instead of killing him was none other than the Joseph that would eventually become an important part of the Egyptian court. He would then accept the Israelites into Egypt to keep them from starving to death during a famine. The famine would lead the Israelites to surrender their birthright of freedom, which would eventually lead to the Moses story. The stories may seem a little tricky at times, but as we will see it will all lead to the same conclusion.

Judah would go on to create his own family, but he tended to have sons that, like their grandfather Jacob, also struggled against the Statist God. Unfortunately, they would often lose the struggle, so God would kill them. The writers have the Jewish struggle with the God of Statism continuing into the next generations of Israel, and it continues to this day.

Genesis 38:7 And Er, Judah's firstborn, was wicked in the sight of the Lord and slew him. 8. And Judah said unto Onan, Go in unto thy brother's wife, and marry her, and raise up seed to thy brother. 9 And Onan knew that the seed should not be his; and it came to pass, when he went in unto his brother's wife, that he spilled it on the ground, lest that he should give seed to his brother. 10. And the thing which he did displeased the Lord: wherefore he slew him also.

The first son already had a wife when God killed him for lack of loyalty, and it was customary for the next brother to take the widow as his wife. The next brother refused to create progeny by his brothers' widow, so God killed him also. Shelah, the next brother in line, wasn't grown yet so Judah told him to go live with his grandfather until he was grown, so maybe God wouldn't kill him too because he was running out of sons.

As luck would have it, it wouldn't be necessary for the next son to have children by his brother's older widow anyway, because on a trip out of town with one of his friends Judah decided a little dalliance might be in order, as his wife had died. He hired a hooker, but which also turned out to be his daughter-in-law. She was the widow of his son which had been killed by God, and who had gone away to live with her own father.

> **Genesis 38:15 When Judah saw her, he thought her to be a harlot; because she had covered her face. 16. And he turned unto her by the way, and said, Go to, I pray thee, let me come in unto thee; (for he knew not that she was his daughter in law.) And she said, What wilt thou give me, that thou mayest come in unto me? 17. And he said, I will send thee a kid from the flock. And she said, Wilt thou give me a pledge, till thou send it?**

So a deal was struck, but he was overly anxious and didn't take the time to remove her veil to see who she actually was. Since that's how his own dad ended up marrying two cousins instead of one, his dad really should have warned him about those darned veils. At any rate, he had twins with his daughter-in-law. At least they managed to keep it in the family.

Keep in mind again that most often in the Old Testament people represent much more than an individual. The daughter-in-law in this case is represented as a whore because that is how God sees a city participating in uncontrolled free market capitalism which is the nemesis of Statism. We saw this same theme in the story of Canaan. The agreement between Judah and the widowed daughter-in-law would have meant Judah was committing the unspeakable act of doing business with a city not under the control of the God of Statism. This would also explain why God had killed the other two sons for their disloyalty.

Meanwhile Joseph, who had been sold into slavery at his brother Judah's suggestion, rather than killing him, was having trouble of his own for not doing enough dallying. The captain of the guard for the Pharaoh, who had purchased Joseph for a slave, had a wife who had been hitting on Joseph when her husband was gone. He had refused to dally, so she falsely accused him anyway for revenge.

> **Genesis 39:12 And she caught him by his garment, saying, Lie with me: and he left his garment in her hand, and fled, and got him out. 13. And it came to pass, when she saw that he had left his garment in her hand, and was fled forth, 14. That she called unto the men of her house, and spake unto them, saying, See, he hath brought in an Hebrew unto us to mock us; he came in unto me to lie with me, and I cried with a loud voice: 15. And it came to pass, when he heard that I lifted up my voice and cried, that he left his garment with me, and fled, and got him out.**

There is no lack of sex, drama, and murder in the Good Book. No doubt the bible still serves as an inspiration for much of our modern literature. I think the writers especially wanted us to know of the intrigues of those who are Statist elites, and how they got where they were. These glimpses inside the families of those favored by God allow the readers to know they were no better than any other social class and were often far worse.

Having been thrown into prison because of the false accusation, Joseph had little to do but while away his time predicting things like how long it would be before the Pharaoh would hang one of his cell mates and the sort. He also got pretty good at things like interpreting dreams, so eventually his reputation reached the Pharaoh, who asked him to interpret some his own dreams. Joseph interpreted some of Pharaohs dreams to mean there would be seven years of famine after seven years of plenty. At this point the Pharaoh was so impressed he took Joseph out of prison and made him his best buddy.

> **Genesis 41:40 Thou shalt be over my house, and according unto thy word shall all my people be ruled: only in the throne will I be greater than thou. 41. And Pharaoh said unto Joseph, See, I have set thee over all the land of Egypt. 42. And Pharaoh took off his ring from his hand, put it upon Joseph's hand, and arrayed**

him in vestures of fine linen, and put a gold chain about his neck; 43. And he made him ruler over all the land of Egypt.

The Pharaoh even gave Joseph one of the high priest's daughters for a wife. All this might seem a little strange at this point because Joseph's predictions still had not come to pass. It would be at least several years before his interpretations of the Pharaoh's dreams could be determined to be accurate, but the point the writers make is still valid.

The point is that once you enter the culture of Statism there are many advantages, which is why it is appealing to so many. So long as you are part of the inner circle of Statism, you end up with riches like gold rings and chains and fine linens at the expense of the rest of the population, and the larger the number of bureaus, departments, and agencies there are, the more inner circles there are to choose from.

In Joseph's case, one of the benefits is that you can invite your families' tribe to come join you when they come for food during a famine. Now we come to understand how Joseph had the influence to allow the Israelites into Egypt. He didn't hold a grudge against his brothers for selling him into slavery because he had done well for himself, and rightly gave the credit to the God of Statism. Being best buddies with a Statist Ultimo like the Pharaoh is a sweet deal. Joseph invited his brothers and the rest of the tribe to live in Egypt to escape the famine where, as we know, they would stay long enough to greatly multiply their number to the point they would eventually become a threat to Egypt, and eventually become unwanted and unwelcome.

We now find the stories have led us back into Egypt, where the Israelites would eventually become a huge problem for the Egyptians, even though they would apparently do jobs the Egyptians wouldn't do. The Egyptians realized too late a foreign insider had brought into their midst an influence of such numbers that they would threaten their own culture, and even their own nation. Joseph would eventually die, but the children of Israel would continue to multiply for generations. The Pharaoh's efforts to prevent the Israelites from taking over his country would result in harsh policies in their attempts to salvage their own culture and would result in the plagues of civil division. One of the desperate measures taken to preserve their own cultural identity would result in Moses being found floating in a basket in the river. This would lead to the greatest story never told of how Statism perpetuates itself through repetitive cycles when Moses creates his own nation as a warlord.

God's Resume

At this point we should take stock of what information the writers of the bible have given us. One way to do this is by identifying the characteristics of God as they are laid out for us in the Old Testament. Here is a list of what we know up till now.

This is a God (The Powers That Be) That:

- Discourages knowing the difference between good and evil, and those who do are ostracized and purged. Yahwists endeavoring to study "the tree of life" would have been particularly annoying and were subjected to a great deal of persecution.

- Creates and uses weapons of mass destruction.

- Separates out the "chosen people" who are given great power in warfare, and usually great wealth, but often wreaks a flood of death, destruction and economic chaos on those not "chosen".

- Is obsessed with taxation and the accumulation of wealth such as gold and silver, and encourages theft by the "chosen", which is justified through elitism.

- Cultural norms are turned into written "Laws", which are passed down from high and inaccessible places, and then "carved into stone". The laws are now untouchable under penalty of death (in ark). The laws are then used by corrupt judges to "witness against the people" when it is convenient to enforce loyalty, instill fear, or to increase dependency.

- Creates a system of punishment consisting of threats, fines, banishment, or death for lack of loyalty.

- Has the same iniquities as man... jealousy, fits of rage, murderous tendencies, greed, etc., for which it gets a pass while dealing out harsh punishments for mere "mortals" (citizens) for the same behavior.

- Allows killing and thievery, but only if you have permission from God.

- Always points to the utopian "promised land" that either doesn't exist or is stolen from others.

- Requires that the people constantly make sacrifices and pay tribute to the elitist insiders who become very wealthy and achieve high status at the expense of the rest of the population.

- Demands loyalty adequate to be willing to sacrifice future generations.

- Promotes nepotism, cronyism, and a strong centralized authority figure.

- Eventually requires a large and elaborate temple to live in, preferably with a large concentration of wealth and ostentation, which cannot be entered except by designated insiders.

- Actively encourages identity politics to divide the people through such methods as job description, birthright, clan, tribe, nation states, class, etc., rather than culture. Once the people are divided politically, they can be turned against each other to impose Statism.

- Actively instigates warfare and genocide, and often targets women and children.

- Creates "manna" that is used to create dependency and is in turn used for economic manipulation such as wealth redistribution to maintain a loyal base of support.

- Protects loyalists, even though they may be criminal in nature.

- Is exalted almost exclusively by those who are authority figures and elitists. These would include warlords, tribal leaders, kings, judges, bureaucrats, high ranking clergy, etc. that benefit directly from Statism.

- Is a direct reflection of a culture we create for ourselves through allowing Statist manipulation to exist, which forces us out of Eden in return for temporary benefits and promises.

We could go on, but I don't think it is necessary. The writers of the bible are describing a Statist political system that has perpetuated itself almost since civilization began, and in virtually every corner of the world. Either that, or the writers are the absolute worst public relations people in history when it comes to promoting a deity.

However, as they point out God is not always Statism. God can come in different forms because The Powers That Be are created by us. It is our culture that allows and most often even encourages Statism to exist because of short term benefits, without thought of future generations. It is the ambitions of a relatively few among us that allows the God of Statism to go on living among us "as a wild man", that divides us and manipulates our culture, so they can rule over us at our expense. Inevitably this leads to cycles of cultural degradation, oppression, warfare, and eventual societal collapse.

The Yahwists are explaining the culture of Statism, just as all culture, comes from within us and will forever create plagues and division until we have the understanding to prevent it. They are warning us and attempting to guide us into a different cultural system not based on craving the temporary benefits of Statism as "chosen" insiders, but into a virtuous culture created by and for all the people that resists God's evil spirit. Creating a culture of Statism banishes us from Eden.

Despite the dangers, Statism will always be very popular to the insiders and to those who believe they are "chosen" but will always be a danger to those not so chosen or favored, and who prefer the freedom of self-determination. The writers recognized how this process happens and describe through parables written in the Bible how the culture of the people is carefully manipulated to benefit the Statist elites. They show how Statism becomes self-perpetuating through cycles that both ends and begins anew in destructive behavior.

The Jewish Yahwists may not have been the first to recognize this but were the first to preserve a warning manual by putting it in writing for future generations in the books of the bible. The Hebrew authors of the time were even instrumental in creating a written language readable by ordinary people through which to pass down this information. The result is that the Jewish people still today are mostly non-Statist. There have been exceptions, such as within the Pharisee and Sadducee clergy that no longer served the people. Self-preservation and the desire for security often trumps virtue.

Even the organization of the Bible is used to make their point. First, you begin with a *Charismatic Leader* who upon obtaining enough followers becomes a *Warlord,* such as Abraham or Moses, whose purpose is to divide the people and turn them against each other. Then the bible continues into the stories where a warlord society often evolves into a larger bureaucracy with many laws and *Judges*. Then someone suggests what you really need are *Kings*. The State continues to grow more powerful through an ever-larger bureaucracy in response to the desire for people to seek security and benefits. You eventually have *Massive Bureaucratic Leviathan* run by a Pharaoh or a Roman Emperor made up of loyal followers that will do whatever they have to do to retain "chosen" status to assure wealth, job security, and power for themselves. Invariably, they now also have the support and protection of armies and bureaucratic Cherubim that are willing to be dependent on the State in exchange for a clear ladder to success, such as witnessed by Jacob.

Once Statism is fully established, new charismatic leaders arise and use the opportunity to break away to create even more nation states, or divide the nation itself, and the cycle begins again. Such is the organization of the bible, and such is the organization of the history of man and our relationship with the God of Statism.

In the end they suggest the obvious solution, which is We the People. Their teachings would eventually lead to the concept of a republic (not to be confused with the Republican party, many of whom do not believe in republicanism), which is representative government, and in which the people are able to claim certain inalienable rights that cannot be taken away by kings and dictators. Unfortunately, the temptations of the Power of Statism is such that the survival of such republics, even when achieved, are still not guaranteed to survive against the vengeful God, and republicanism has been defeated many times. Greece was once a republic and was defeated by Statism. Even the Roman Empire was once a republic, but also was replaced by Statism. Modern day republics are still under siege and are now often republics in name only. The Statist God is still winning through the same tactics described and warned about in the bible. If only we could heed their warnings!

In fact, the experiences of the writers of the bible would not be so different today in many parts of the world. There is nothing the God of Statism did in the Old Testament that has not recently been in the news in some part of the modern world. Political correctness, fear of the Powers That Be, financial insecurity which encourages dependency, and propaganda to influence and manipulate the culture of the population is always a huge part of Statist Culture and continues even today.

It also continues that anyone being politically incorrect by voicing opposition is seen as a threat. Any threat is subject to being purged and vilified, and mob mentality is still encouraged. Criticism against the State (The Powers that Be) often is not even allowed in many cases, because debate and open thinking and "the tree of knowledge of good and evil" is the first enemy of Statism and is one of the first things singled out for attack in the bible by this God. Even today, in the most Statist of societies around the world, open opposition is often illegal, just as in the bible stories.

The writers of the bible were very familiar with the issues of Statism, and their stories are still very relevant because "The Powers that Be" under which they labored to write the books are still hard at work. Will the Powers That Be even break down the Republic of the United States into smaller nation states, and turn us against each other as in the bible? The process is ongoing. It was already attempted once and resulted in the Civil War. The only solution is to struggle against the God of Statism as did

Jacob/Israel. Once achieved, it becomes our responsibility to protect a culture that rejects Statism.

Had the writers been allowed the freedom to write openly, the bible might possibly have been written as something similar to the United States Constitution, instead of parables warning of an oppressive god. The bible is the story of why we need a system of representation that opposes the God of Statism.

Many of the Islamic countries today are examples of contemporary victims of a Statist God that persecutes anyone not following the tenets of those in power. Their God is still a jealous and vengeful Statist God, and the turmoil, oppression, and suffering in this part of the world are examples of what life was like when the Old Testament was being written. We see through their troubles how difficult it is to openly promote the concept of individual freedom and collective cultural cooperation in these regions. Their prisons remain full of political prisoners, and their executions and wars are many. This has been more common than not in most societies throughout history. The fear of God is still being used by their elitists to force their version of culture onto others by telling their own "chosen" people that others are inferior and are a threat that must be slaughtered. This is a necessary part of assuring the authorities remain in power, and to continue to expand their influence to retain their positions of privilege. For these regions, the existence of a Statist God assures continued banishment from Eden and guarantees continued social turmoil. It is this type of culture that continues to be dominant not just in the Middle East, but many areas around the world. The public warning message of the bible is still being ignored.

It is ironic the Islamic religions of the Middle East originate from writings in the Koran, which were in turn derived from the original bible, whose very purpose is to warn of the cultural phenomenon of Statism. That message has been ignored, and because of religious and political Statism, the land capable of producing philosophers, mathematicians, linguists, astronomers, and the like now produce mostly warfare, terrorism, and refugees, just as when the bible was being written.

That many of the people in these regions want to find a better way and are expressing that desire through rebellion against their leadership, and through migration, is a testament to true human nature. Despite the fear and endemic propaganda, they still have an instinctive desire to determine the course of their own lives. Unfortunately, some of them are still ideological victims of their Statist version of religion and politics, and use their hatred, frustration, and confusion to plague other cultures by becoming terrorists, just as happened so often in the bible. They victimize others, but we should remember they are the first victims, just as were the young people who followed Joshua into Canaan, and the young people who followed Hitler to become Nazis in Germany. Whether the "promised land" is a Reich, a Caliphate, or simply a lifetime of security at the expense of the taxpayers, it is still the same monotheistic God.

The God of Statism Claims His "Inheritance"

Let's continue to follow the stories in the bible. We have gone back to the beginning and have now been brought back up to date where we left off at the time of Moses and Aaron, who have died never having enjoyed the utopia to which they were leading their people. To this day, there has never been a single charismatic leader of any kind in history that gains power by telling his people of a utopian "promised land" whose followers have lived to see it, and the bible emphasizes this point.

Still, unlike the previous generation, dependency and the fear of God has been instilled in this next generation since childhood, so they will obey when told to go to war. They will do this even though it is already known that most wealth will be confiscated and placed in the hands of those most chosen.

> **Numbers 3:44 And the Lord spake unto Moses saying, 45. Take the Levites instead of all the firstborn among the children of Israel, and the cattle of the Levites instead of their cattle; and the Levites shall be mine: I am the Lord. 46. And for those that are to be redeemed of the two hundred and threescore and thirteen of the firstborn of the children of Israel, which are more than the Levites; 47. Thou shalt even take five shekels apiece by the poll, after the shekel of the sanctuary shalt thou take them: (the shekel is twenty gerahs:) 48. And thou shalt give the money, wherewith the odd number of them is to be redeemed, unto Aaron and his sons. 49. And Moses took the redemption money of them that were over and above them that were redeemed by the Levites: 50. Of the firstborn of the children of Israel took he the money; a thousand three hundred and threescore and five shekels, after the shekel of the sanctuary: 51. And Moses gave the money of them that were redeemed unto Aaron and to his sons, according to the word of the Lord, as the Lord commanded Moses.**

I suppose the rest of the population should appreciate that the Powers That Be would no longer charge the price of their actual firstborn children and cattle above the number owned by the Levites but would instead accept redemption cash. Also, the cash from the population that exceeded the amount of tax collected by Levites would now be transferred to them. As God's employees, who are clearly the most chosen, they are allowed benefits not available to mere citizens. Once the general population has been suitably oppressed, impoverished, and demoralized, then becoming a Statist to become more "chosen" starts looking pretty good, and so the process of cultural decline continues as more and more of the population seek to be a chosen insider. A culture of individuality and self-determination so necessary for the existence of a successful culture suffers as a result, and there is now a new kind of poverty, which is a poverty of virtue.

We can continue with the invasion of Canaan. After forty years, nearly all the original followers of Moses were dead, as they had spent much of their lives wandering and warring against various other tribes. But no matter, there is a new generation who are now not so stiff-necked and have grown up being totally dependent on and fearful of God. They apparently have good reason to be fearful, because before beginning the reign of terror on the Canaanites, God warns them...

Joshua 1: 18 Whosoever he be that doth rebel against thy commandment and will not hearken unto thy words in all that thou commandest of him, he shall be put to death: only be strong and of a good courage.

With indoctrination and fear of god in full effect, the preparations for terror can now begin. Joshua sent some spies into the city of Jericho, which is their first target. Not surprisingly, since the writers made their point in clever ways, they decided to stay in the home of a hooker named Rahab. She assured the spies that the population of the city were in fact fearful of the Israelites, because just as Sodom and Gomorrah, they had been weakened by recent raids and warfare, and it should be no problem to defeat the city.

Just as for Lot in earlier times, in return for aiding and abetting the spies, the hooker and her family were promised protection from the mayhem about to fall upon Jericho. The spies returned to Joshua with the news, and the army was made ready.

Joshua 4:13. About forty thousand prepared for war passed over before the Lord unto battle, to the plains of Jericho.

But now the Israelites also had a new incentive to succeed in battle, in addition to God's previous threats.

Joshua 5:12 And the manna ceased on the morrow after they had eaten of the grain of the land; neither had the children of Israel manna any more; but they did eat of the fruit of the land of Canaan that year.

The free manna had served its purpose to create dependency and loyalty with this generation and besides, to Statists the fruits of other people's productivity always taste the best. But the battle would not be allowed to begin until this new generation of Israel had confirmed their loyalty through their own circumcision, which had not taken place yet.

Bringing Down the Walls of Resistance

There is a very fascinating story attached to Joshua's attack on Jericho. We've all heard the story of how the trumpets of ram's horns, done exactly according to direction from God, brought down the walls of Jericho.

> **Joshua 6:8 And it came to pass, when Joshua had spoken unto the people, that the seven priests bearing the seven trumpets of rams' horns passed on before the Lord, and blew with the trumpets: and the ark of the covenant of the Lord followed them. 9. And the armed men went before the priests that blew with the trumpets, and the rereward came after the ark, the priests going on, and blowing with the trumpets. 10. And Joshua had commanded the people, saying, Ye shall not shout, nor make any noise with your voice, neither shall any word proceed out of your mouth, until the day I bid you shout; then shall ye shout.**

The reason they had ram's horns is because they were used for communication purposes. The ram's horns were the only method of mass communication available at the time, and were used to summon gatherings, broadcast messages, and provide direction. The story is that they would march around the city and blow the horns exactly in unison in the same manner each day as directed by God, until a given signal when they would all shout together.

This story is incredibly prophetic, because this is exactly how messages are still spread today through what we now refer to as the media. The media, such as newspapers, network news on TV and the like, have replaced ram's horns but serve the same purpose. At regular intervals, an agreed-upon message is promulgated through various Statist propaganda outlets with a carefully controlled and unified messaging process until everyone is of the same mind. We can then all shout the same narrative together on cue. This is especially useful when used against political opponents, such as represented by Jericho.

The number of walls of resistance brought down with this method is probably incalculable and is still used effectively in every Statist society even today. Narrative control through the media could even be considered another weapon of mass destruction. You can say it is a stretch to compare their methods with propaganda style media campaigns, but the similarities cannot be ignored, and bringing down walls of resistance through creating fear, doubt, and hysteria to defeat the enemy is the goal in both cases. Either those writing the bible already knew how this took place, or else they predicted it with uncanny accuracy. The use of unified messaging to control the narrative would be used more than once in the bible to route the enemy and is still a common feature of Statism. The method worked then just as it does now, and the walls of resistance came tumbling down.

> **Joshua 6:19 But all the silver, and gold, and vessels of brass and iron, are consecrated unto the Lord: they shall come into the treasury of the Lord.**

Unfortunately for the general population, God already had dibs on the most valuable items, as the invading army was informed ahead of time. Nevertheless, the invasion was successful.

> **Joshua 6:21. And they utterly destroyed all that was in the city, both man and woman, young and old, and ox, and sheep, and ass, with the edge of the sword.**

It seems the women, the children, and animals usually didn't fare well from these terror attacks instigated by God. They would all usually be put to the sword on general principles, but at least the hooker who betrayed her merchant neighbors by protecting the spies was saved, along with her family. One individual had the gall to take some of the stolen wealth home for himself and his own family but was discovered.

> **Joshua 7:23. And Joshua, and all Israel with him, took Achan the son of of Zerah, and the silver, and the garment, and the wedge of gold, and his son, and his daughters, and his oxen, and his asses, and his sheep, and his tent, and all that he had: and they brought**

them unto the valley of Achor. 25. And Joshua said, Why hast thou troubled us? The Lord shall trouble thee this day. And all Israel stoned him with stones, and burned them with fire, after they had stoned them with stones.

Economic terror is just as important as physical terror, so you just don't mess with God and his warlord by stealing the wealth they had just stolen after a successful day of slaughtering. Once again, the elitists seeking control would encourage mob mentality. The smiting and genocide against the Canaanites would continue until most of the tribes of Israel had received their "inheritance" which The Powers That Be had encouraged the Israelites to steal. Eventually Joshua became too old to keep it up. He finally died before the job was done because, again, you can do just so much slaughtering in one lifetime. After that, the job would fall to Judah.

Judah Changes the Paradigm

Unfortunately for the Powers That Be, Judah just didn't have the knack for genocide the way Joshua and Moses had, so after some initial success things began to change for this God. Rather than continue the wave of terrorism, Judah began to allow some of the other tribes to survive, and the Israelites sometimes even chose to live among them. This is how they eventually became intermingled with the Canaanites. This was a huge annoyance to God, because other tribes had their own culture, and their own versions of God, many of which encouraged the freedom and self-determination of open markets. Under Judah, the Israelites began to experiment with different types of cultures and politics. They attempted to move away from a terrorist warlord society and into something different. These first attempts did not go well because of God's resistance to that trend.

> **Judges 2:14 And the anger of the Lord was hot against Israel, and he delivered them into the hands of spoilers that spoiled them, and he sold them into the hands of their enemies round about, so that they could not any longer stand before their enemies. 15. Whithersoever they went out, the hand of the Lord was against them for evil, as the Lord had said, and as the Lord had sworn unto them: and they were greatly distressed. 16. Nevertheless the Lord raised up judges, which delivered them out of the hand of those that spoiled them.**

Just as in Babel, God once again punished and scattered the Israelites to prevent them from living peacefully among themselves and their neighbors. However, thanks to stiff-necked Judah and his attempts to change the nature of God's relationship with the people, this is where the experiment with Judges begins. This was initially a source of great distress to God, but he quickly took credit for the judges, and soon found the judges would be just as useful in promoting his agenda as were the warlords.

There would be many times throughout history that Statist Gods would sell out the people of their own countries, just as in the bible. This too is still happening today. If foreigners are more likely to maintain the Powers That Be within the State because of the independent nature and rebelliousness of the original citizens, then selling out their own population is one solution. It can be useful to import people who are more likely to be loyal, usually in exchange for offering benefits such as welfare assistance at the expense of the current residents. Also, you can banish, subjugate, or simply impoverish those current citizens not seen as loyal to purge their rebellious influence, even as they are being replaced with new demographics. These tactics are often used by God in the Old Testament, so this type of cultural manipulation is also nothing new.

What Judah discovered is that just because they attempt to shed their own conquering warlord society, that doesn't mean others have done the same. Disbanding their armies and moving towards living peacefully among other cultures now means they are susceptible to invasion from tribes still victimized by Statism. There follows a series of times that they would be conquered, become servile to other kings, followed by revolt and returning peace, only to be made submissive again to the next conqueror.

These early attempts at a true civilization would be hampered repeatedly by surrounding Statist societies that did not live by the same standards. This is still true of all peace-loving societies. Despite constant negotiations, freedom-loving societies are still under constant attack by the God of Statism and if history is any indication, then The Powers That Be will continue to win more often than not and self-determination will most often lose. The message is that we can stop the cycles, but only if we are willing to work to prevent it. Nevertheless, the experiments by the people to gain peace through having a cultural mediator and negotiator, rather than a warlord, had some initial success. In response, God adapted by working through the judges as he did with warlords, which quickly led to corrupt judges. As predicted, it is often Judges who are the first to become corrupt.

Judges 3:18 And when the Lord raised them up judges, then the Lord was with the judge, and delivered them out of the hand of their enemies all the days of the judge. For it repented the Lord because of their groanings by reason of them that oppressed them and vexed them.

Inevitably, the judges would soon be the new face of Statism because, as it says, the Lord was with the judges—not the people. Each time they would begin a peaceful period of existence, they would begin to no longer be dependent on the God of Statism, which would make him angry again. The people would become "evil in the sight of the Lord", so God would repeatedly use warfare to retain the influence of the Powers That Be.

Being "evil in the sight of the Lord" meant the Israelites tried other forms of Statism that existed in other cultures. Replacing one kind of Statism for another never works and has been tried without success throughout history. The bible warns of the dangers of worshiping other people's Gods with good reason. Failed kings, czars, or dictators have often been removed, only for the experiment to fail again with their replacements, who also often promise a land of milk and honey. This process would eventually result in many political "isms".

Thanks to the bible, we now know to beware of all plans accompanied by the lure of a "promised land". Following a leader always leads to a Statist society, which then requires a heavy-handed State bureaucracy to maintain because of the persistence of top down culture. Many are still paying a high price for that mistake. The Israelites discovered this early on. They were learning the hard way that a truly successful God is when the Powers that Be are the people themselves which requires representatives, not "exalted" leaders.

Thanks to Judah, the most promising development during this time is that some "judges" would at least assume an overall attitude of defense and reprisal, rather than outright conquering and terrorism as their culture had dictated up to this point. Outwardly, little would change because so long as there is a single nation on earth that is controlled by Statism, all other nations have no choice but to maintain their own defense against attacks.

The authors would also make their point by writing stories that show, as with all types of Statist leadership, judges would be susceptible to corruption, greed, and other iniquities. There is a long series of judges with varying degrees of success, but the writers would use many of them as examples of corruption, and some judges often resorted to the same open hostility towards others as the warlords before them. True civilization would have to wait, and to a large degree we are still waiting.

That the judges could be used by God to perpetuate war just as well as warlords would be demonstrated in their parables. One of the judges, called Gideon, provides an abject lesson in Statist manipulation. Once again, the Israelites had been sold out by God as punishment for their iniquities, and had been conquered by their enemies...

Judges 6:1 And the children of Israel did evil in the sight of the Lord: and the Lord delivered them into the hand of Midian seven years.

It appears Midian finally took revenge for the slaughter that took place under Moses. After doing some suffering and slavery at the hands of the people they had been sold out to, God chose a new surrogate insider called Gideon to begin another cycle of war and division to rebuild the State he had destroyed.

Judges 6:12 And the angel of the Lord appeared unto him, and said unto him, The Lord is with thee, thou mighty man of valor. 13. And Gideon said unto him, Oh my Lord, if the Lord be with us, why then has all this befallen us? And where be all his miracles which our fathers told us of, saying Did not the Lord bring us up from Egypt? But now the Lord has forsaken us, and delivered us into the hands of the Midianites. (16. And the Lord said unto him, Surely I will be with thee, and thou shalt smite the Midianites as one man.)

Never mind about the failed promises of the past, and no one even mentions the original "promised land" anymore. However, this is a God who is always willing to return with more promises when there is a war to be fought and there are loyal followers to be gained. War is always a useful tool when the loyalty of the citizens is in question. You need to keep people busy, otherwise they might go around checking out other Gods. The writers show how easy it is for a Statist God to become reestablished through the parable of Gideon. God demonstrates his power by limiting the number of participants in promoting the next war.

> **Judges 7:2 And the Lord said unto Gideon, the people that are with thee are too many for me to give the Midianites into their hands, lest Israel vaunt themselves against me, saying, Mine own hand has saved me.**

You never want the people, especially the Israelites, giving credit to themselves. Instead, you want the propaganda value of crediting the insiders of The Powers that Be, so most of the army was sent home. But God still had a point to make, so there was another test to further limit the number of warriors.

> **Judges 7:5 So he brought down the people unto the water: and the Lord said unto Gideon, Every one that lappeth of the water with his tongue, as a dog lappeth, him shalt thou set by himself; likewise every one that boweth down upon his knees to drink. 6. And the number of that lapped, putting their hand to their mouth, were three hundred men: but all the rest of the people bowed down upon their knees to drink water. 7. And the Lord said unto Gideon, By the three hundred men that lapped will I save you, and deliver the Midianites into thine hand: and let all the other people go every man unto his place.**

God would show Gideon it was not necessary to have large armies to begin a new cycle of Statism. Here the writers make the point with surprising irony that all a Statist needs to regain power is a small inside group of loyal lapdogs to start the next conflict.

Gideon and the three hundred surrounded the enemy camp and used the same method as Joshua with the coordinated messaging, represented once again through trumpet blasts and coordinated shouting to send the enemy running as they were being slaughtered. The rest of the Israelites then happily joined in the chase.

Most will be willing participants when there is plunder at stake and victory appears certain. However, a few of the Israelites were reluctant to contribute to the cause once war did break out, so were burnt to death or put to the sword. Fear instilled in those not inclined to voluntarily contribute resources or participate in mob mentality is always a trademark of a Statist God.

Nevertheless, peace prevailed for a time which once again caused the stiff-necked Israelites to forget about the God of Statism, and which of course caused them to become evil again in the sight of the Lord. God (The Powers that Be) being the culprit for frequent wars is portrayed in a different way by the writers through the story of one of the most famous judges called Samson. This is another story of strength obtained through the backing of the State, and even tops the last story by showing how easy it is to start another war using a single individual. This war would be against the Philistines {[36]}.

Samson was a "judge" given great strength and power so God could make a comeback among the stubborn Israelites. Upon becoming an adult, Samson asked his parents to obtain a Philistine woman for him to marry, even though they were not friendly towards the Israelites. The parents were understandably upset because cultural preservation is especially important among tribal communities.

Judges 14:3 Then his father and his mother said unto him, Is there never a woman among the daughters of thy brethren, or among all my people, that thou goest to take a wife of the uncircumcised Philistines? And Samson said unto his father, Get her for me; for she

[36] https://en.wikipedia.org/wiki/Philistines

pleaseth me well. 4. *But his father and his mother knew not that it was of the Lord, that he sought an occasion against the Philistines:* **for at that time the Philistines had dominion over Israel.**

God needed another war, and Samson would be the tool. Although often wrongly depicted as a hero, or even a victim himself, Samson was a Statist subversive who would serve to start the next conflict. Samson was made to be a Nazarite from birth by his parents, which meant he would be totally indoctrinated to be a devoted tool for the God of Statism. He was subject to a vow of loyalty, so couldn't do things like drink alcohol, have anything to do with dead bodies, or cut his hair. Women, on the other hand, would be his weakness, and the catalyst for war on more than one occasion. His first wife, taken over protests from his parents was a Philistine which, out of loyalty to her own clan, promptly betrayed him by leaking the answer to a riddle he had made up at his wedding.

Calculated information leaks are a great method of promoting a Statist agenda, which in most cases is to create conflict and division when there is too much peace going on. God knew the leak of information would provide Samson with a good excuse for him to serve his purpose. The leak obligated Samson to make good on a boastful bet he had made over thirty sheets and thirty garments, which he would have to pay if the Philistines could solve the riddle. Somehow, they knew the answer. Samson knew they could not have known the answer without help from his wife, who had secretly leaked the information to embarrass him. Just as with many intelligence leaks today, it was all part of God's plan.

Judges 14:18 ...And he said unto them, If ye had not plowed with my heifer, ye had not found out my riddle.

Samson was very angry because of his big mouthed heifer, so he made good on his bet by going into a Philistine town and killing thirty men, stealing their garments, and then using the spoils to pay off the bet to the other Philistines. Samson was, after all, a man of honor that paid his debts. The writers again make the point that

Statists always resort to thievery to pay their debts. This is usually done in the form of taxation and can sometimes be used as an excuse for dividing the people and promoting conflict, as between Cain and Abel.

He then went back to claim his wife but his father-in-law, assuming he no longer wanted her and knowing of Samson's volatile personality, had given her back to another Philistine. Samson responded by tying a bunch of foxes together by their tails with torches between them and turned them lose to burn the crops and vineyards of the Philistines. We can assume burning the crops was successful judging by their response. There is no word on the foxes.

The Philistines, knowing Samson was deliberately attempting to start another war, and knowing he was backed by the Powers That Be, tried to make amends to Samson by burning his father-in-law and wife to death. That may have helped assuage Samson's offended sensibilities some, but he still wasn't satisfied because his express purpose was to claim to be triggered to start a war. No matter how extreme your efforts, trying to placate Statist subversives by pandering to them never works, and simply leads to even more extreme efforts on their part. Just as Samson, they often falsely claim to be the victim.

> **Judges 15:7 And Samson said unto them, Though ye have done this, yet will I be avenged of you, and after that will I cease. 8. And he smote them hip and thigh with a great slaughter: and he went down and dwelt in the top of the rock Etam.**

God's ploy to create war would be successful, and Samson did a lot of smiting. Deciding the terrorism of having their citizens murdered and their crops burned was a little too much, the Philistines determined a larger war might now be appropriate despite their reluctance and began gathering against the Israelites. But the Israelites, knowing they were outnumbered and not being anxious for another war anyway, wanted to turn Samson over to the Philistines to prevent the escalation of hostilities. After promising they wouldn't kill Samson, he allowed them to tie him up and be delivered over to the Philistine neighbors. Once he was in their hands, he got lose.

> **Judges 15:15 And he found a jawbone of an ass, and put forth his hand and took it, and slew a thousand men therewith. 16. And Samson said, With the jawbone of an ass, heaps upon heaps, with the jaw of an ass have I slain a thousand men.**

This is another example of the writers using irony in their message and is also another example of God creating a weapon of mass destruction. There have probably been at least as many deaths caused by the jawbones of asses than by any other weapon in history. Just as in their story, the jawbone of a single ass, if used effectively by a Statist God, is a weapon of mass destruction even more dangerous than God's other invention—the sword.

Now we know why the riddle had to do with the sweetness of honey he found within the carcass of a lion he had torn apart. The writers almost always represent the general population as a lion, and Samson's purpose was to rip them apart through creating conflict. Successfully tearing apart the lion was sweet to Samson because that was his mission.

There is another episode where Samson was almost trapped and ambushed while patronizing a hooker but escaped by moving the gate and confusing the enemy, much as Lot and the angels had done in Sodom. If you fear your enemies are onto you, it helps to have the strength to move the goalposts, or in this case the "gate". But the most notorious story is with his new lady friend—Delilah. Being very resentful against Samson, the Philistines now worked behind his back again with the new woman who, after much badgering, learned his strength came from being in God's employment as a Nazarite, which included the vow of not cutting his hair. Learning this led to his getting a haircut as he slept, which broke his link with God because of his vow. Through Delilah's deceit, this led him to being captured again by the Philistines. Seeing he had lost the protection of God, the Philistines used the opportunity to blind him, and then sent him to prison because of his terrorism. Eventually his hair grew back, so his vow to God became valid again.

Judges 16:28 And Samson called unto the Lord, and said, O Lord God, remember me, I pray thee, and strengthen me, I pray thee, only this once, O God, that I may be at once avenged of the Philistines for my two eyes.

Once again, he became strong with the favor of God through his blind loyalty, and he destroyed the Philistine temple by pulling the pillars down and collapsing the roof, killing himself and about three thousand men and women as a suicide terrorist.

The point here is that having the backing of a Statist God has its advantages when you want to be strong enough to do things like killing people and starting wars and maintaining job security, but that strength can disappear if the covenant is broken. In a Statist culture, the chosen often acquire great power, but live with the fear of losing their strength of status and security by having their connection broken from the State.

Only with a vow of dedication and blind loyalty, and the avoidance of breaking the covenant, can that strength be maintained. For some in extremely Statist societies it becomes preferable to die than to risk breaking the contract, and to prove loyalty they often will take those considered enemies with them in death and is the principle behind most suicide terrorist attacks. Samson had served his purpose to God as a subversive terrorist. Another three thousand people in New York City would later die of a similar terrorist suicide attack bringing down the Twin Towers. Those deaths would be the result of the jawbone of another ass called Bin Laden.

Other judges would follow, almost all of which would result in more war, more corruption, murders, intrigue, etc. Before the experiment of rule by Judges ends, there is another story that is a reversal of the usual story of Israelites being "evil in the sight of the Lord" by adopting other people's Gods. Instead, this would be the reverse story of their God being unknowingly adopted by

100

others. It is both sad, but again somewhat ironic, in the way the story is depicted by the writers. It is a story which involves Eli, the judge presiding at the time, and Samuel the prophet.

Eli has brought disfavor from the people by passing his Judgeship down to sons that were not loyal to God. Along with their disloyalty, they were also unpopular to the people because they were openly corrupt, which is always an unfortunate side effect of nepotism with progeny raised in privilege. But thanks to God, the war with the Philistines continues, so once again the Israelites appeal to their God by bringing out the Ark of the Covenant, originally built by Moses the Statist, to help with the war effort. However, God feels the need to punish the Israelites because of their disloyalty to Eli's corrupt sons. There is discontent among the stiff-necked Israelites so as punishment God allows the Israelites to lose two major battles, resulting in the deaths of thirty-four thousand Israelites in two separate battles. God must sometimes find it exhausting at the necessity of having to mete out so much death and destruction on his own people to keep them distracted from the real problem, which is himself. During one battle...

I Samuel 4:10 And the Philistines fought, and Israel was smitten, and they fled every man into this tent: and there was a very great slaughter; for there fell of Israel thirty thousand footmen. 11. And the ark of God was taken; and the two sons of Eli, Hophni and Phinehas, were slain.

During the battles, Eli's two sons are killed, and the Ark of the Covenant is taken by the Philistines. When Eli, who was elderly and had grown fat serving God, learned of these calamities, he fell and broke his neck, and died also. Had he lived, he may have lamented the loss of his two corrupt sons, but he needn't have been concerned about the Ark, as it would soon be returned.

The importance of this story centers around the Philistine's new-found ownership of the Ark. They took the Ark to their city of Ashdod and brought it into the house of Dagon, their own God, which then fell and was broken. This signified they gave up Dagon to make a covenant with this new God, but as they would soon find, the Ark of the Covenant wouldn't work well for them and brought plagues to them just as it had for the Israelites.

> **Samuel 5:6 But the hand of the Lord was heavy upon them of Ashdod, and he destroyed them, and smote them with emerods, even Ashdod and the coasts thereof. 7. And when the men of Ashdod saw it was so, they said, The ark of the God of Israel shall not abide with us: for his hand is sore upon us, and upon Dagon our god.**

The people of Ashdod realized the mistake of giving up their own God and decided to pass the Ark off to other cities to get rid of it, but it plagued them as well. At this point they were wishing they had just kept the God they had.

> **I Samuel 5:9 And it was so, that, after they had carried it about, the hand of the Lord was against the city with a very great destruction: and he smote the men of the city, both small and great, and they had emerods in their secret parts.**

It should be noted that "emerods" are hemorrhoids, so the Ark with its laws carved into stone, and manna used to create a covenant of dependency, was literally a pain in their "secret parts". I'm willing to bet the writers got in a few chuckles as they wrote this story.

As the new owners of the ark, they knew they had to get rid of the thing before it destroyed them all. So, they packed in some gifts consisting of gold reproductions of their hemorrhoids and the mice that had plagued their crops as a bribe to the Israelites if they would just please take it back. They put it on a cart pulled by oxen, so when it arrived in Bethshemesh the Israelites celebrated by sacrificing the oxen and made a barbecue with the wood of the cart. Unfortunately, the Levites opened the Ark to celebrate, and victoriously displayed the golden ornaments to the people, which must have brought much laughter, but which greatly angered God.

I Samuel 6:19 And he smote the men of Bethshemesh, because they had looked into the ark of the Lord, even he smote of the people fifty thousand and threescore and ten men: and the people lamented, because the Lord had smitten many of the people with a great slaughter.

God's ark is back, but don't think for one moment you can violate protocol by openly revealing the purpose of the contents. The manna and laws carved into stone protected in the Ark are the tools of God's power over the people and is untouchable and cannot be questioned or ridiculed without some smiting and slaughter. Besides, a sense of humor is very much discouraged in any Statist society. If you are not currently either smiting or being smitten you must believe you soon will be, and so must live in constant fear of God and forego humor. The writers make it clear it was just as unfortunate for the Israelites that the ark was returned, as it was for those who had tried to adopt it.

We Want a King!

We now have another judge called Samuel who, just as Samson, had also been indoctrinated from childhood, and would help God lead his people into more warfare, would win some battles, and for then for a while peace would return. Unfortunately, just as Eli before him, he would eventually grow old and once again his sons would also be corrupt. Nepotism has always been a bad aspect of Statism, and the resulting corruption has resulted in the failure of many States and the suffering of many people.

> **I Samuel 8:3 And his sons walked not in his ways, but turned aside after lucre, and took bribes, and perverted judgment.**

The repeated corruption, and the nepotism of a parade of Statist judges handing down power to their progeny, would lead to the next social experiment. Deciding this whole judge thing just wasn't working out, the people of Israel decided to try something else. The people determined to find themselves a king, which was becoming all the rage because all the neighbors were being ruled by them at the time. Some of them weren't so bad, and many were good Statist warriors who led the people into successful battles, especially against the Israelites when God felt the need to punish them. Samuel was disappointed his sons were being rejected, so he told the people what the result would be if they insisted on having a king.

> **I Samuel 8:11 And he said, This will be the manner of the king that shall reign over you: He will take your sons, and appoint them for himself, for his chariots, and to be his horsemen; and some shall run before the chariots. 12. And he will appoint him captains over thousands, and captains over fifties; and will set them to ear his ground, and to reap his harvest, and to make his instruments of war, and instruments of his chariots. 13. And he will take your daughters to be confectionaries, and be cooks, and to be bakers.**

14. And he will take your fields and your vineyards, and your oliveyards, even the best of them and give them to his servants. **15.** And he will take the tenth of your seed, and of your vineyards, and give to his officers, and to his servants. **16.** And he will take your menservants, and your maidservants, and your goodliest young men, and your asses, and put them to his work. **17.** He will take the tenth of your sheep: and ye shall be his servants. **18.** And ye shall cry out in that day because of your king which ye shall have chosen you: and the Lord will not hear you in that day. **19.** Nevertheless the people refused to obey the voice of Samuel: and they said, Nay; but we will have a king over us; **20.** That we also may be like all the nations; and that our king may judge us, and go out before us, and fight our battles.

The story of Samuel gave the writers the perfect opportunity to openly describe Statism as they knew it. Nevertheless, in their desperation the people apparently believed their odds would be better if they could at least choose their own king, rather than accepting the nepotism of the corrupt sons of the judge to rule over them. Through Samuel, the writers would express more clearly than ever how they felt about their cultural system under Statism, and how one version is no better than the other, as they would go on to demonstrate. The writers would make clear their opinion not only of corrupt judges, but also of kings and their monarchies, because they knew their nature from personal experience. Regardless, the experiment would continue with the move away from judges to an even more political system with the search for a king. Predictably, that also would not work out for the Israelites, but thanks to stiff necked free thinkers like Judah, culture continued to evolve. They had learned allowing an "exalted" leader as their judge was a system that also did not work for the benefit of the people any better than a warlord. Now they would learn the next lesson from the search for a king.

Saul—The Naive Newbie

The next story is yet another example of how the writers insert a sense of hilarity and irreverence into the bible. So how do the writers illustrate the search for a king, and again not so subtly insert their own opinions? They begin by having the story of the search for a king coincide with the story of a search for asses.

A man by the name of Kish couldn't find his asses. He sent his son Saul to search for them, but the job was arduous. They traveled through the land extensively, but even though they searched with both hands and both feet, they simply could not find their asses.

I Samuel 9:3 And the asses of Kish Saul's father were lost. And Kish said to Saul his son, Take now one of the servants with thee, and arise, go seek the asses. 4. And he passed through mount Ephraim, and passed through the land of Shalisha, but they found them not: then they passed through the land of Shalim, and there they were not: and he passed through the land of the Benjamites, but they found them not. 5. And when they were come to the land of Zuph, Saul said to his servant that was with him Come, and let us return; lest my father leave caring for the asses, and take thought for us. 6. And he said, unto him, Behold now, there is in this city a man of God, and he is an honorable man; all that he saith cometh surely to pass: now let us us go thither; peradventure he can shew us our way that we should go.

If you are looking for asses, there is no better place to consult than with a loyal man of the God of Statism. In their search they find themselves in the vicinity where Samuel is still judge, and where the people are, coincidentally, searching for a king because of Samuel's corrupt sons. Samuel saw an opportunity when he was approached by Saul regarding the asses, and a deal is struck between them. First, Samuel reassures Saul and invites him to dine with him and give him prophetic news regarding the search.

I Samuel 9:18 Then Saul drew near to Samuel in the gate, and said, Tell me, I pray thee, where the seer's house is. 19. And Samuel answered Saul, and said, I am the seer: go up before me unto the high place; for ye shall eat with me to-day, and to-morrow I will let thee go, and will tell thee all that is in thine heart. 20. And as for thine asses that were lost three days ago, set not thy mind on them: for they are found. And on whom is all the desire of Israel? Is it not on thee, and on all thy father's house? 21. And Saul answered and said, Am not I a Benjamite, of the smallest tribes of Israel? And my family the least of all the families of the tribe of Benjamin? Wherefore then speakest thou so to me?

The people may have rejected his two sons, but Samuel would find a way to provide the people with a king of his own choosing, and still maintain power through his influence over the young and naive king. He would groom his new surrogate through flattery and compliments. There was more than one way to continue to hold sway over the people. Through this parable the writers demonstrate how the first of what would be a long lineage of royal asses had been found.

I Samuel 9:22 And Samuel took Saul and his servant, and brought them into the parlor, and made them sit in the chiefest place among them that were bidden, which were about thirty persons.

Saul would be made to feel very important. The next day, Samuel would speak to Saul in secret.

I Samuel 9:27 And as they were going down to the end of the city, Samuel said to Saul, Bid the servant pass on before us, (and he passed on,) but stand thou still awhile, that I may shew thee the word of God.

I Samuel 10:1 Then Samuel took a vial of oil, and poured it upon his head, and kissed him, and said, Is it

not because the Lord hath anointed thee to be captain over his inheritance?

By the time Samuel had secretly explained all the benefits of his plan to make him a king, the young impressionable Saul would never want to give it up, and the corruption of wealth and power and the desire to keep it for himself would soon take over his life. As a result, he would soon learn of God's evil spirit. Being captain over the Lords "inheritance" is a sweet deal. First, Samuel would tell Saul of others who would cooperate, and with whom he should now be seen, as he was being groomed for the public.

I Samuel 10:3 Then shalt thou go on forward from thence, and thou shalt come to the plain of Tabor, and there shall meet thee three men going up to God to Beth-el, one carrying three kids, and another carrying three loaves of bread, and another carrying a bottle of wine: 4. And they will salute thee, and give thee two loaves of bread; which thou shalt receive of their hands. 5. After that thou shalt come to the hill of God, where is the garrison of the Philistines: and it shall come to pass, when thou art come thither to the city that thou shalt meet a company of prophets coming down from the high place with a psaltery, and a tabret, and a pipe, and a harp, before them; and they shall prophecy: 6. and the spirit of the Lord will come upon thee, and thou shalt prophesy with them, and shall be turned into another man.

If one is to become king, you must be seen with the right people, know who to trust, from whom to accept bribes, and know how to create an image acceptable to both the insiders and the public. Being carefully guided by the prophets "coming down from the high place", Saul would indeed become "another man" with the help of his new friends, and others would not fail to notice.

I Samuel 10:11 And it came to pass, when all that knew him beforetime saw that, behold, he prophesied among the prophets, then when the people said to one another, What is this that is come unto the son of

Kish? Is Saul also among the prophets? 12. And one of the same place answered and said, But who is their father? Therefore is became a proverb, Is Saul also among the prophets?

This method of installing surrogates is still being used today in most Statist political organizations, regardless of which type of government is claimed. The people are manipulated by insiders into believing they are choosing their own leaders, when in fact they are being carefully chosen and groomed by insiders who want to retain influence and job security. This happens particularly in democracies where public manipulation becomes a full-time endeavor. Samuel would call a meeting among the tribes and announce triumphantly that the first king to "rule" the people had been found.

I Samuel 12:1 And Samuel said unto all Israel, Behold, I have hearkened unto your voice in all that ye said unto me, and have made a king over you. 2. And now, behold, the king walketh before you: and I am old and grayheaded; and, behold, my sons are with you: and I have walked before you from my childhood unto this day.

It is important to present oneself as just one of the people. Even though the people have had nothing to say of who becomes their king, Samuel reassured them that God had made the right choice for them—with his help.

I Samuel 12:13 Now therefore behold the king whom ye have chosen, and whom ye have desired! And, behold, the Lord hath set a king over you. 14. If ye will fear the Lord, and serve him, and obey his voice, and not rebel against the commandment of the Lord, then shall both ye and also the king that reigneth over you continue following the Lord your God: 15. But if ye will not obey the voice of the Lord, but rebel against the commandment of the Lord, then shall the hand of the Lord be against you, as it was against your fathers.

There would follow more threats, intimidation, and admonishment, but not to worry—even though in their wickedness they had asked for a king rather than be subject to his corrupt sons, he would still be with them to guide them as to how best to "serve" the king and "obey his voice".

> **I Samuel 12:23 Moreover as for me, God forbid that I should sin against the Lord in ceasing to pray for you: but I will teach you the good and the right way: 24. Only fear the Lord, and serve him in truth will all your heart; for consider how great things he hath done for you. 25. But if ye shall still do wickedly, ye shall be consumed, both ye and your king.**

Unfortunately, nothing would change for the Israelites under their new king, and the fear of God would still be with them. Samuel would guide Saul through many battles, but in his naivete Saul would sometimes take his own initiative and not do things according to instructions from his handler Samuel, especially in the ever-vital slaughtering and plundering department. As the new warlord-king, Samuel would tell Saul to slaughter the people of another tribe with strict directions from God.

> **I Samuel 15:3 Now go and smite Amalek, and utterly destroy all that they have, and spare them not; but slay both man and woman, infant and suckling, ox and sheep, camel and ass.**

Being a novice regarding the God of Statism, Saul would unwittingly violate his orders. He had no problem smiting "man and woman, infant and suckling" in return for good benefits from God, but he made a couple of judgment errors.

> **I Samuel 15:8 And he took Agag the king of the Amalekites alive, and utterly destroyed all the people with the edge of the sword. 9. But Saul and the people spared Agag, and the best of the sheep, and of the oxen, and of the fatlings, and the lambs, and all that was good, and would not utterly destroy them: but every thing that was vile and refuse, that they**

110

destroyed utterly. 10. Then came the word of the Lord unto Samuel, saying, 11. It repenteth me that I have set up Saul to be king: for he is turned back from following me, and hath not performed my commandments.

Saul would apologetically explain to Samuel he was allowing his people to save the livestock from the senseless slaughter for sacrifice to God and had allowed the Amalekite king alive to present to Samuel as a prize.

I Samuel 15:21 But the people took of the spoil, sheep and oxen, the chief of the things which should have been destroyed, to sacrifice unto the Lord thy God in Gilgal.

By allowing the king and some animals to survive the slaughter, Saul was severely criticized by Samuel because he had displeased God.

I Samuel 15:22 And Samuel said, Hath the Lord as great delight in burnt offerings and sacrifices, as in obeying the voice of the Lord? Behold, to obey is better than sacrifice, and to hearken than the fat of rams.

I Samuel 15:24 And Saul said unto Samuel, I have sinned: for I have transgressed the commandment of the Lord, and thy words: because I feared the people, and obeyed their voice.

Not having had political experience, Saul had committed the cardinal sin of listening to the people, which is not acceptable to the God of Statism. God had now decided if you want complete blind obedience you had better not call Saul. The leaders must only be loyal and obey God without question, while claiming to save, serve, and protect. Listening to the people, and to "obey their voice", was not part of the plan. Saul would be purged of his chosen status, and things would have to be set right in the eyes of the Lord.

I Samuel 15:32 Then said Samuel, Bring ye hither to me Agag the king of the Amalekites. And Agag came unto him delicately. And Agag said, Surely the bitterness of death is past. 33. And Samuel said, As thy sword hath made women childless, so shall thy mother be childless among women. And Samuel hewed Agag in pieces before the Lord in Gilgal.

Just as Samson when his vow was broken because of his haircut, Saul had also lost his covenant with God. In this case it was a result of falling short in his task to slaughter all the Amalekites, along with the women and children and livestock—without exception. As a result, he would no longer have the full power of the State behind him, and there would be a search for a new king to replace him. Saul would now have competition for power, which would come from a newly "chosen" and handsome young man named David, but he would not give in easily. Meanwhile, Samuel lamented that his hand-picked surrogate had chosen to listen to the people instead of God.

I Samuel 16:1 And the Lord said unto Samuel, How long wilt thou mourn for Saul, seeing I have rejected him from reigning over Israel? Fill thine horn with oil, and go, I will send thee to Jesse the Bethlehemite: for I have provided me a king among his sons.

Far from what the people had hoped for, the God of Statism and his minions "anoint" kings of their choosing—not the people. David is introduced to Samuel by his father, Jesse.

I Samuel 16:12 And he sent, and brought him in. Now he was ruddy, and withal of a beautiful countenance, and goodly to look to. And then the Lord said, Arise, anoint him: for this is he. 13. Then Samuel took the horn of oil, and anointed him in the midst of his brethren: and the spirit of the Lord came upon David from that day forward. So Samuel rose up, and went to Ramah. 14. But the spirit of the Lord departed from Saul, and an evil spirit from the Lord troubled him.

15. And Saul's servants said unto him, Behold now, an evil spirit from God troubleth thee.

Not yet knowing that David has been chosen over him, David is brought into Saul's court by insiders. They tell Saul that David can calm him by playing a harp. Saul is unaware that David has been brought in to undermine him. David would serve to create conflict and division, and part of that plan would be to ultimately replace Saul with someone more obedient to God.

I Samuel 17:23 And it came to pass, when the evil spirit from God was upon Saul, that David took an harp, and played with his hand: so Saul was refreshed, and was well, and the evil spirit departed from him.

At first, the deception that he was there to help Saul by providing reassuring relief from God's evil spirit gained David favor, but that would soon change when Saul discovered God now preferred David over himself. The evil spirit is manifested in the desire to retain power, just as "hardening the heart" was for the Pharaoh in the days of Moses. Both were inflicted by God into the hearts of those whose main goal in life was to retain their position of power over the people.

King David—A Perfect Bureaucrat For the God of Statism

The Story of Saul continues into the next story, which is the story of how even those of weak character and inexperience can achieve great Power once they express loyalty to the State. This, as we know, is always one of the great temptations of God's evil spirit. Once "chosen", David now has this power and volunteers to go up against a giant Philistine called Goliath in battle. The Philistines were a tribe that originated in Greece and had a very similar history to the Israelites except that, unlike the Israelites, ultimately failed to resist the God of Statism, so were permanently absorbed into the larger State of Babylon. The stiff-necked Jewish people were never absorbed even during multiple diaspora (scattering of the Jews) as a result of God's punishment. Because of their own lack of resistance, the people of Philistinia (or Palestine) would eventually be replaced by Arabs. Relatively speaking, the Arabs are newcomers. Meanwhile, the Philistine State was still represented by the metaphorical giant called Goliath.

David volunteered to battle Goliath and won easily by bringing a slingshot to a sword fight and killed the giant, which was followed by another great slaughter against the Philistines. The successful slaughter by David against the Philistines made Saul even more jealous, so he determined to kill David. He began to fear the more successful slaughtering done by David would earn him a higher status in the eyes of God, which proved to be correct. Once you have been among the chosen it often becomes unthinkable to give up the sense of security, status, and feeling of superiority the power of the State offers. At one point, Saul even apologized for listening to the people, and begged Samuel to once again make him one of the chosen, but was unsuccessful because of his connection with the people.

Since receiving the evil spirit, Saul had developed an impolite habit of throwing a javelin at people when he felt the benefits of having his own kingdom were being threatened and made several attempts on David's life over dinner in such manner. With the help of Saul's son Jonathon, who had befriended him, David escaped into the surrounding areas ruled by other kings. First, David escaped to the land of Nob, where the priests of king Ahimelech helped by providing him with food and by returning the sword he had captured from Goliath. He then left there and fled to Gath, where king Achish knew of David and his exploits in battle and wondered why David would be traveling alone. Rather than admit he was on the run from his own countrymen led by Saul, David feigned being a crazy person by clawing at doors and drooling on himself, so Achish sent him away in disgust. David then journeyed to a large cave called Adullam, where he met up with his family and other members of his tribe.

> **I Samuel 22:2 And every one that was in distress, and every one that was in debt, and every one that was discontented, gathered themselves unto him: and he became captain over them: and there were with him about four hundred men.**

As Moses had discovered much earlier, and pandering politicians ever since, it is never hard to create followers from the victim groups described here, which is why they always become the core of the "chosen" for Statists just coming into power. The need to create a following is also why it is so common to create as much distress, debt, and discontent as possible during the process of molding a nation into a Statist culture. This is a main reason why nations ruled by Statism will not allow prosperity without strict State control. It is from the victim groups that are found the followers who allow Statists to attain power; because victim groups have no problem turning to Statism as their savior if benefits are offered in return for a covenant of loyalty and obedience.

During Saul's chase after David, there would be more slaughter. Discovering the priests had helped David by providing him with food and giving him the sword of Goliath, king Saul ordered their deaths.

> **I Samuel 22:16 And the king said, Thou shalt surely die, Ahimelech, thou, and all thy fathers' house. 17. And the king said unto the footmen that stood about**

him, Turn, and slay the priests of the Lord; because their hand also is with David, and because they knew when he fled, and did not shew it to me. But the servants of the king would not put forth their hand to fall upon the priests of the Lord.

Saul had forgotten it was now David who had been chosen by The Powers That Be, and not himself, so the people followed their own will. But he still had a loyal insider called Doeg, who was the head over the footmen, and had him give the order instead.

Samuel 22:18 And the king said to Doeg, Turn thou, and fall upon the priests. And Doeg the Edomite turned, and he fell upon the priests, and slew on that day fourscore and five persons that did wear a linen ephod. 19. And Nob, the city of the priests, smote he with the edge of the sword, both men and women, children and sucklings, and oxen, and asses, and sheep, with the edge of the sword.

This story shows that even if you no longer have God's power to back you up, you can still use sympathetic and powerful insiders to inflict mayhem and terror to profit from the State. Today, this is often done through lobbying. Insiders approached by those who otherwise have no influence are paid large sums to act as a go-between to influence those who still retain favor from The Powers That Be. One of David's sons would eventually use this to great advantage for himself.

Saul was determined to regain his power and wealth and all the benefits of being an elitist and would continue to seek David's death. David, however, now had enough followers to become a warlord in his own right, thanks to the help of his victim groups, and used his reputation to instill the fear of God in other tribes. He now had the ability on his own to defeat villages and inflict great slaughter and demand tribute.

On at least two occasions David had the opportunity to kill Saul in his sleep but refrained from doing so because he knew Saul had also at one point been anointed by God. David had, in effect, extended one of the first recorded political pardons to a former insider in deference to his having previously been among the chosen. This often works to gain loyal followers from those sympathetic to the previous leader.

Knowing Saul would continue the pursuit, David took his small army into the land of the Philistines, with whom he had previously been warring, and now joined forces with them. At one point, under king Achish the Philistines had decided that in response to Saul's attacks they would again be forced into war with the Israelites. Although David had volunteered to help go up against his own people as an ally to the Philistines, the princes understandably decided David couldn't be trusted because of his history of slaughtering them and was sent away.

He returned to the city of Ziklag, which had been given to him by king Achish. While gone, the city had been invaded by Amalekites and destroyed. So instead of joining in the slaughter of his fellow Israelites, David spent his time slaughtering Amalekites.

Among the Israelites killed in war with the Philistines during his absence were Saul and his son Jonathan. Jonathan had been a good friend to David and had helped him escape from his father. After Saul's death, another of Saul's sons called Rehoboam inherited the kingdom of Israel except for the tribe of Judah, because God had decided to make David their king. As is often the way with monarchies, there were multiple intrigues and murders and wars among the tribes of Israel until finally God decided to have David be king over all the tribes because of his continued success in warfare. David eventually became king over all Israel and celebrated by bringing the Ark of the Covenant to his house to be blessed by its power. As usual, it would not be without incident, and the writers would once again point out the dangers of the Ark.

II Samuel 6:6 And when they came to Nachon's threshingfloor, Uzzah put forth his hand to the ark of God, and took hold of it; for the oxen shook it. 7. And the anger of the Lord was kindled against Uzzah; and God smote him there for his error; and there he died by the ark of God.

117

Uzzah means "strength". As we have seen before, there is no tolerance to the strength of commoners for touching the power of God in the protected ark. Uzzah paid dearly for his "error" of touching the ark, just as those before him. Being reminded to be fearful of God, but nevertheless craving the power it would give him, the death merely caused a delay before king David would bring the ark to the city he had named after himself as he celebrated.

II Samuel 6:16 And as the ark of the Lord came into the city of David, Michal Saul's daughter (David's first wife) looked through a window, and saw king David leaping and dancing before the Lord: and she despised him in her heart.

After making lots of burnt offerings and peace offerings and much celebrating...

Samuel 6:20 Then David returned to bless his household. And Michal the daughter of Saul came out to meet David, and said, How glorious was the king of Israel today, who uncovered himself today in the eyes of the handmaids of his servants, as one of the vain fellows shamelessly uncovereth himself! 21. And David said unto Michal, It was before the Lord, which chose me before all his house, to appoint me ruler over the people of the Lord, over Israel: therefore will I play before the Lord 22. And I will yet be more vile than thus, and will be base in mine own sight: and of the maid-servants which thou hast spoken of, of them shall I be had in honour. 23. Therefore Michal the daughter of Saul had no child unto the day of her death.

Who needs a complaining wife when you are the king and can allow all the maid-servants to have you "in honour". Like Samson, David's lack of character and a weakness for women would be useful to The Powers That Be. At one point, from his rooftop he saw a woman bathing, and decided he wanted her. Inquiring who she was, it was determined she was Bathsheba, the wife of a loyal man in his military called Uriah. Despite the fact she was married, a king wants what a king wants. He brought her into his house whereupon she became pregnant. Upon learning of it, Uriah would no longer enter his own house to be with her and this became an embarrassment to David. He solved the problem with instructions to send Uriah into one of many battles to be killed.

II Samuel 11:15 And he wrote in the letter, saying, Set ye Uriah in the forefront of the hottest battle, and retire ye from him, that he may be smitten, and die.

The ploy worked, Uriah died in battle, and King David kept Uriah's wife for himself—along with his many other wives. A powerful insider called Nathan knew of the matter and pointed out he knew of David's lack of character, but not to worry, God would protect him. He would, however, now spend his life fighting God's battles and smiting other tribes in exchange for keeping the truth hidden. Just for good measure, and possibly to prevent further scandal, God killed the illegitimate child. Killing the child was necessary because it is important to outwardly maintain a proper image to the public as much as possible, especially to the stiff-necked Israelites who are always looking for an excuse to be rebellious anyway.

Samuel 12:14 Howbeit, because by this deed thou hast given great occasion to the enemies of the Lord to blaspheme, the child also that is born unto thee shall sure die. 15. And Nathan departed unto his house. And the Lord struck the child that Uriah's wife bare unto David, and it was very sick.

After seven days of suffering the child died, but David soon got over it. After the child's death David would no longer have to fast or mourn.

Samuel 13:23 But now he is dead, wherefore should I fast? Can I bring him back again? I shall go to him, but he shall not return to me. 24. And David comforted Bathsheba his wife, and went in unto her: and she bare a son, and he called his name Solomon: and the Lord loved him.

119

The scandal was covered up, and a now a not-so-legitimate new son was destined to be the next king. David would not be as lucky with his other progeny. Apparently his weak character was passed on to his sons, one of which would rape his own sister, whereupon another son called Absalom would kill the son that had done the raping. After going into exile for some time, thinking he would no longer be welcome in the family, Absalom would eventually return. Happily, his father would forgive him for murdering his incestuous rapist brother. Holiday gatherings must have been interesting for this family.

Upon returning, Absalom acquired great power inside the kingdom by serving as his father's handler. All those wanting to see the king would have to go through Absalom, who used his position to curry favor with powerful people by selling access to his father. As a result, he eventually had a great following. As mentioned earlier, insiders manipulating access to leaders in ways that benefit themselves is still common in the world of politics. Eventually, he would even have enough influence to conspire to take over the kingdom from his father. The conspiracy would also necessarily include murdering his father, so it seems the temptations of God's evil spirit would be as much an issue among David's family as it had been for Saul.

Because his own son was now trying to kill him, King David went on the run again with what were his few remaining loyal followers. Absalom now controlled the armies, the bureaucrats, and most servants. Once again finding himself with few loyal followers, David once again fled to other cities in his kingdom, where generally he was not welcomed. He approached a town called Bahurim.

Samuel 16:5 And when king David came to Bahurim, behold, thence came out a man of the family of Saul, whose name was Shimei, the son of Gera: he came forth, and cursed still as he came. 6. And he cast stones at David, and at all the servants of king David: and all the people and all the mighty men were on his right hand and on his left. 7. And thus said Shimei when he

cursed, Come out, come out, thou bloody man, and thou man of Belial: 8. The Lord hath returned upon thee all the blood of the house of Saul, in whose stead thou hast reigned; and the Lord hath delivered the kingdom into the hand of Absalom thy son: and, behold, thou art taken in thy mischief, because thou art a bloody man.

The people still remembered Saul as someone who, unlike David, would listen to the people on occasion and hadn't done nearly as much slaughtering. Meanwhile, Absalom was back home on the rooftop of his father's palace, publicly violating his concubines who were left behind to keep the house in order. Not surprisingly, monarchies have been known to produce somewhat dysfunctional families, where most arguments are over who has the power to rule the People. Meanwhile, the people tend to produce warriors, servants, concubines, taxpayers—and body counts. Oh well, you can't say Samuel didn't warn them about kings.

Through plunder and war, David would finally once again acquire warriors sufficient to fight back against his son Absalom, and there would be a battle between David's loyalists and the other Israelite tribes following Absalom.

Samuel 18:6 So the people went out into the field against Israel: and the battle was in the wood of Ephraim; 7. Where the people of Israel were slain before the servants of David, and there was there a great slaughter that day of twenty thousand men. 8. For the battle was there scattered over the face of all the country: and the wood devoured more people that day than the sword devoured.

Understandably, not too many of the warriors were in favor of a war deciding which corrupt family member would rule over them, and most of them deserted the battlefield into the forest. Regardless, a lot of people paid the price for a family argument. During the battle, Absalom would accidentally hang himself in a tree by the neck in a humiliating manner, whereupon some of David's loyal followers would then finish him off. Then David would have the loyal followers murdered for killing his murderous son as he bewailed his miserable son's death. Nevertheless, the death of his son would mean the competition had been eliminated, and David would now have full power over all the tribes as king.

The Powers That Be were impressed, but although David was a devoted Statist who managed to do great slaughtering and gather great wealth from his spoils of war and taxes, God decided he had done too much slaughtering to be worthy of building a Great House of God as David promised. It isn't that God didn't love him for all his loyalty and slaughtering and plunder—it just wouldn't look good. Thanks to the stubborn Israelites, God was being forced to pay more attention to his image as culture evolved.

Again, Statist rulers do grow old, and then they often can't keep up with their occupation, that mostly consists of warfare, and King David was no different. Even though he had an older son called Adonijah from one of his wives who was now the rightful heir to his throne, he had made a promise to his stolen wife Bathsheba that their second son Solomon would be king. As we recall, his first illegitimate son with Bathsheba had been killed by God. Adonijah was in the process of proclaiming his rightful heritage when David instead proclaimed Solomon would be king at the insistence of Bathsheba. Solomon then took the reins of power, and to clinch the deal he had his older brother Adonijah murdered. It's easy to understand why Sunday school teachers are tempted to use comic books instead of telling the truth about what the bible says.

Kings 2:24 Now therefore, as the Lord liveth, which hath established me, and set me on the throne of David my father, as he promised, Adonijah shall be put to death this day. 25. And king Solomon sent by the hand of Benaiah the son of Jejoiada; and he fell upon him that he died.

During the illegitimate transition of power, Solomon fired the high priest and a general called Joab, who thought Adonijah should be ruler instead of Solomon because of birthright laws. Solomon then had Joab murdered just to make sure his power would not be questioned. Such are the necessities of securing Statist power. The evil spirit placed by God always stays busy. Despite a rough beginning, most of Solomon's rule would be peaceful. All the slaughtering had mostly been done for Solomon by Saul and his own father, David.

The Judahites and other Israelite tribes would now be subservient to Solomon. There was no one left offering any real resistance, so for now there would be peace. Solomon could concentrate on things other than warfare. He had a dream where he asked God for wisdom, which he believed God rewarded him in great abundance, and as a bonus for loyalty God would, as usual, reward him with great riches and a long life despite his corruption. One of his most famous acts of wisdom concerned two hookers, who were arguing over who had claim to a baby. His solution was to cut the baby in half and give half to each. When only one released claim to save the baby's life, he knew that was the mother. There would apparently be many more examples of his great wisdom. Also, now that there was peace, Solomon could focus on using his vast inheritance from his father's spoils of war for construction projects. In addition, he would continue amassing even more wealth through even more taxes.

> **I Kings 4:21 And Solomon reigned over all kingdoms from the river unto the land of the Philistines, and unto the border of Egypt: they brought presents and served Solomon all the days of his life.**

He would use the wealth for building great buildings for himself, his wife, and of course for the God of Statism that had put him in power. The purpose of the construction projects would be to create a legacy for himself. Just as the Great Pyramids, the monuments would be of no benefit to the general population.

> **I Kings 4:26 And Solomon had forty thousand stalls of horses for his chariots, and twelve thousand horsemen. 27. And those officers provided victual for king Solomon, and for all that came unto king Solomons' table, every man in his month: they lacked nothing.**

Other than for the forced labor, times were good for the civil servants that worked for the king, and although taxes were high for the rest of the people as they paid the bill for Solomon's palaces and temples, they at least had respite from constant warfare. Peacetime for the Powers That Be means time for public works projects to serve as monuments to their greatness. Solomon would become famous for his building projects, so instead of working to improve their own lives, many of his subjects would now be conscripted for building egotistical monuments to Solomon, and of course to the God of Statism. This is a concept that has gained wide acceptance, and so this God now has opulent homes and monuments in virtually every capital city in every nation. All devoted Statists still want to copy Solomon in building monuments with their name attached.

> **I Kings 5:13 And king Solomon raised a levy out of all Israel; and the levy was thirty thousand men. 14. And he sent them to Lebanon, ten thousand a month by courses: a month they were in Lebanon, and two months at home: and Adoniram was over the levy 15. And Solomon had threescore and ten thousand that bare burdens, and fourscore thousand hewers in the mountains; 16. Beside the chief of Solomon's officers which were over the work, three thousand and three hundred, which ruled over the people that wrought in the work. 17. And the king commanded and they brought great stones, costly stones, and hewed stone, to lay the foundation of the house.**

Meanwhile, The Powers That Be are always happy to have a permanent home and express their pleasure, but with conditions as usual.

> **I Kings 6:11 And the word of the Lord came to Solomon, saying, 12. Concerning this house which thou art in building, if thou wilt walk in my statutes, and execute my judgments, and keep all my commandments to walk in them; then will I perform my word with thee, which I spake unto David thy**

father: 13. And I will dwell among the children of Israel, and will not forsake my people Israel. 14. So Solomon built the house, and finished it.

However, the Powers That Be do not believe in austerity so the house would not be cheap and there would no doubt be many cost over-runs. Solomon had no concern for such things.

I Kings 6:21 So Solomon overlaid the house within with pure gold: and he made a partition by the chains of gold before the oracle; and overlaid it with gold. 22. And the whole house he overlaid with gold, until he had finished all the house: also the whole altar that was by the oracle he overlaid with gold.

It had taken awhile, but under Solomon the people were finally being subjected to the full brunt of Statist wealth and power centralization just as in Egypt. It had taken generations of slaughtering and divisive nation building under direction from the God of Statism, but they were finally back where they started. This God is always impressed with the opulence and wealth collected from the people, so he welcomed the new house, but there would continue to be warnings of destruction if Israel strayed after other Gods. No doubt the gods of Egypt had experienced the same fears.

Unfortunately, this would become a problem because of the fact Solomon would have seven hundred wives and three hundred concubines. The women were often abducted from different countries that had their own cultures and to keep the peace Solomon felt obligated to allow them to worship other Gods as they pleased. It could be he was just willing to do anything to avoid being nagged by a thousand wives and concubines...

I Kings 11:4 For it came to pass, when Solomon was old, that his wives turned away his heart after other gods: and his heart was not perfect with the Lord his God, as was the heart of David his father.

David may not have had much character, and was a psychotic mass murderer, but was a devoted bureaucrat that loved all of God's laws that kept him in power. In return God loved him. On the other hand, his son Solomon's great wisdom would not be enough to protect him from being caught between the wishes of his wives and the wishes of God. The story continues with God allowing Solomon to keep his kingdom all his days. After all, he had built God a nice home with all that gold and all. But his punishment for allowing other ideas from other Gods (which, along with all his wives, was no doubt the source of much of his wisdom) would be that his son would pay the price for his father's disloyalty by having the kingdom taken away except for only a fraction of what Solomon had.

Again, the writers emphasize the benefits of this God are only temporary, and usually only last a generation or two before another cycle of failure begins.

"The Powers That Be" Continue to Divide the People

The progression of Statism would continue with more division. As we know, constant division is always an indicator of Statism. Speaking of Solomon's son Rehoboam, who would be the new king, through the prophet Ahijah, God said...

I Kings 11:35 But I will take the kingdom out of his son's hand, and will give it unto thee, even ten tribes (to Jeroboam). 36. And unto his sons will I give one tribe, that David my servant may have a light always before me in Jerusalem, the city which I have chosen me to put my name there. 37. And I will take thee, and thou shalt reign according to all that thy soul desireth, and shalt be king over Israel. 38. And it shall be, if thou wilt hearken unto all that I command thee, and wilt walk in my ways, and do that is right in my sight, to keep my statutes and my commandments, as David my servant did; that I will be with thee, and build thee a sure house, as I built for David, and will give Israel unto thee. 39. And I will for this afflict the seed of David, but not for ever.

God would continue to "afflict the seed of David" with his statutes and commandments, but there is a hint there could be a way out someday.

Hearing Jeroboam would rule over most of the tribes of Israel instead of his son Rehoboam, Solomon naturally tried to kill him as he had killed his brother, but Jeroboam would escape into Israel. We can see a very important point made in this story by the writers, other than the fact that all powerful leaders become corrupt. First, the authors were clearly proud to establish that they and their ancestors were never very good at walking in the ways of a Statist God. That their ancestors were constantly being punished by this God of Statism is a testament to that point, but now they are setting up a new focal point. This is made clear in the statement, "And I will for this afflict the seed of David, but not forever." Despite the mayhem inflicted by God and his hand-chosen judges and kings, the writers always manage to suggest there is room for optimism in the future. Without that optimism and hope, there would be no reason for the bible to exist. The Bible is an instruction manual to understand Statism and why escaping that system is necessary to regain the knowledge of good and evil and eat from the tree of life.

The Israelite descendants may continue to have reason for optimism and are now independent and successful, but thanks to the God of Statism, Jerusalem is still today one of the most cursed cities on earth. The inhabitants must live with constant cultural tension and turmoil with their Statist neighbors. The God of Statism is still a threat to Israel and Jerusalem to this day as punishment for their defiance and so long as that threat exists, there will be no lasting cultural paradise or Eden for anyone in the Middle East.

They now describe in the following story how it came about that all the tribes are stripped from the kingdom of Solomon by God and given to his servant Jeroboam. The exception would be a small kingdom ruled by Rehoboam, who would rule over Jerusalem. The rebellion which followed would eventually lead to a different kind of nation, which would eventually stand alone and have a different kind of culture, while the other tribes would be absorbed into larger nation states.

The stories warn us of common ways power is gained through manipulation of the people. The bible stories of the powerful elite always include insider intrigue, corruption, lack of empathy, and murder. They also show how having a centralized State always results in social chaos, usually driven by the elites. The writers demonstrate the fallacy of following such leaders into wars against other nations. This is usually a ploy for the "chosen" to gain even more power, or to maintain their authority.

Just as his father Solomon, and his grandfather David before him, Rehoboam would prove to be a true Statist that would oppress and eventually lose the support of the people but would of course be loved by God. Once Solomon had died, and his servant Jeroboam could be sure he wouldn't be killed, he returned to eventually become the leader chosen to rule over the ten remaining tribes. Upon his return, Jeroboam would speak to Solomon's son, king Rehoboam. This would offer another opportunity for the authors to speak through their characters. King Rehoboam would meet with a delegation of the people to speak to the corrupt king Jeroboam.

I Kings 12:3 That they sent and called him. And Jeroboam and all the congregation of Israel came, and spake unto Rehoboam, saying, 4. Thy father made our yoke grievous: (speaking of Solomon and his forced labor and taxes) **now therefore make thou the grievous service of thy father, and his heavy yoke which he put upon us, lighter, and we will serve thee. 5. And he said unto them, Depart yet for three days, then come again to me. And the people departed. 6. And king Rehoboam consulted with the old men, that stood before Solomon his father while he yet lived, and said, How do ye advise that I may answer this people? 7. And they spake unto him, saying, If thou wilt be a servant unto this people this day, and wilt serve them, and answer them, and speak good words to them, then they will be thy servants for ever.**

Serving the people in return, what a novel idea! It's easy to see why Jeroboam {[37]} (which means the people contendeth) ended up ruling over most of the tribes instead of Rehoboam {[38]}(which means the people are enlarged). When "the people are enlarged" the tide tends to turn against many rulers.

I King 12:8. But he forsook the counsel of the old men, which they had given him, and consulted with the young men that were grown up with him, and which stood before him: 9. And he said unto them, What counsel give ye that we may answer this people, who have spoken to me, saying, May the yoke which thy

---

[37] https://www.behindthename.com/name/jeroboam
[38] https://www.behindthename.com/name/rehoboam

father did put upon us lighter? 10. And the young men that were grown up with him spake unto him, saying, Thus shalt thou speak unto this people that spake unto thee, saying, Thy father made our yoke heavy, but make thou it lighter unto us; thus shalt thou say unto them, My little finger shall be thicker than my father's loins. 11. And now whereas my father did lade you with a heavy yoke, I will add to your yoke: my father hath chastised you with whips, but I will chastise you with scorpions.

The announcement that Rehoboam would ignore the wisdom of the older men and Jeroboam and be an even bigger d**k than his father Solomon did not go over well with the people. So, this is the story of how most of Israel abandoned king Rehoboam, son of Solomon.

I Kings 12:16 So when all Israel saw that the king hearkened not unto them, the people answered the king, saying, What portion have we in David? neither have we inheritance in the son of Jesse: to your tents, O Israel: now see to thine own house David. So Israel departed unto their tents. 17. But as for the children of Israel which dwelt in the cities of Judah, Rehoboam reigned over them. 18. Then king Rehoboam sent Adoram, who was over the tribute; and all Israel stoned him with stones, that he died. Therefore king Rehoboam made speed to get him up to his chariot, to flee to Jerusalem. 19. So Israel rebelled against the house of David unto this day. 20. And it came to pass, when all Israel heard that Jeroboam was come again, that they sent and called him unto the congregation, and made him king over all Israel: there was none that followed the house of David, but the tribe of Judah only.

And to this day Israel still "rebels against the house of David", which is yet another declaration of independence. As the wiser of the two, it isn't surprising Jeroboam would also eventually become evil in the site of the Lord. This would in turn provide another opportunity to divide the people even further. Just as at other times, if there is insufficient strife between other cultures and there is no one left to slaughter, then you must again divide and set the people within a nation against each other. It won't be necessary to go through all the various kingdoms and the usual corruption and warfare and intrigue. The writers of the bible have made their point that even the best kingdoms are always Statist, and therefore inherently nepotist and corrupt. And just as with Samuel's speech warning of kings, the meeting between Rehoboam and Jeroboam shows the authors were clearly familiar with the issues of the relationship between the rulers and the people, and how that relationship affects culture. They continue to emphasize through repetition.

The pattern has been established. The kings chosen by God could commit any atrocity and still be loved. The only exceptions were that you must never worship other Gods or idols, and you must love the multitude of laws, statutes, precepts, and commandments that create and protect the bureaucracy. Transgression would happen repeatedly, and in response God would destroy, or at least punish the Jewish people by selling them into slavery. There would be unending suffering of the people at the hands of the God of Statism, either through warfare with foreigners or among the people themselves, but there would always be another king waiting that was chosen by God. The wisdom of the Yahwists is in pointing out the nature of this monotheistic God of Statism.

Somewhere in this conveyor belt of kings, the people of Jerusalem would of course gain a bad reputation. Their rebellious nature would result in their suffering destruction several times. The writers include a letter sent to one of the ruling kings regarding the stiff necked people of Jerusalem.

Ezra 4:12 Be it known unto the king, that the Jews which came up from thee to us are come unto Jerusalem, building the rebellious and the bad city, and have set up the walls thereof, and joined the foundations. 13. Be it known now unto the king, that, if this city be builded, and the walls set up again then they not pay toll, tribute, and custom, and so thou shalt endamage the revenue of the kings. 14. Now because we have maintenance from the kings palace, and it was not meet for us to see the kings dishonour, therefore have we sent and certified the king; 15. That search may be made in the book of the records of thy fathers: so shalt thou find in the book of records, and know that this city is a rebellious city, and hurtful unto kings and provinces, and that they have moved sedition within the same of old time: for which cause was this city destroyed.

The Jewish ancestors in Jerusalem became famous for their lack of cooperation, which was hurtful to the income of the larger State and would "endamage the revenue of the kings" to support the king's palaces and pay for their wars. It is no wonder this God must focus so much punishment on those stiff-necked Israelites in Jerusalem. Jerusalem would be rebuilt, but not by God and not without controversy, or without further tragedy at the hands of the God of Statism.

Job—Unmasking God's Address

The story of Job departs from the norm of teaching by example in earlier parables to a more philosophical approach. The story of Job takes the form of a conversation with some of his friends and is very similar in style to dialogues attributed to Socrates or Plato and may be indicative of Greek influence. In this story they point out a common misunderstanding of the nature of God. They use dialogue to show the folly of thinking our relationship with God is always that of subservience to an "exalted" figurehead, who is watching from a distance. In opposition to this concept, they use the story of Job to make the point that God is within us and is the culture we choose for ourselves.

If you choose a cultural God of Statism then you will come to believe in a reward and punishment system from the top and will believe that those more fortunate must therefore be more "chosen" by God, and those who are less fortunate are not as "chosen". This is a Statist ideology and has often been used to manipulate us. The story of Job points out that our culture should be a God chosen by and for We The People and should provide strength from within us as individuals as well as a collective culture. Job shows we should never allow ourselves to be subjected to manipulation by outside forces other than nature, and especially from a reward and punishment system from which we must seek to be more favored or "chosen".

Job is a man that is very successful, and so is considered by most to be blessed by God because of his great riches and good fortune. God even brags about Job to his assistant Satan.

> **Job 1:8 And the Lord said unto Satan, Hast thou considered my servant Job, that there is none like him in the earth, a perfect and an upright man, one that feareth God, and escheweth evil? 9. Then Satan answered the Lord, and said, Doth Job fear God for nought? 10. Hast not thou made an hedge about him, and about his house, and about all that he hath on every side? Thou hast blessed the work of his hands,**

and his substance is increased in the land. 11. But put forth thine hand now, and touch all that he hath, and he will curse thee to thy face.

God then gave his assistant permission to deprive Job of everything important in his life. Job lost his servants, his considerable wealth, and even his children. Many of those who had been close to Job and trusted and admired him when he was successful now looked down on him. Yet, Job was able to remain loyal to his own version of God.

Job 1:21 And said, Naked came I out of my mother's womb, and naked shall I return thither: the Lord gave, and the Lord hath taken away; blessed be the name of the Lord. 22. In all this Job sinned not, nor charged God foolishly.

God pointed out to Satan that although they had deprived Job of everything which brought him joy, he had not been deprived of his inner character.

Job: 2:3 And the Lord said unto Satan, Hast thou considered my servant Job, that there is none like him in the earth, a perfect and an upright man, one that feareth God, and escheweth evil? And still he holdeth fast his integrity, although thou movedst me against him, to destroy him without cause.

Satan (which means adversary), was still convinced he could cause Job to lose his inner strength and self-confidence.

Job 2:4 And Satan answered the Lord, and said, Skin for skin, yea, all that a man hath will he give for his life. 5. But put forth his bone and his flesh, and he will curse thee to thy face.

In response, God gave permission to do even further damage to Job. When Satan gives Job horrible boils and fever as he sets in ashes mourning his losses, his wife tells him to give up on God.

Job 2:9 Then said his wife unto him, Dost thou still retain thine integrity? Curse God and die. 10. But he said unto her, Thou speakest as one of the foolish

women speaketh. What? Shall we receive good at the hand of God, and shall we not receive evil? In all this did not Job sin with his lips.

Job didn't think it made sense to curse God because of adversity, because there can be both good and bad in life, and both come from God. His character gave him the inner strength and understanding not to blame his version of God for his problems. Then three of Job's buddies came to console him in his sorrow, and after seven days of not speaking while mourning, Job finally broke the silence by cursing the day he had ever been born because of his misery.

Job 3:25 For the thing which I greatly feared is come upon me, and that which I was afraid is come unto me. 26. I was not in safety, neither had I rest, neither was I quiet; yet trouble came.

He knew he had done nothing wrong, yet everything had fallen apart for him, so he complained bitterly about his circumstances—but not about his God. Then one of his buddies called Eliphaz suggested to him that he must have done something to be punished in such a way and is being purified by God. He told Job...

Job 4:7 Remember, I pray thee, who ever perished, being innocent? Or where were the righteous cut off? 8. Even as I have seen, they that plow inequity, and sow wickedness, reap the same. 9. By the blast of God they perish, and by the breath of his nostrils are they consumed.

Eliphaz told Job he should not question that he was subject to the wisdom and blessing of God's punishment.

Job 5:17 Behold, happy is the man whom God correcteth: therefore despise him not thou the chastening of the Almighty: For he maketh sore, and bindeth up: he woundeth, and his hands make whole.

Eliphaz told Job he should not complain, because it was God's will to purify through judgment and punishment. Job responded by pointing out he would be happy if it were that simple. If his experience was God's punishment, he would be happy to die.

Job 6:8 Oh that I might have my request; and that God would grant me the thing that I long for! 9. Even that it would please God to destroy me; that he would let loose his hand, and cut me off! 10. Then should I yet have comfort; yea, I would harden myself in sorrow: let him not spare; for I have not concealed the words of the Holy One. 11. What is my strength, that I should hope? And what is mine end, that I should prolong my life?

Making it clear that he would be happy to accept God's punishment for purifying if that was the purpose, but he challenged them to show where he had gone wrong, and why he should be punished.

Job 6:24 Teach me, and I will hold my tongue: and cause me to understand wherein I have erred. 25. How forcible are right words! But what doth your arguing reprove? 26. Do ye imagine to reprove words, and the speeches of one that is desperate, which are as wind? 27. Yea, ye overwhelm the fatherless, and ye dig a pit for your friend. 28. Now therefore be content, look upon me; for it is evident unto you if I lie. 29. Return, I pray you, let it not be iniquity; yea, return again, my righteousness is in it. 6.30 Is there iniquity in my tongue? Cannot my taste discern perverse things?

If Job had done evil, he insisted he would know it, and would speak the truth of it. He also expressed he had every right to complain and not passively accept adversity as beyond his control.

Job 7:11 Therefore I will not refrain my mouth; I will speak in the anguish of my spirit; I will complain in the bitterness of my soul.

Job was a person who knew himself, and his self-image was not dependent on judgment from The Powers That Be, because to him God was his own inner strength and character. Then his other

136

friend, called Bildad, suggested maybe adversity had come because his servants and children were being punished for their bad behavior, rather than Job.

Job 8:3 Doth God pervert judgment? Or doth the Almighty pervert justice? 4. If thy children have sinned against him, and he have cast them away for their transgression; 5. If thou wouldest seek unto God betimes, and make thy supplication to the Almighty; 6. If thou wert pure and upright; surely now he would awake for thee, and make the habitation of thy righteousness prosperous.

Bildad suggested that people only grow because of punishments wisely and justly placed by God upon man to guide them. God had probably decided to punish Job's children and servants, and to deprive Job of his happiness and prosperity to punish the children while improving Job.

Job 8:19 Behold, this is the joy of his way, and out of earth shall others grow. 20. Behold, God will not cast away a perfect man, neither will he help the evildoers: 21. Till he fill thy mouth with laughing, and thy lips with rejoicing. 22. They that hate thee shall be clothed with shame; and the dwelling place of the wicked shall come to nought.

His friend thought God would judge how to make things right by causing Job and his family to suffer, and he should willingly accept the punishment brought to him. Job's response was basically to say alright fine, if he or his family is being judged by God, then exactly how does he plead on his own behalf of his innocence, and in the end, why would it even matter if God predetermined their fate anyway?

Job 9:19 If I speak of strength, lo, he is strong: and if of judgment, who shall set me a time to plead? 20. If I justify myself, mine own mouth shall condemn me: if I say I am perfect, it shall also prove me perverse. 21. Though I were perfect, yet would I not know my soul:

I would despise my life. 22. This is one thing, therefore I said it, He destroyeth the perfect and the wicked. 23. If the scourge slay suddenly, he will laugh at the trial of the innocent. 24. The earth is given into the hand of the wicked: he covereth the faces of the judges thereof; if not, where and who is he? 25. Now my days are swifter than a post: they flee away, they see no good. 26. They are passed away as the swift ships: as the eagle that hasteth to the prey. 27. If I say, I will forget my complaint, I will leave off my heaviness, and comfort myself: 28. I am afraid of all my sorrows, I know that thou wilt not hold me innocent. 29. If I be wicked, why then labor I in vain? 30. If I wash myself with snow water, and make my hands never so clean; 31. Yet shalt thou plunge me in the ditch, and mine own clothes shall abhor me. 32. For he is not a man, as I am, that I should come together in judgment. 33. Neither is there any daysman betwixt us, that might lay his hand upon us both. 34. Let him take his rod away from me, and let not his fear terrify me: 35. Then would I speak, and not fear him; but it is not so with me.**

Through these conversations and Job's responses, the writers are pointing out the absurdity of thinking of God as an outside entity that watches and judges us. That is a concept in which there is no way to win, or even to understand why things happen. Simply put, good and bad happens to both good and bad people. Why would God be so fickle? That kind of God would make no sense. He goes on to point out that there was much evil in life that went unpunished, so how is one supposed to learn how to be righteous if there is a reward and punishment system taking place at random? Job did not believe in a Statist God judging over him. His God was his own culture.

Job 12:6 The tabernacles of robbers prosper, and they that provoke God are secure; into whose hand God bringeth abundantly. 7. But ask now the beasts, and

they shall teach thee; and the fowls of the air, and they shall tell thee: 8. Or speak to the earth, and it shall teach thee: and the fishes of the sea shall declare unto thee. 9. Who knoweth not in all these that the hand of the Lord hath wrought this? 10. In whose hand is the soul of every living thing, and the breath of all mankind?

Job thought most of what he learned to gain wisdom was not from worshiping, but from observing nature. He did not learn righteousness from an arbitrary system of reward and punishment that was inconsistent. He especially rejected judgment from those who saw themselves as self-righteous and judged others through their fortune or misfortune. He told his buddies in no uncertain terms what he thought of their wise opinions.

Job 13:4. But ye are forgers of lies, ye are all physicians of no value. 5. O that ye would altogether hold your peace! And it should be your wisdom. 6. Hear now my reasoning, and hearken to the pleadings of my lips. 7. Will ye speak wickedly for God? And talk deceitfully for him? 8. Will ye accept his person? Will ye contend for God? 9. Is it good that he should search you out? Or as one man mocketh another, do ye so mock him?

Job felt it was ridiculous for his buddies to presume to speak for the God he knew was within him. Again, to further make his point, Job emphasized the capricious nature of a God that manipulated and guided the lives of people, because he had witnessed that fallacy himself through his own observations of human nature.

Job 21:7 Wherefore do the wicked live, become old, yea, are mighty in power? 8. Their seed is established in their sight before them, and their offspring before their eyes. 9. Their houses are safe from fear, neither is the rod of God upon them. 10. Their bull gendereth, and faileth not; their cow calveth, and casteth not her calf. 11. They send forth their little ones like a flock,

and their children dance. 12. They take the timbrel and harp, and rejoice at the sound of the organ. 13. They spend their days in wealth, and in a moment go down to the grave. 14. Therefore they say unto God, Depart from us; for we desire not the knowledge of thy ways. 15. What is the almighty, that we should serve him? And what profit should we have, if we pray unto him? 16. Lo, their good is not in their hand: the counsel of the wicked is far from me.

Job explained there was no way to learn to be righteous by whether one achieved success or failure in their lifetime because many that were evil became successful, and many good people experienced misfortune, so what his friends were saying made no sense. He knew he should remain true to himself, and what he believed was right, despite all the afflictions that had befallen him.

Job 27:3 All the while my breath is in me, and the spirit of God is in my nostrils; 4. My lips shall not speak wickedness, nor my tongue utter deceit. 5. God forbid that I should justify you: till I die I will not remove integrity from me. 6. My righteousness I hold fast, and will not let it go: my heart shall not reproach me so long as I live. 7. Let mine enemy be as the wicked, and he that riseth up against me as the unrighteous. 8. For what is the hope of the hypocrite, though he hath gained, when God taketh away his soul? 9. Will God hear his cry when trouble cometh upon him? 10. Will he delight himself in the Almighty? Will he always call upon God?

He refused to either condemn God or plead to God to cure his problems. He knew salvation, if forthcoming, would reside within himself and his own sense of self-worth. He still refused to believe that his adversities were a form of punishment to improve him, because he knew he had done no wrong. He argued against that kind of logic, because he knew himself and his own character, and still would not accept their idea of God's judgment.

Job 31:4 Doth not he see my ways, and count all my steps? 5. If I have walked with vanity or if my foot hasted to deceit; 6. Let me be weighed in an even balance, that God may know mine integrity. 7. If my step hath turned out of the way, and mine heart walked after mine eyes, and if any blot hath cleaved to mine hands; 8. Then let me sow, and let my offspring be rooted out. 9. If mine heart have been deceived by a woman, or if I have laid wait at my neighbour's door; 10. Then let my wife grind unto another, and let others bow down upon her. 11. For this is a heinous crime; yea, it is an iniquity to be punished by the judges.

He clearly did not believe God worked the way his friends thought he did. But the last friend to speak was Elihu, who was angry his other friends had eventually given up on defending God and condemning Job. He was also angry with Job for insisting on his own innocence. Elihu insisted that God was an all-powerful force judging us all. Those who were kings were anointed because God had chosen them to be kings, and those who were poor God had chosen to be poor, because all were subject to his judgment.

Job 36:5 Behold, God is mighty, and despiseth not any: he is mighty in strength and wisdom. 6. He preserveth not the life of the wicked: but giveth right to the poor. 7. He withdraweth not his eyes from the righteous: but with kings are they on the throne; yea, he doth establish them for ever, and they are exalted. 8. And if they be bound in fetters, and be holden in cords of affliction; 9. Then he sheweth them their work, and their transgressions that they have exceeded. 10. He openeth also their ear to discipline, and commandeth that they return from inequity. 11. If they obey and serve him, they shall spend their days in prosperity, and their years in pleasure. 12. But if they obey not, they shall perish by the sword, and they shall die without knowledge.

According to Elihu, God determined lives and judged and rewarded according to whether they pleased him, just as his friends believed. Elihu believed in worshiping a Statist God that would deliberately manipulate the people to serve his own agenda. Finally, the writers introduce God into the dialogue with both a rebuke against Job's three friends, and a confession. The writers show God no longer being able to stand the blather.

> **Job 38:1 Then the Lord answered Job out of the whirlwind, and said, 2. Who is this that darkeneth counsel by words without knowledge? 3. Gird up now thy loins like a man; for I will demand of thee, and answer thou me. 4. Where wast thou when I laid the foundations of the earth? Declare, if thou hast understanding. 5. Who hath laid the measure thereof, if thou knowest? Or who stretched the line upon it? 6. Whereupon are the foundations thereof fastened? Or who laid the corner stone thereof;**

God admonishes Job's friends for their lack of knowledge and wisdom. The writers then have God acknowledging the many wonders of nature as a primary source of understanding, and pointed out that the three friends, unlike Job, had no knowledge of the nature of things. His friend's version of culture seeks guidance and judgment from The Powers That Be, which has the character of an opportunistic bird of prey who hunts from a lofty place.

> **Job 39:28 She dwelleth and abideth on the rock, upon the crag of the rock, and the strong place. 29. From thence she seeketh the prey, and her eyes behold afar off. 30. Her young ones also suck up blood: and where the slain are, there is she.**

A Statist God is almost always associated with blood and war and deprives people of their inner culture from a "strong place" that is sheltered from the prey. God explains to Job he was right all along, and that he is right to be his own judge.

> **Job 40:10 Deck thyself now with majesty and excellency; and array thyself with glory and beauty.**

11. Cast abroad the rage of thy wrath: and behold every one that is proud, and bring him low; and tread down the wicked in their place. 13. Hide them in the dust together, and bind their faces in secret. 14. Then will I also confess unto thee thine own right hand can save thee.

After admitting Job is in fact his own judge and has every right to be angry against both his accusers and his circumstances, the writers then have God making another astounding confession. God points out that Job was right all along, and his salvation would only be by "thine own right hand". Job had correctly refused to buy into the false notion of a reward and punishment system from a fickle God outside himself, and therefore how pointless it would be to blame God for his troubles. He chose to believe that God, whether good, bad, or indifferent, is of his own choosing, dwelt inside him all along, and did not guide with a punishment and reward system outside his own actions and the actions of nature. He knew his God was in the culture he chose for himself, and it was his responsibility to be his own judge in that regard. The God his friends believed in was arbitrary and confusing, because his actions were either completely random, or more often even malicious. Then God further reprimands the friends for their ignorance.

Job 42:7 And it was so, that after the Lord had spoken these words unto Job, the Lord said to Eliphaz the Temanite, My wrath is kindled against thee, and against thy two friends: for ye have not spoken of me the things that is right, as my servant Job hath. 8. Therefore take unto you now seven bullocks and seven rams, and go to my servant Job, and offer up for yourselves a burnt offering; and my servant Job shall pray for you: for him will I accept: lest I deal wih you after your folly, in that ye have not spoken of me the thing which is right, like my servant Job.

Job knew himself, and therefore his own God, much better than his friends. Then Job once again becomes successful by "thine own right hand". The lesson is that God does not respond with reward

143

or punishment, but is within our own culture, and is something we determine for ourselves. God does not determine the nature of man, man determines the nature of God. It is not our inner god that is dishonest, it is the God created by Statism that is dishonest.

God then makes another revelation. Culture is man's most powerful force, which is why Statists, as represented by Job's friends, want to determine our culture for us by telling us it is God's will what happens to us. In the story of Job, the writers end the story by having God make yet another important confession. He explains it is through the misguided actions of the people seeking temporary benefits that he creates a Statist culture in the form of a fearsome Behemoth or Leviathan. A Statist God is the culture that creates the Leviathan, and we must be our own judge in that regard also.

> **Job 41:10 None is so fierce that dare stir him up: who then is able to stand before me? 11. Who hath prevented me, that I should repay him? Whatsoever is under the whole heaven is mine. 12. I will not conceal his parts, nor his power, nor his comely proportion. 13. Who can discover the face of his garment? Or who can come to him with his double bridle? 14. Who can open the doors of his face? His teeth are terrible round about. 15. His scales are his pride, shut up together as with a close seal. 16. One is so near to another, that no air can come between them. 17. They are joined one to another, that they cannot be sundered.**

If no one stands up to prevent its creation, then the Leviathan soon becomes so fearsome no one can stand up it, and it now determines our actions and culture for us. Those who benefit from Statism now stick together closely as scales and become an establishment that cannot be penetrated as "They are joined one to another, that they cannot be sundered", and the Leviathan becomes self-perpetuating.

> **Job 41:11 Canst thou draw out leviathan with an hook? Or his tongue with a cord which thou lettest down? 2. Canst thou put an hook into his nose? Or**

bore his jaw through with a thorn? 3. Will he make many supplications unto thee? 4. Will he make a covenant with thee? Wilt thou take him for a servant forever? 5. Wilt thou play with him as a bird? Or wilt thou bind him for thy maidens? 6. Shall the companions make a banquet of him? Shall they part him among the merchants? 7. Canst thou fill his skin with barbed irons? Or his head with fish spears? 8. Lay thine hand upon him him, remember the battle, do no more. 9. Behold, the hope of him is in vain: shall not one be cast down even at the sight of him?

Once we create him, the God of Statism can then manipulate his Leviathan in many ways. Once this Leviathan is created by those who want to rule or benefit from being ruled, all their hopes are in vain. They lose their wisdom and virtue and live in fear of their own creation. Meanwhile, the rulers and their surrogates wait to feed on the blood of those who are ruled. God continues to describe a Leviathan State created by those who desire to rule over others in their search for security and power.

Job 41:33 Upon earth there is not his like, who is made without fear. 34. He beholdeth all high things: he is a king over all the children of pride.

As the writers point out, allowing the creation of this Leviathan in the belief that our cultural interests will be served to our benefit is always a fallacy. God should be the culture we choose for ourselves individually as did Job, and it does not have to be the Leviathon created by the God of Statism, which always includes being "king over all the children of pride". Job's friends were not able to demoralize him through criticism, because of his strength of character. Satan will always be our adversary by imposing punishment for believing in ourselves, and that instead we must be subservient to an external God that judges and punishes us. Unlike his friends, Job was not a servant to the God of Statism. Rather, God was his servant, and gave him strength of character.

Psalms—The Curse of Bureaucratic Dependency

In Psalms the writers show the stark differences between Job, who is a self-made man who knows himself, as opposed to King David, who owes everything to the God of Statism. Unlike Job, king David is a man that has no character of his own. His is a story of a man that begins adulthood having the power of the State behind him which allows him to kill Goliath, and then goes on to slaughter many others in his lifetime. He goes to war because God wants him to go to war, and never questions why. He uses his power and influence to steal and plunder, including the wife of one of his own personal allies and generals. He is unable to regret his actions, and instead orders that the betrayed general be placed into battle and abandoned so he would be killed to avoid embarrassment.

When David's illegitimate son with his stolen wife Bathsheba is killed by God, he was incapable of mourning his death. He is unwanted by his own people and despised by some of his wives. He passed his weakness down to his children, and even when his own son betrays him and tries to kill him, he never questioned the God of Statism and the evil spirit that was the source of all his problems. After fleeing in fear of being killed by his own son, he volunteered to help the Philistines go to war against his own tribes of Israel. He has no loyalty to his own people, but he remains loyal to his God of Statism, and therefore this God loves him. Without character of his own, David is completely dependent on The Powers That Be, and uses written laws to maintain power and authority. King David is the opposite of Job, who is self-reliant, has his own sense of self-worth, and does not become wealthy through Statism, but by his own hand. King David repeatedly shows his blind loyalty and pleads for his own sake even as his people abandon him.

Psalm 6:1 O Lord, rebuke me not in thine anger, neither chasten me in thy hot displeasure. 2. Have mercy upon me, O Lord; for I am weak: O Lord, heal

me; for my bones are vexed. 3. My soul is also sore vexed: but thou O Lord how long? 4. Return, O Lord, deliver my soul: oh save me for thy mercies' sake. 5. For in death there is no remembrance of thee: in the grave who shall give thee thanks? 6. I am weary with my groaning; all the night make I my bed to swim; I water my couch with my tears. 7. Mine eye is consumed because of grief; it waxeth old because of all mine enemies. 8. Depart from me, all ye workers of iniquity; for the Lord hath heard the voice of my weeping.

Having no inner soul to give him strength as does Job, King David must repeatedly turn to God for salvation and grieves selfishly whenever he brings misfortune upon himself.

Psalm 8:1 O Lord my God, in thee do I put my trust: save me from all them that persecute me, and deliver me: 2. Lest he tear my soul like a lion, rending it in pieces, while there is none to deliver.

Like Job's friends, David believes in a God that rewards and punishes according to how devoted he is to Statist laws, commandments, statutes, and precepts handed down from above.

Psalm 18:19 He brought me forth also into a large place; he delivered me, because he delighted in me. 20. The Lord rewarded me according to my righteousness; according to the cleanness of my hands hath he recompensed me. 21. For I have kept the ways of the Lord, and have not wickedly departed from my God. 22. For all his judgments were before me, and I did not put always his statutes from me.

David loved the God of Statism whose favor allowed him success, mostly in battle, which is the specialty of this God.

Psalm 18:39 For thou hast girded me with strength unto the battle: thou hast subdued under me those that rose up against me. 40. Thou hast also given me the necks of mine enemies; that I might destroy them that

hate me. 41. They cried, but there was none to save them: even unto the Lord but he answered them not. 42. Then did I beat them small as the dust before the wind: I did cast them out as the dirt in the streets. 43. Thou hast delivered me from the strivings of the people; and thou hast made me the head of the heathen: a people whom I have not known shall serve me. 44. As soon as they hear of me, they shall obey me: the strangers shall submit themselves to me. 45. The strangers shall fade away, and be afraid out of their close places. 46. The Lord liveth; and blessed be my rock; and let the God of my salvation be exalted.

King David loved the power over others that God gave him, but just as others discovered, a Statist God is a fickle God.

Psalm 22:1 My God, my God, why hast thou forsaken me? Why art thou so far from helping me, and from the words of my roaring? 2. O my God, I cry in the daytime, but thou hearest not; and in the night season, and am not silent. 3. But thou art holy, O thou that inhabitest the praises of Israel. 4. Our fathers trusted in thee: they trusted, and thou didst deliver them. 5. They cried unto thee, and were delivered: they trusted in thee, and were not confounded. 6. But I am a worm, and no man; a reproach of men, and despised of the people. 7. All they that see me laugh at me to scorn: they out the lip, they shake the head, saying, 8. He trusted on the Lord that he would deliver him: let him deliver him, seeing he delighted in him.

Not understanding that the One True God is the culture inside us that gives us a sense of self-worth, David is often confused and full of despair. It also means David is a danger to those around him, because he will always turn to the God of Statism to achieve power, wealth, and prestige that are the outward trappings that give him a false sense of identity and a feeling of success. That David is a conflicted person is made clear by the writers. He alternates between pleading to God and debasing himself when things are not going well, to exalting God—and himself, when things are working out for him. His entire sense of self-worth is invested in the superficial successes of achieving wealth and power over the people through Statism, because to him that shows God's favor.

It is as though those writing the bible are openly mocking him for his superficiality. We can only hope David is simply used as a metaphor, because as a person he would have been hopelessly neurotic. But, like so many other neurotic psychopaths throughout history, David would be a strong Statist ruling over others. Character weakness and a lack of empathy for others because of self-absorption is a common characteristic of Statist leaders and has often been to the detriment of the people who are subject to their whims. Unfortunately, they come to power because many are willing to follow because of fear, greed, or faith in false idols that provide temporary benefits. Like David, these are the people whose faith in The Powers That Be never waivers.

> **Psalm 119:108 Accept, I beseech thee, the freewill offerings of my mouth, O Lord, and teach me thy judgments. 109. My soul is continually in my hand: yet do I not forget thy law. 110. The wicked have laid a snare for me: yet I erred not from thy precepts. 111. Thy testimonies have I taken as an heritage for ever: for they are the rejoicing of my heart. 112. I have inclined mine heart to perform thy statutes always, even unto the end.**

> **Psalm 119:141 I am small and despised: yet do not I forget thy precepts. 142. Thy righteousness is an everlasting righteousness, and thy law is the truth. 143. Trouble and anguish have taken hold on me: yet thy commandments are my delights. 144. The righteousness of thy testimonies is everlasting: give me understanding, and I shall live.**

King David is a person who needs laws to guide him because he does not have enough character to use his own good judgment or to make good decisions. David was a very imperfect man, but he was a near perfect Statist. Through David, the writers make the point that all the laws, statutes, regulations, precepts, and commandments; and whether they are created by God, Government, or the Great Goober in the sky will never replace a culture of virtue.

Replacing culture with laws, no matter how voluminous, is always a fallacy. The culture of a nation *is* the nation, and it does not have to be a nation cowered by the Leviathan created by the God of Statism. King David never received understanding. Those who collected the books and put them together to create the bible did a good job. Even though the process may have been haphazard in some ways, it is appropriate that Job is followed by Psalms so that we can compare Job's calm culture of self-reliance and self-determination to King David's neurotic dependency on laws and bureaucracy.

Proverbs—A Conflicted King

As we recall in I Kings, in his later years king Solomon, son of David, began to seek other gods which made him evil in the sight of the Lord. We can refer to this passage in I Kings.

I Kings 11:9 And the Lord was angry with Solomon, because his heart was turned from the Lord God of Israel, which had appeared unto him twice, 10. And had commanded him concerning this thing, that he should not go after other gods: but he kept not that which the Lord commanded. 11. Wherefore the Lord said unto Solomon, Forasmuch as this is done of thee, and thou hast not kept my covenant and my statutes, which I have commanded thee, I will surely rend the kingdom from, and will give it to thy servant. 12. Notwithstanding in thy days I will not do it for David thy father's sake: but I will rend it out of the hand of thy son. 13. Howbeit I will not rend away all the kingdom; but will give one tribe to thy son for David my servant's sake which I have chosen. 14. And the Lord stirred up an adversary unto Solomon, Hadad the Edomite: he was of the king's seed in Edom.

As always, the God of Statism divides at every opportunity. Through Proverbs we see why Solomon lost favor in God's eyes. For most of his years Solomon participated wholeheartedly in Statist corruption, greed, and oppression. He had murderous tendencies using his father, king David, as a role model. But as so often happens with us humanoids, in his later years his culture began to change, and he turned away from the God of Statism and began to pursue another cultural state called natural wisdom. The Proverbs are alleged to be his writings, and here are some of the results.

Proverbs 4:5 Get wisdom, get understanding: forget it not; neither decline from the words of my mouth. 6. Forsake her not, and she shall preserve thee: love her, and she shall keep thee. 7. Wisdom is the principal

**thing; therefore get wisdom: and with all thy getting
get understanding. 8. Exalt her, and she shall bring
thee to honour, when dost embrace her. 9. She shall
give to thine head an ornament of grace: a crown of
glory shall she deliver to thee. 10 Hear, O my son, and
receive my sayings; and the years of thy life shall be
many. 11. I have taught thee in the way of wisdom; I
have led thee in right paths.**

As he gained natural wisdom near the end of his life, some of
his writings would be seriously in breach of his covenant with the
God of Statism. He began to believe in self-reliance and self-
accountability.

**Proverbs 6:5 Deliver thyself as a roe from the hand of
the hunter, and as a bird from the hand of the fowler.
6. Go to the ant, thou sluggard; consider her ways, and
be wise: 7. *Which having no guide, overseer, or ruler, 8.
Provideth her meat in the summer, and gathereth her
food in the harvest.* 9. How long wilt thou sleep, O
sluggard? When wilt thou arise out of thy sleep?**

Even the suggestion that one should wake up and go through
life without a "guide, overseer, or ruler" would have been radical
or even blasphemous at the time. Turning away from the God of
Statism will bring punishment in ways such as depriving you of
your kingdom and giving it to your servant, which is exactly what
happened when Solomon's son came to power. This is how his
servant, Jeroboam, ended up with ten tribes taken from Solomon's
son, Rehoboam. Rehoboam would pay the price for his father's
insolence and his own corruption.

At any rate, whether it is true or not, Solomon would be given
credit for writing many other proverbs in his later years, most of
which refer to wisdom regarding the creation of a virtuous culture.
It's ironic how the bible always keeps coming back to the same
thing. Here is one example.

**Proverbs 6:20 My son, keep thy father's
commandment, and forsake not the law of thy mother:**

21. Bind them continually upon thine heart, and tie them about thy neck. 22. When thou goest, it shall lead thee; when thou sleepest, it shall keep thee; and when thou awakest, it shall talk with thee.

As it says, the family and the larger society should be the teacher—not the State with its centralized control and indoctrination. The point is, we should never allow the State to influence our children by abdicating our right to raise our own child. We should try to avoid State programs that take over child rearing responsibilities from the parent, and we should be very wary of State subsidized educational facilities. Don't forget the terrorism perpetrated by the second generation of Moses' followers; indoctrinated into dependency by the first generation. And don't forget Hitler's youth programs that led to Nazism. Statism always charges a heavy price, especially when it's free.

The Proverbs get to the heart of the issue by addressing personal culture and relationships, instead of the laws and commandments from above that were so loved by Moses and king David. Very few problems are solved through studying Proverbs, because all the advice is subject to conditions just as God is subject to conditions. Culture is always changing. Nevertheless, what they write causes us to stop and think and consider our own culture, which leads us to improve ourselves and hopefully facilitate the eventual resurrection of Eden.

If the lessons of Proverbs are to be taken seriously, then lawyers taught to interpret Statist laws should not exist. What should replace them are Culturalists who are taught to interpret cultural virtue, and genuinely care about the whole of society rather than the interests of a single client. Then they could use that cultural wisdom to help guide violators back into society instead of searching for loopholes in poorly written laws that allow criminals back onto the streets. This method does nothing to encourage cultural success. Whether individuals are released back into the public or sent to prison with others who are also culturally dysfunctional, I don't think a large percentage of those that go through our legal system come out feeling they have learned why virtue and respect for oneself and others is important in their lives.

Maybe instead of prisons we should consider Virtue Villages, where inmates can learn the rewards of healthy interaction with others who have been trained in virtue. Those who are not successful would not be allowed back into society to threaten those more culturally successful. To prevent indoctrination, success or failure would be determined not by the State, but by We The People. It may be wishful thinking, but hey, we can consider new ideas. The purpose of the bible is to encourage us to think for ourselves rather than waiting for gods and kings to do it for us.

Unfortunately, many cultural crimes revolve around the greed for State-printed script, which is used as a tool of manipulation, so we would probably have to work on that issue first. Maybe cryptocurrency or some other method of exchange could someday help in this regard, once it has sufficiently matured and evolved in a way that can resist State regulation and manipulation. Most importantly, we should at all costs avoid turning to more laws and bureaucracies that invariably lead to creating a Statist Leviathan based on laws instead of cultural virtue.

Ecclesiastes—The Sad Result of Bureaucratic Power

We still have more to learn from Solomon. Ecclesiastes was also supposedly written by Solomon, but we know the writers were simply using Solomon to show the failures of Statism. The writers return to Solomon in Ecclesiastes for the same reason they return to king David in Psalms, and that is to further their message. Whereas in Proverbs they would emphasize the value of cultural wisdom, they would now use Solomon's own Ecclesiastes {39} (which means a collector or gatherer) to demonstrate the follies of ignoring that wisdom in preference to the vanity of power as he did in his younger days.

> **Ecclesiastes 2:8 I gathered me also silver and gold, and the peculiar treasure of kings and of the provinces: I gat me men singers and women singers, and the delights of the sons of men, as musical instruments, and that of all sorts. 9. So I was great, and increased more than all that were before me in Jerusalem: also my wisdom remained with me. 10. And whatsoever mine eyes desired I kept not from them, I withheld not my heart from any joy; for my heart rejoiced in all my labour: and this was my portion of all my labour. 11. Then I looked on all the works that my hands had wrought, and on the labour that I had laboured to do: and, behold, all was vanity and vexation of spirit, and there was no profit under the sun.**

Unfortunately for Solomon, just as most Statists he had spent most of his life thinking success would be gained by accumulating power, material wealth, and building monuments, rather than a virtuous culture for himself and his citizens. His wisdom, or rather his elitist intellectualism and imagined enlightenment which he mistook for wisdom in his early days, had all come to nothing.

---

39 http://www.abarim-publications.com/Meaning/Qoheleth.html#. W2CKwNJKjIU

Ecclesiastes 2:16 For there is no remembrance of the wise more than of the fool forever; seeing that which now is in the days to come shall all be forgotten. And how dieth the wise man? As the fool. 17. Therefore I hated life; because the work that is wrought under the sun is grievous unto me: for all is vanity and vexation of spirit.

Ecclesiastes 12:12 And further, by these, my sons, be admonished: of making many books there is no end; and much study is a weariness of the flesh. 13. Let us hear the conclusion of the whole matter: Fear God, and keep his commandments: for this is the whole duty of man. For God shall bring every work into judgment, with every secret thing, whether it be good, or whether it be evil.

In the beginning, Solomon thought his elite intellectualism and his power and wealth made him special in some way, but in the end realized that was not true. Everything Solomon had done in his life had the purpose of bringing pleasure and power to himself. He never did anything to help himself or others to achieve anything close to Eden, and instead had exalted himself over serving the people by collecting knowledge without purpose and building worthless monuments. Towards the end, he decided all the knowledge in the world is worthless compared to cultural understanding (God), and whether it be good or evil. Our culture, "whether it be good, or whether it be evil" would be our true judge. We can tell from this story of the richest man on earth at the time that the stiff-necked people who wrote the bible understood this perfectly. His elitism had produced nothing but vanity.

Isaiah—A Bipolar God And His Problem Child

Isaiah is a prophet in the Old Testament that at times seems to predict the evolution of a new God. The books take on the form of criticisms of Israel, Judah, and Jerusalem, who combined are always the problem child for the God of Statism, because they continue to turn away from him.

> **Isaiah 1:2 Hear, O heavens, and give ear, O earth: for the Lord hath spoken, I have nourished and brought up children, and they have rebelled against me. 3. The ox knoweth his owner, and the ass his master's crib: but Israel doth not know, my people doth not consider.**

As the book of Isaiah appears to be going through the stubbornness of Israel, it shows how the God of Statism prevents man from creating Eden. In the process, it also appears to be suggesting that may change in the future. The purpose is apparently to show how God can evolve over time with cultural improvements, and to demonstrate the possibilities that could take place. However as problem solvers, first all the obstacles preventing us from creating Eden are openly examined in Isaiah by the writers, and their findings are still relevant to our culture today. Recall that Eden is not a location, but a state of cultural paradise and delight. These are some of the problems laid out in Isaiah that show the difficulties that must be overcome before achieving Eden.

Degradation of Culture Under Statism

As we now know, it is a characteristic of those forced to live under Statist culture that the citizens eventually lose respect not only for their Statist God, but also for themselves and others. This pattern is demonstrated many times in the Old Testament and can still be detected in many societies. Statism causes a poverty of culture and loss of virtue, and this has been demonstrated all through history. The Statism forced upon Israel has failed the people once again and has brought cultural degradation.

> **Isaiah 1:4 Ah sinful nation, a people laden with iniquity, a seed of evildoers, children that are corrupters: they have forsaken the Lord, they have provoked the Holy One of Israel unto anger, they are gone away backwards. 5. Why should ye be stricken anymore? Ye will revolt more and more: the whole head is sick, and the whole heart faint.**

This book shows what happens when the people realize the utopian "promised land" offered by The Powers That Be have not materialized, which results in God no longer getting respect. They may still fear God but losing their faith and having nowhere to turn causes cultural decay. Inevitably, those who supported Statism lose the delusion of feeling chosen or special because in the end their sacrifices have gained them nothing. The benefits promised by the God of Statism may increase material wealth for elitists, but never creates fruitfulness for most of the people. The people grow tired of going through the motions and rituals, and their culture eventually becomes listless and corrupt. The writers speak of the lamentations by the God of Statism, who must find new ways to maintain loyalty when there is a loss of faith.

> **Isaiah 1:11 To what purpose is the multitude of your sacrifices unto me? Saith the Lord: I am full of the burnt offerings of rams, and the fat of fed beasts; and I delight not in the blood of bullocks, or of lambs, or of he goats. 12. When ye come to appear before me, who hath required this at your hand, to tread my courts? 13. Bring no more vain oblations; incense is an abomination unto me; the new moons and sabbaths, the calling of assemblies, I cannot away with; it is iniquity, even the solemn meeting. 14. Your new moons and your appointed feasts my soul hateth: they are a trouble unto me; I am weary to bear them.**

The writers point out this God may oppress and control the people and force outward obeisance, but it becomes insincere and pointless. In the end, this control over the people has never been successful because either there is rebellion and chaos, or the culture of the people devolves into the corruption of mindless rituals and a lack of virtue where the people no longer have hope or self-respect. Eden cannot be created until virtue is restored. Now for the next reason.

The Law and Order Fallacy Leads to a Police State

God condemns the people for their iniquities but promises to bring back law and order desperately needed because of the decay of culture. These promises are made despite the fact God created the problems to begin with. A culture of virtue can never exist under the God of Statism regardless of threats and promises and new laws. The writers know from experience that larger emphasis on laws will only result in laws being enforced that are mostly politically motivated and will be used primarily to protect the God of Statism and its loyal followers. Nevertheless, God now wants to regain strength by taking society backwards to reinstate the fear of God, just as in the bad old days. At first, the God of Statism tries to reassert power through cajoling and threats, along with negotiating and patronizing to solve the problems of cultural degradation.

> **Isaiah 1:18 Come now, and let us reason together, saith the Lord: though your sins be as scarlet, they shall be white as snow; though they be red like crimson, they shall be as wool. 19. If ye be willing and obedient, ye shall eat the good of the land: 20. But if ye refuse and rebel, ye shall be devoured with the sword: for the mouth of the Lord has spoken it. 21. How is the faithful city become an harlot! It was full of judgment; righteousness lodged in it; but now murderers. 22. Thy silver is become dross, thy wine mixed with water: 23. Thy princes are rebellious, and companions of thieves: every one loveth gifts, and followeth after rewards: they judge not the fatherless, neither doth the cause of the widow come unto them. 24. Therefore saith the**

Lord, the Lord of hosts, the mighty One of Israel, Ah, I will ease me of mine adversaries, and avenge me of mine enemies: 25. And I will turn my hand upon thee, and purely purge away thy dross, and take away all thy tin: 26. And I will restore thy judges as at the first, and thy counsellors as at the beginning: afterward thou shalt be called, The city of righteousness, the faithful city. 27. Zion shall be redeemed with judgment, and her converts with righteousness. 28. And the destruction of the transgressors and of the sinners shall be together, and they that forsake the Lord shall be consumed.

God argues he can bring back law and order through strict enforcement and more written laws, which always fails. There are many examples today of this misconception. One glaring example is how some cities pass strict gun laws which do nothing to prevent gun deaths, and often they are even increased. On the other hand, in areas where gun laws are very lax there are fewer gun deaths. The difference is in the culture, not the number of laws or the number of guns. Laws can never replace cultural virtue. More stringent enforcement and more laws result in more oppression.

Isaiah now skips ahead to another vision. He hearkens back to Jacob/Israel, who you will recall struggled with God. He then saw the truth, which caused his relationship with God to change, whereupon he was renamed Israel (struggles with God). Just as Jacob changed after his struggle, Isaiah now hints an entire nation could also change, but the transition may be long and difficult just as Jacob's struggle had been. He predicts that if there could be an end to the Statist social system of authoritarian control people would come from other lands to learn of this new God of the People. Before this can happen the Powers That Be must relinquish power and become a God that teaches peace rather than war. If this were to occur, it could be the last days of The God of Statism.

Isaiah 2:2 And it shall come to pass in the last days, that the mountain of the Lord's house shall be established in the top of the mountains, and shall be

exalted above the hills; and all nations shall flow into it. 3. And many people shall go up and say, Come ye, and let us go up to the mountain of the Lord, to the house of the God of Jacob; and he will teach us of his ways, and we will walk in his paths: for out of Zion shall go forth the law, and the word of the Lord from Jerusalem. 4. And he shall judge among the nations, and shall rebuke many people; and they shall beat their swords into plowshares, and their spears into pruning hooks: nation shall not lift up sword against nation, neither shall they learn war any more. 5. O house of Jacob, come ye, and let us walk in the light of the Lord.

Isaiah predicts a new society could be born resulting in a new relationship with God but knows it can only be achieved through the same determination of the house of Jacob who struggled with God in the past. This prophecy is a dramatic change from the God of the past. Until now, God has always been a vengeful God of war and oppression. It was the God of Statism that created nations to war against each other beginning with Abraham. The growth of those most victorious in war would eventually result in a Leviathan Behemoth controlled by God.

The swords being beaten into plowshares would not even exist had they not been invented by the God of Statism in the beginning to prevent Adam and Eve from reentering Eden. The sword had been made even more necessary by his endless wars. This had been a god that had on occasion even suggested using farm implements to create weapons—not the other way around. The Yahwist writers would have a real task on their hands to suggest a way to completely change the nature of society if their writings were to be useful for future generations. They knew the God of Statism would prevail until we stop the endless cycles. The struggle would never be easy because, as we have seen, this God has many tools to maintain power and control. We can also see this from the next parable with Isaiah showing the next reason Eden had not yet been rebuilt.

Isaiah 6:1 In the year that king Uzziah died I saw also the Lord sitting upon a throne, high and lifted up, and his train filled the temple. 2. Above it stood the seraphims: each one had six wings: with twain he covered his face, and with twain he covered his feet, and with twain he did fly. And one cried unto another, and said Holy, holy, holy, is the Lord of hosts: the whole earth is full of his glory.

Unlike Cherubim working directly with the public and having many faces, there are other loyal assistants to the God of Statism who don't want anyone to see their faces, or know where they are going, hence the covering of their faces and feet. The secretive Seraphim {[40]} (which means burners or destroyers) do not appear publicly. There have been many "burned" by them. The Seraphim are the secretive manipulators of society, and many of their victims are not even aware they are being manipulated until it is too late. The Seraphim are depicted as praising the God of Statism and plotting for his success.

These Seraphim are still today comfortably residing within various State bureaucracies and agencies, are usually concentrated within upper level law enforcement and intelligence communities, and strongly wish to maintain Statism to benefit themselves. Their work is mostly anonymous, but their activities have a huge influence in the workings of the State because of their ability to manipulate the people, as well as other bureaucrats. Today these are sometimes referred to in the U.S. as the Deep State. Seraphim are useful to God when determining loyalty and are adept at punishing those who are not. One of their favorite methods of manipulation is the use of "media propaganda" departments, where they install false prophets. Even today, no modern society of

---

[40] http://www.abarim-publications.com/Meaning/Seraphim.html#.XaJ4g0ZKjIU

Statism could exist without the assistance of the Seraphim. Isaiah envisions receiving his instructions from them.

> **Isaiah 6:8 Also I heard the voice of the Lord, saying, Whom shall I send, and who will go for us? Then said I, Here am I; send me. 9. And he said, Go, and tell this people, Hear ye indeed, but understand not; and see ye indeed but perceive not. 10. Make the heart of this people fat, and make their ears heavy, and shut their eyes; lest they see with their eyes, and hear with their ears, and understand with their heart, and convert, and be healed. 11. Then said I, Lord, how long? And he answered, Until the cities be wasted without inhabitant, and the houses without man, and the land be utterly desolate, 12. And the Lord have removed men far away, and there be a great forsaking in the midst of the land. 13. But yet in it shall be a tenth, and it shall return, and shall be eaten: as a teil tree, and as an oak, whose substance is in them, when they cast their leaves: so the holy seed shall be the substance thereof.**

The insider Seraphim want to rid their population of any who are not loyal to the God of Statism and are determined to retain power through the purging and subjugation process. They discourage citizens wanting to "convert and be healed" and "see with their eyes". They only want to retain those who remain loyal, so that "the holy seed shall be the substance thereof". The exclusion of most of the people prevents Eden from appearing. Under these conditions, society instead starts another cycle of failure. Because of the self-serving efforts of the Seraphim insiders, this brings us to the next reason Eden has not yet appeared.

The Purging Process

The purpose of purging is to create a core made up of only the most faithful so the God of Statism can reassert and strengthen itself. This is usually a defensive act by a degraded Statist society and can be expressed through methods such as ethnic cleansing, propaganda and purging political opponents but can also result a in revolution or civil war. This turns the people within a nation against each other in the hope that only the loyal remain, and the disloyal become displaced or subjugated. After the purging process has been accomplished, it is hoped those remaining will once again be consumed with Statist utopian idealism. You don't want people that can see, hear, or "understand with their heart", because those are the people that cause trouble in a Statist society. It is for these reasons Adam and Eve were tossed out of Eden in the beginning. Again, Eden cannot be created under these conditions.

> **Isaiah 13:13 Therefore I will shake the heavens, and the earth shall remove out of her place, in the wrath of the Lord of hosts, and in the day of his fierce anger. 14. And it shall be as the chased roe, and as a sheep that no man taketh up: they shall every man turn to his own people, and flee every one into his own land. 15. Every one that is found shall be thrust through; and every one that is joined unto them shall fall by the sword. 16. Their children also shall be dashed to pieces before their eyes; their houses shall be spoiled, and their wives ravished.**

The purging process can often be very violent. What follows indicates a contest between two philosophies. Isaiah predicts there will continue to be destruction and wars between the kings, along with continued attacks on Jerusalem and Judah to punish them because of their cultural resistance to God. It doesn't take a prophet to predict these things. As a response to the relentless attacks on their non-Statist tendencies, the Judahites turn to another possibility and a new philosophy. They begin to solidify the concept of a God with a different personality. Because of their efforts, they envision a God that would provide salvation rather than Statism, and understanding rather than perpetual punishment.

> **Isaiah 12:1 And in that day thou shalt say, O Lord, I will praise thee: though thou wast angry with me thine anger is turned away, and thou comfortedst me.**

Behold God is my salvation, I will trust, and not be afraid: for the Lord Jehovah is my strength and my song; he also is become my salvation. 3. Therefore with joy shall ye draw water out of the wells of salvation. 4. And in that day shall ye say, Praise the Lord, call upon his name, declare his doings among the people, make mention that his name is exalted. 5. Sing unto the Lord; for he hath done excellent things: this is known in all the earth. 6. Cry out and shout, thou inhabitant of Zion: for great is the Holy One of Israel in the midst of thee.

As we can see, the Yahwists, (This is the first time YHWH is pronounced Jehovah) in their search for truth and understanding of the role of culture, have been waiting for an opportunity to suggest an alternative. A solution would be the creation of a new Lord Jehovah (YHWH, or Yahwism) which would represent a new emphasis on the people instead of the rulers, and which would encourage self-determination because he is "in the midst of thee" and will appear as one with the people.

Isaiah predicts that this new ideology could be the savior of Israel, but that the God of Statism would still reign in other regions and would lead to their own continued devastation. The ravages of Statism still continues to take its toll in every society wherever it exists and thus confirms their predictions. It is the cycles of cultural upheaval created by Statism that often leads to conflict. This leads to the next reason Eden has not yet reappeared.

Civil War or Revolution within Nations

Isaiah 19:2 And I will set the Egyptians against the Egyptians: and they shall fight every one against his brother, and every one against his neighbor; city against city, and kingdom against kingdom. 3. And the spirit of Egypt shall fail in the midst thereof; and I will destroy the counsel thereof: and they shall seek to the

idols, and to the charmers, and to them that have familiar spirits, and to the wizards. 4. And the Egyptians will I give over into the hand of a cruel lord; and a fierce king shall rule over them, saith the Lord, the Lord of hosts.

Even Egypt, where control and oppression of the people had been institutionalized, would have to face uprisings and would no longer be immune to revolution. The relevancy of these stories is still being demonstrated today. Meanwhile, the Statists who still ruled the people of Judah were depicted as having become so corrupt they are no longer capable of maintaining their bureaucracy or the loyalty of the population. This breakdown of culture always occurs in societies with centralized rule and is also usually the last stage of a Statist system. Unfortunately, the normal pattern is that another cycle of Statist culture will appear from the chaos, or there will be an exodus of some of the population to begin their own Statist society. Because of cultural degradation this cannot be prevented from happening. This is the process demonstrated by the story of Moses and is another obstacle to the appearance of Eden.

Corruption and Degradation of the Bureaucracy

Isaiah 28:3 The crown of pride, the drunkards of Ephraim, shall be trodden under feet: 4. And the glorious beauty, which is on the head of the fat valley, shall be a fading flower, and as the hasty fruit before the summer; which when he that looketh upon it seeth, while it is yet in his hand he eateth it up. 5. In that day shall the Lord of hosts be for a crown of glory, and for a diadem of beauty, unto the residue of his people, 6. And for a spirit of judgment to him that sitteth in judgment, and for strength to them that turn the battle to the gate.

To those that continue to benefit from Statism, it is still a "crown of glory", but the flower has begun to fade as corruption and sloth overtake those at the "head of the fat valley". There will be a "spirit of judgment to him that sitteth in judgment". People will begin to question the authority of their own leadership. Modern day versions of decadence would be issues such as drug and alcohol abuse, criminality, cronyism, and corruption, which will begin to rise within the bureaucracy which further damages any possibility of creating heaven or Eden. Once they no longer even believe in themselves, the authorities fall into self-destructive habits. Even as they continue to exalt themselves, their culture becomes weak and defenseless.

> **Isaiah 28:7 But they also have erred through wine, and through strong drink are out of the way; the priest and the prophet have erred through strong drink, they are swallowed up of wine, they are out of the way through strong drink; they err in vision, they stumble in judgment. 8. For all tables are full of vomit and filthiness, so that there is no place clean. 9. Whom shall he teach knowledge? And whom shall he make to understand doctrine? Them that are weaned from the milk, and are drawn from the breasts. 10. For precept must be upon precept, precept upon precept; line upon line, line upon line; here a little, and there a little: 11. For with stammering lips and another tongue will he speak to his people. 12. To whom he said, This is the rest wherewith ye may cause the weary to rest; and this is the refreshing: yet they would not hear. 13. But the word of the Lord was unto them precept upon precept, precept upon precept; line upon line, line upon line; here a little, and there a little; that they might go, and fall backward, and be broken, and snared, and taken.**

To maintain a Statist society, it is vital for the strength of the bureaucracy to be maintained. You must continue to push the false idol that all doctrine is for the benefit of the people and therefore must be strictly applied through "precept upon precept; line upon line" and expanded and enforced at the will of the State. You must continue to make promises and increase benefits. There must be new laws applied with regularity to increase the size and power of bureaucracy to "serve the people" and pretend to be protecting. But the rulers are not taking care of business, and as a result they are falling away from the strength of the God of Statism and allowing their bureaucracy to die, along with their culture. They have become comfortable in their position of power, but virtue becomes nonexistent, which leaves them open to becoming a failed state subject to invasion. They have ignored their prospects of reaching the Sabbath, where there "is the rest wherewith ye may cause the weary to rest; and this is the refreshing: yet they would not hear."

> **Isaiah 28:14 Wherefore hear the word of the Lord, ye scornful men, that rule this people which is in Jerusalem. 15. Because ye have said, We have made a covenant with death, and with hell are we at agreement; when the overflowing scourge shall pass through, it shall not come unto us: for we have made lies our refuge, and under falsehood have we hid ourselves: 16. Therefore thus saith the Lord God, Behold, I lay in Zion for a foundation a stone, a tried stone, a precious corner stone, a sure foundation: he that believeth shall not make haste. 17. Judgment also will I lay to the line, and righteousness to the plummet: and the hail shall sweep away the refuge of lies, and the waters shall overflow the hiding place. 18. And your covenant with death shall be disannulled, and your agreement with hell shall not stand; when the overflowing scourge shall pass through, then ye shall be trodden down by it.**

The elites live in a state of denial of their own iniquities and, as always, believe they are still justified to rule over their subjects. Eventually the people will themselves begin to build upon the foundation stone, recognized as the rebelliousness of the people of Judah against Statism. Judgment and righteousness will be reevaluated. Some seven hundred years later the book of Isaiah will serve as an inspiration for a Jewish radical called Jesus. For now, the battle would be far from over. In fact, the battle would never end until the last days of Statism, which still has not yet arrived. The corruption and degradation of leadership, and the activities of bureaucrats to continue to protect their own interests, lead to the next reason Eden cannot appear.

Stop the People from Creating Heaven Themselves

Isaiah 34:1 Come near, ye nations, to hear; and hearken, ye people: let the earth hear, and all that is therein; the world, and all things that come forth of it. 2. For the indignation of the Lord is upon all the nations, and his fury upon all their armies: he hath utterly destroyed them, he hath delivered them to the slaughter. 3. Their slain also shall be cast out, and their stink shall come up out of their carcases, and the mountains shall be melted with their blood. 4. And all the host of heaven shall be dissolved, and the heavens shall be rolled together as a scroll: and all their host shall fall down, as the leaf falleth off from the vine, and as a falling fig from the fig tree. 5. For my sword shall be bathed in heaven: behold, it shall come down upon Idumea, and upon the people of my curse, to judgment. 6. The sword of the Lord is filled with blood, it is made fat with fatness, and with the blood of lambs and goats, with the fat of the kidneys of rams: for the Lord hath a sacrifice in Bozrah, and a great slaughter in the land of Idumea. 7. And the unicorns shall come down with them, and the bullocks with the bulls; and their land shall be soaked with blood, and their dust made fat with fatness. 8. For it is the day of the Lord's vengeance, and the year of recompences for the controversy of Zion.

You just know you're going to be trouble when even the unicorns of heaven are going to be destroyed. You cannot allow the people to ignore or attempt to go around the bureaucracies to create their own culture, no matter the level of corruption. God will not relent easily, and will find cause for warfare among nations or between nations, as they are repeatedly divided and turned against each other. The God of Statism fears a heavenly culture and has a desire that "all the host of heaven shall be dissolved," and "all their host shall fall down", "For my sword shall be bathed in heaven". There is no desire for the State to create a higher level of cultural heaven among the people, as it would necessarily exclude the God of Statism. And so the "controversy of Zion" continues today with Jewish stiff-necked resistance to Statism. Israel continues to survive, even though their culture has been under continuous attack, both from inside and out, since the beginning. They have even been scattered around the world and persecuted on many occasions and in horrible ways. This is not a phenomenon totally specific to the Jews, but again—they wrote the book. Fortunately, both they and the book have survived.

While the book of Isaiah acknowledges the possibilities of the creation of Eden through self-governance and self-rule, it also continues to demonstrate the difficulties and realities of doing so. For one thing, the God of Statism can be temporarily useful and will even be invited to return when a nation is under attack from the enemies of other Statist societies bent on their destruction. Very often, there are attempts to takeover those seen as weaker and unable to defend themselves. A state of degraded culture always invites invasion, which requires the return of Statism in response. So, we now have yet another reason Eden has not yet appeared.

War and The Military Industrial Complex

Returning to Statism for salvation in difficult times is pleasing to God. This is the story of Hezekiah, king of Judah, pleading to the god they thought they had abandoned, because of the eminent destruction of Jerusalem at the hands of the Assyrians and others who have decided to besiege Jerusalem. Because of their cultural weakness they appeared vulnerable and ripe for invasion. In response, King Hezekiah of Judah pleads to God to return and offer aid.

Isaiah 37:15 And Hezekiah prayed unto the Lord, saying, 16. O Lord of hosts, God of Israel, that dwellest between cherubims, thou art the God, even thou alone, of the kingdoms of earth: thou hast made heaven and earth. 17. Incline thine ear, O Lord, and hear; open thine eyes, O Lord, and see: and hear all the words of Sennacherib, which hath sent to reproach the living God. 18. Of a truth, Lord, the kings of Assyria have laid waste all the nations, and their countries, 19. And have cast their gods into the fire: for they were no gods, but the work of mens hands, wood and stone: therefore they have destroyed them. 20. Now therefore, O Lord our God, save us from his hand, that all the kingdoms of the earth may know that thou art the Lord, even thou only. 21. Then Isaiah the son of Amoz sent unto Hezekiah, saying, Thus saith the Lord God of Israel, Whereas thou hast prayed to me against Sennacherib king of Assyria: 22. This is the word which the Lord hath spoken concerning him; The virgin, the daughter of Zion, hath despised thee, and laughed thee to scorn; the daughter of Jerusalem hath shaken her head at thee. 23. Whom hath thou reproached and blasphemed? And against whom exalted thy voice, and lifted up thine eyes on high? Even against the Holy One of Israel.

As usual, this is a God that shows contempt when the people return to him because of impending catastrophe, because he knows he is scorned by the stiff-necked Israelites.

Isaiah 37:28 But I know thy abode, and thy going out, and thy coming in, and thy rage against me. 29. Because thy rage against me, and thy tumult, is come up into mine ears, therefore will I put my hook in thy nose, and my bridle in thy lips, and I will turn thee back by the way by which thou camest. 30. And this shall be a sign unto thee, Ye shall eat this year such as groweth of itself; and the second year that which

171

springeth of the same: and in the third year sow ye and reap, and plant vineyards, and eat the fruit thereof. 31. And the remnant that is escaped of the house of Judah shall again take root downward, and bear fruit upward: 32. For out of Jerusalem shall go forth a remnant, and they that escape out of mount Zion: the zeal of the Lord of hosts shall do this. 33. Therefore thus saith the Lord concerning the king of Assyria, He shall not come into this city, nor shoot an arrow there, nor come before it with shields, nor cast a bank against it. 34. By the way that he came, by the same shall he return, and shall not come into this city, saith the Lord. 35. For I will defend this city to save it for my own sake, and for my servant David's sake. 36. Then the angel of the Lord went forth, and smote in the camp of the Assyrians a hundred and fourscore and five thousand: and then they arose early in the morning, behold, they were all dead corpses. 37. So Sennacherib king of Assyria departed, and went and returned, and dwelt at Nineveh. 38. And it came to pass, as he was worshiping in the house of Nisroch his god, that Adrammelech and Sharezer his sons smote him with the sword; and they escaped in to the land of Armenia: and Esarhaddon his son reigned in his stead.

As it turns out, people are often willing to put a hook in their nose, and a bridle in their lips, and go backwards whenever survival is an issue. If you want 185,000 warriors of a threatening army to wake up dead, and your worst enemy to be murdered by his own sons to preserve your own turf, then you have little choice but to turn to the God of Statism for protection. Herein lies one of the biggest obstacles to the creation of Eden. It is almost impossible to put Statism back into its bottle once he has been released again in times of war. Therefore, constant warfare is useful to the God of Statism.

Those who have struggled to raise their culture to a new level are under constant attack from other Statists and must repeatedly return the war-like god of Statism to protect them. This is how the military industrial complex stays in business, even in freedom loving societies that reject war. Even worse, as we see in the next parable, if the military can become politicized it usually spells trouble for the people but is usually a good thing for reestablishing the State. As we have seen, sometimes God will even start wars for no other purpose.

Elitists such as Hezekiah discover that returning to this God extends benefits for themselves even after the war. God grants life to the king for another fifteen years, which allows him time to accumulate more wealth and power, even though he had been on his death bed politically. This is his reward for calling on God to return and save them.

> **Isaiah 38:9 Go, and say to Hezekiah, Thus saith the Lord, the God of David thy father, I have heard thy prayer, I have seen thy tears: behold, I will add unto thy days fifteen years. 6. And I will deliver thee and this city out of the hand of the king of Assyria: and I will defend this city. 7. And this shall be a sign unto thee from the Lord, that the Lord will do this thing that he hath spoken; 8. Behold, I will bring again the shadow of degrees, which is gone down in the sun dial of Ahaz, ten degrees backward. So the sun returned ten degrees, by which degrees it was gone down.**

Warfare has always been a strong incentive for Statist leadership, as shown in the previous stories, but in returning to the God of Statism one must be prepared to go backwards, metaphorically represented here by the sun. Once the war is over, the extension of his term in office by God provides Hezekiah an opportunity to reassert his power and boast of his wealth to some visiting dignitaries from Babylon. He welcomes his fellow elitists and shows them his proudest possessions.

> **Isaiah 39:2 And Hezekiah was glad of them, and shewed them the house of his precious things, the silver and the gold, and the spices, and the precious ointment, and all the house of his armour, and all that**

was found in his treasures: there was nothing in his house, nor in all his dominion, that Hezekiah shewed them not. 3. Then came Isaiah the prophet unto king Hezekiah, and said unto him, What said these men? And from whence came thee unto thee? And Hezekiah said, They are come from a far country unto me, even from Babylon. 4. Then said he, What have they seen in thine house? And Hezekiah answered, All that is in mine house have they seen: there is nothing among my treasures that I have not shewed them. 5. Then said Isaiah to Hezekiah, Hear the word of the Lord of hosts: 6. Behold, the days come, that all that is in thine house, and that which thy fathers have laid up in store until this day, shall be carried to Babylon: nothing shall be left, saith the Lord. 7. And of thy sons that shall issue from thee, which thou shalt beget, shall they take away; and they be eunuchs in the palace of the king of Babylon. 8. Then said Hezekiah to Isaiah, Good is the word of the Lord which thou hast spoken. He said moreover, For there shall be peace and truth in my days.

As Hezekiah returns his people to Statism, he becomes one more bureaucrat that is willing to sacrifice the future generations for benefits today through having his political life extended. Just as young Solomon, he believed the treasures of his land were what he had accumulated in his storehouses. If he had understood that true treasure lies in the potential of his people and had shared that with his visitors instead of showing them his storehouses, he might have altered history. Instead, he returned to a fickle God that, although reassuring to him in wartime, as usual would charge a heavy price for his services and take culture backwards. And as usual, the actions of a few at the top would determine which God would determine the culture of the people. Through his actions and his greed for benefits, Hezekiah would give the God of Statism new strength, resulting in his nation once again being sold into slavery to a more powerful State. The price you pay for Statism is very high. However, "And the remnant that is escaped of the house of

Judah shall again take root downward, and bear fruit upward". Once the noblemen of Judah have been exiled to Babylon, the people remaining are relatively free to consider their own cultural evolution.

I Am You and You Are Me

Another very telling story comes out of the parables of Isaiah as God makes another confession.

> **Isaiah 45:5 I am the Lord, and there is none else, there is no God beside me: I girded thee, though thou hast not known me: 6. That they may know from the rising of the sun, and from the west, that there is none beside me. I am the Lord, and there is none else. 7. I form the light, and create evil: I the Lord do all these things.**

Again, the writers point out that God is both good and evil, and his nature is determined by the culture of We The People, and vice versa. They point out the futility of creating false idols and worshiping them as though a God is something outside of our nature. Any image of god is a false idol, simply because you cannot form an image of a cultural concept or human nature.

> **Isaiah 40:18 To whom then will ye liken God? or what likeness will ye compare unto him? 19. The workman melteth a graven image, and the goldsmith spreadeth it over with gold, and casteth silver chains. 20. He that is so impoverished that he hath no oblation chooseth a tree that will not rot; he seeketh unto him a cunning workman to prepare a graven image, that shall not be moved. 21. Have ye not known? have ye not heard? hath it not been told you from the beginning? have ye not understood from the foundation of the earth? 22. It is he that sitteth upon the circle of the earth, and the inhabitants thereof are as grasshoppers; that stretcheth out the heavens as a curtain, and spreadeth them out as a tent to dwell in: 23. That bringeth the princes to nothing; he maketh the judges of the earth as vanity. 24. Yea, they shall not be planted; yea, they shall not be sown: yea, their stock shall not take root in the earth: and he shall blow upon them, and they shall wither, and the whirlwind shall take them away as stubble.**

Statism, with its princes and judges and other graven idols, will all eventually wither and blow away. Different political systems may come and go, but culture is eternal and will still be determined by our nature, and God reflects our nature. We are responsible for determining what our culture and nature will be, including the nature of God. However, if we so choose, then the God of Statism will still be with us, and the cycles of failure will repeat themselves. We can bring him back as often as we want, and he will be happy to oblige.

Isaiah 41:13 For I the Lord will hold thy right hand saying unto thee, Fear not, thou worm Jacob, and ye men of Israel; I will help thee, saith the Lord, and thy redeemer, the Holy One of Israel.

The writers portray a God that, although recognizing the people of Jacob have resisted, still turn to him in time of trouble, so he questions the ability of man to ever have the courage to stand up for themselves to change his nature. He challenges those who make false idols designed to show his nature, or to be able to bring about both good and evil as he does.

Isaiah 41:21 Produce your cause, saith the Lord; bring forth your strong reasons, saith the King of Jacob. 22. Let them bring them forth, and shew us what shall happen: let them show the former things, what they be, that we may consider them, and know the latter end of them; or declare us things for to come. 23. Shew the things that are to come hereafter, that we may know that ye are gods: yea, do good, or do evil, that we may be dismayed, and behold it together. 24. Behold, ye are nothing, and your work of naught: an abomination is he that chooseth you. 25. I have raised up one from the north, and he shall come: from the rising of the sun shall he call upon my name: and he shall come upon princes as upon mortar, and as the potter treadeth clay. 26. Who hath declared from the beginning, that we may know? And beforetime, that we may say, He is righteous? Yea there is none that

sheweth, yea, there is none that declareth, yea there is none that heareth your words. 27. The first shall say to Zion, Behold, behold them: and I will give to Jerusalem one that bringeth good tidings. 28. For I beheld, and there was no man; even among them, and there was no counsellor, that, when I asked of them; could answer a word. 29. Behold, they are all vanity; their works are nothing: their molten images are wind and confusion.

Those who believe they will be saved by another false redeemer, rather than receive the message they can save themselves, are worshiping a false idol. "For I beheld, and there was no man; even among them, and there was no counsellor; that, when I asked of them; could answer a word. 29. Behold, they are all vanity; their works are nothing: their molten images are wind and confusion." The god that will be our redeemer is in ourselves and in our ability to reshape our culture. In the meantime, the people continue to evolve culturally and, not surprisingly, so does God.

> **Isaiah 43:18 Remember ye not the former things, neither consider the things of old. 19. Behold, I will do a new thing; now it shall spring forth; shall ye not know it? I will even make a way in the wilderness, and rivers in the desert. 20. The beast in the field shall honor me, the dragons and the owls: because I give waters in the wilderness, and rivers in the desert, to give drink to my people, my chosen. 21. This people have I formed for myself; they shall shew forth my praise. 22. But thou hast not called upon me, O Jacob; but thou hast been weary of me, O Israel.**

The writers show a God that is willing to have a different nature and to "do a new thing" if we claim our power, but we must first call on the God of We The People. We can be encouraged that at some point the rebellious Jewish people did call on their own abilities to save themselves, but not before great suffering. The writers also show that a weak and corrupt culture can leave the people vulnerable. To a large extent we are seeing this in the U.S. and Western Europe today. This development is not an entirely natural or accidental degradation of culture. Statism abhors freedom of the people, just as nature abhors a vacuum, and there will always be powerful forces that prefer the secure profitability and elitism offered through Statism, which requires the accompanying degraded and divided culture to begin to build power. On the other hand, the god within us only requires we call upon our own ability to create a virtuous culture. This would be a culture which could have everlasting life rather than the turmoil of the cycles of failure.

We know a new God described here can be accomplished, because the Jewish people in Israel today have created a strong culture capable of resisting Statism to serve as an example. We once had the same strong culture in the U.S., but our culture is being deliberately degraded to weaken us to reimpose Statism, which is why the warnings in the bible have become urgently important. The Jewish people have always known this instinctively, and they have become survivors that are strong on defense but are no longer ruled by warlords as were their ancestors or their current neighbors.

We shouldn't despise people who have been victimized by Statism. We should understand their status as victims, while offering a strong defense against their influence on a more successful culture. As an example, the Nazis in World War II were not our enemy. The enemy was their degraded culture that created the Nazi movement from impoverished shopkeepers, farmers, and students by offering them the temptations of Statism, which is God's evil spirit. They surrendered their birthright of self-determination in return for a steady paycheck and snappy uniforms. Eden cannot be created until we can find a way to prevent this sort of thing from happening again. Until then, the God of Statism will continue to be an ever-present threat.

Jeremiah—More Wrath and More Promises

Jeremiah continues with the already age-old story of Jewish resistance. The Powers That Be complain bitterly at how the people of Israel and Judah consistently turn away from him. The condemnation of his "children" has again turned into a lengthy rant of their inequities. This is a petulant God that admonishes the people to return and pledge obedience to the God of Statism, or else there will continue to be punishment. His negotiation with the people also continues, because without active participation from the people, The Powers That Be have no power.

Jeremiah 4:1 If thou wilt return, O Israel, saith the Lord, return unto me: and if thou wilt put away thine abominations out of my sight then shalt thou not remove. 2. And thou shalt swear, The Lord liveth, in truth, in judgment, and in righteousness; and the nations shall bless themselves in him, and in him shall they glory. 3. For thus saith the Lord to the men of Judah and Jerusalem, Break up your fallow ground, and sow not among thorns. 4. Circumcise yourselves to the Lord, and take away the foreskins of your heart, ye men of Judah and inhabitants of Jerusalem: lest my fury come forth like fire, and burn that none can quench it, because of your doings.

At this point, Jeremiah breaks in with a response.

Jeremiah 4:10 Then said I, Ah, Lord God! Surely thou has greatly deceived this people and Jerusalem, saying, Ye shall have peace; whereas the sword reacheth unto the soul.

The deception that God will bring peace has been recognized, and so they continue to resist. But the nature of this God is still Statism, and therefore the destructive nature of man will continue.

Jeremiah 4:17 As keepers of a field, are they against her round about; because she (Jerusalem) **hath been**

180

rebellious against me, saith the Lord. 18. Thy way and thy doings have procured these things unto thee; this is thy wickedness, because it is bitter, because it reacheth unto thine heart. 19. My bowels, my bowels! I am pained at my very heart; my heart maketh a noise in me; I cannot hold my peace, because thou hast heard, O my soul, the sound of the trumpet, the alarm of war. 20. Destruction upon destruction is cried; for the whole land is spoiled: suddenly are my tents spoiled and my curtains in a moment. 21. How long shall I see the standard, and hear the sound of the trumpet? 22. For my people is foolish, they have not known me; they are sottish children, and they have none understanding: they are wise to do evil, but to do good they have no knowledge. 23. I beheld the earth, and, lo, it was without form, and void; and the heavens and they had no light. 24. I beheld the mountains, and lo, they trembled, and all the hills moved lightly. 25. I beheld, and, lo, there was no man, and all the birds of the heavens were fled. 26. I beheld, and, lo, the fruitful place was a wilderness, and all the cities thereof were broken down at the presence of the Lord, and by his fierce anger. 27. For thus has the Lord said, The whole land shall be desolate; yet will I not make a full end. 28. For this shall the earth mourn, and the heavens above be black: because I have spoken it, I have purposed it, and will not repent, neither will I turn back from it.

The God of Statism cannot change its nature or go away of its own volition, and can only change through our own actions, which is difficult because of all the reasons laid out in Isaiah. "For my people is foolish, they have not known me; they are sottish children, and they have none understanding: they are wise to do evil, but to do good they have no knowledge." The temptations of Statism are strong, and the result is like an addiction that forces the victim to be "wise to do evil", and to steal from culture to support the habit, and cannot stop. Or is like a train that can only go where the tracks lead it, unless the tracks are rerouted. Only culture can change the nature of God, and that must be done by We The People, because we are the tracks. The addiction will continue until We The People who resist Statism decide to have an intervention to stop it.

As for themselves, the stubborn people of Judah and Israel still refuse to be the enabler, even though they often suffer the consequences.

> **Jeremiah 11:9 And the Lord said unto me, a conspiracy is found among the men of Judah, and among the inhabitants of Jerusalem. 10. They are turned back to the iniquities of their forefathers, which refused to hear my words; and they went after other gods to serve them: the house of Israel and the house of Judah have broken my covenant which I made with their fathers. 11. Therefore thus saith the Lord, Behold, I will bring evil upon them, which they shall not be able to escape; and though they shall cry unto me, I will not hearken to them. 12. Then shall the cities of Judah and the inhabitants of Jerusalem go, and cry unto the gods unto whom they offer incense: but they shall not save them at all in the time of their trouble.**

An addict deprived of drugs will often become unstable or seek out another source. That the Israelites were still struggling to find another way in those times is evident. Their trial and error continued, and although they paid a price for every mistake, they were still evolving culturally. This does not make God happy.

> **Jeremiah 14:10 Thus sayeth the Lord unto this people, Thus have they loved to wander, they have not refrained their feet, therefore the Lord doth not accept them; he will not remember their iniquities, and visit their sins. 11. Then said the Lord unto me, Pray not for this people for their good. 12. When they fast, I will not hear their cry; and when they offer burnt offerings and an oblation, I will not accept them: but I will**

consume them by the sword, and by the famine, and by the pestilence.

Again, Jeremiah breaks in with a response.

Jeremiah 14:13 Then said I, Ah, Lord God! Behold, the prophets say unto them, Ye shall not see the sword, neither shall ye have famine; but I will give you assured peace in this place.

There are those who see the deceitfulness and try to determine an escape mechanism. There are those among the people that are suggesting optimism and change for the future, and these are becoming a threat to God. Optimism is not beneficial to the Powers That Be. That there are those out there suggesting there can be a future with no more war and pestilence and famine upsets God, who needs these hardships so that the people will return for protection and a sense of security.

Jeremiah 14:14 Then the Lord said unto me, The prophets prophesy lies in my name: I sent them not, neither have I commanded them, neither have spake unto them: they prophesy unto you a false vision and divination, and a thing of nought, and the deceit of their heart. 15. Therefore thus saith the Lord concerning the prophets that prophecy in my name, and I sent them not, yet they say, Sword and famine shall not be in this land; By sword and famine shall those prophets be consumed. 16. And the people to whom they prophesy shall be be cast out in the streets of Jerusalem because of the famine and the sword; and they shall have none to bury them, their wives, nor their sons, nor their daughters: for I will pour their wickedness upon them.

No one can question the use of plagues such as war and famine which cause the people return to God for salvation. Those who show a lack of loyalty and speak of other ways will face consequences. However, being the stiff-necked Israelite people, they are seeing the problems this God has brought through selling them out to slavery to the Babylonians and others because of their own corrupt leadership, and some of the wiser citizens begin to speak up. Despite all the punishment, or no doubt because of it, they are still evolving culturally and begin to speak more often of a new philosophy toward life.

Being exiled to Babylon, some of them have recognized what has brought them to their current state of affairs in their slavery and punishment. They begin speaking publicly about the accomplishments of their stiff-necked brethren that escaped. The escapees had remained in Israel, rather than obey God and submit to slavery. They apparently also speak openly to others of what they have learned of God, and their message begins to spread among other cultures. The Powers That Be must stop this behavior.

Jeremiah 29:15 Because ye have said, The Lord hath raised us up prophets in Babylon; 16. Know that thus saith the Lord of the king that sitteth upon the throne of David, and of all the people that dwelleth in this city, and of your brethren that are not gone forth with you into captivity; 17. Thus saith the Lord of hosts; Behold, I will send upon them the sword, the famine, and the pestilence, and will make them like vile figs, that cannot be eaten, they are so evil. 18. And I will persecute them with the sword, and with the famine, and with the pestilence, and will deliver them to be removed to all the kingdoms of earth, to be a curse, and an astonishment, and an hissing, and a reproach, among all the nations whither I have driven them: 19. Because they have not hearkened to my words, saith the Lord, which I sent unto them by my servants and the prophets, rising up early and sending them; but would not hear, saith the Lord. 20. Hear ye therefore the word of the Lord, all ye of the captivity, whom I have sent from Jerusalem to Babylon: 21. Thus saith the Lord of hosts, the God of Israel, of Ahab the son of Kolaiah, and of Zedekiah the son of Maaseiah, which prophesy a lie unto you in my name; Behold, I will

deliver them into the hand of Nebuchadnezzar king of Babylon; and he shall slay them before your eyes; 22. And of them shall be taken up a curse by all the captivity of Judah which are in Babylon, saying, The Lord make thee like Zedekiah and like Ahaab, whom the king of Babylon roasted in the fire;

If you are so "evil in the sight of the Lord" that you won't even accept the slavery you have been sold into by your Statist God, and even openly suggest another way of life, then there's not much God can do but have you killed unpleasantly or at least have you publicly discredited, vilified, or enslaved. The writers use these stories to make the point that they are aware it is through the actions of their leadership that they have been sold into slavery. Not only had their elites allowed Statism to become their religion, but the people had also experienced the resulting corruption and moral decay that weakened their culture to the point they had become defenseless.

It is through learning from their experiences that Yawhism produced the wisdom and knowledge necessary to see the need for a culture of self-determination. They had the ability to learn from their own sinfulness, and so were able to evolve socially and morally. The alternative to cultural evolution is they would continue to suffer the cycles of God's wrath. They began to realize change could only come through their own actions, and through the natural and living flow of culture. They had seen that seeking new kings to save them was just another fallacy. A living god is a god that can change and evolve and improve through the virtue and wisdom of the people. But how do you make the people understand they must resist the temptations of Statism? If you are a Yahwist then you write books with parables that evoke wisdom, in the hope the people will someday understand. Those books now speak to We The People.

185

Israel Remains a Stiff-Necked Bastion of Resistance

The writers knew any culture emphasizing the power of the people, rather than the Powers of the State, would make them an outcast and cause them to have many enemies among the Powers of other States fearful of the effects their message would have on their own citizens. However, the Yahwists must have been optimistic by nature, and time and again the authors demonstrate how fast God can change with culture. That, of course, is because they are essentially the same thing, because our culture creates God in our image. The question to them is, how do The Powers That Be of the State become the Power of the People? As they begin to imagine what such a culture would look like, their idea continues to take shape. This is demonstrated by the next statement concerning politics and self-rule.

> **Jeremiah 30:21 And their nobles shall be of themselves, and their governor shall proceed from the midst of them; and I will cause him to draw near, and he shall approach unto me: for who is this that engaged his heart to approach unto me? Saith the Lord. 22. And ye shall be my people, and I will be your God.**

Their view is that God is always willing to be a God of the People, but only if we defy the God of Statism and discuss the iniquities of our culture openly and demand freedom. We can only achieve Eden by teaching we are responsible for maintaining a virtuous culture that will allow it to exist. Governance must come "from the midst of them", and not be anointed by a Statist God. If not, we will always allow ourselves to be sold into slavery by God and suffer the repetitive cycles of Statism.

The real danger is we will eventually no longer have stiff-necked people to show us the lesson of resistance to the God of Statism. If that ever happens, we are lost and the entire planet could become Statist under a single centralized Global God of Statism and a heavenly Eden would then never exist, because that centralized system would no longer allow cultural experimentation and evolution for fear it would lose power and control. Any suggestions of a new way would make the people "evil in the sight of the Lord", then division, war, famine, and pestilence would follow.

Ezekiel—The Threat From Within

It seems that every generation of writers contributing to the books of the bible felt the need to include their version of how Statist cultural manipulation plays such an important role in society. There is the usual theme of the rebellion of the stiff-necked people of the Jewish ancestors, and of course the continuous punishment meted out by the God of Statism for their lack of loyalty.

Most stories also deal with how God never loses the opportunity to blame the victims of his wrath on the iniquities of the people as they receive his punishment. Of course, this is the truth because it is always the culture of the people that allows this God to exist. Their iniquities are in turn largely the result of Statism the people create because of the accompanying degradation of society. The cycles become self-perpetuating. The Yahwists see this happening in all kingdoms, not just their own. As they recognized, the God of Statism is a monotheistic god. The writers then continue to point out all the various ways Statism can creep into any society. The writers use Ezekiel as a more detailed example of how subversion can come from within and is one way a weakened and degraded society can be targeted.

The story of Ezekiel accurately describes a method of Statist social engineering that avoids open warfare against a stronger culture. First, you begin by working from within a society to establish a foothold, and then expand that influence until control is achieved. Using this method, the culture of an entire nation can be fundamentally transformed through creating internal strife, economic chaos, social degradation, division through identity politics, and terrorism which are all drawn from the Ark of Statism toolbox.

Since Statism encourages elitism, the general population is always considered to be inferior and profane, so it is always justifiable to turn citizens against each other to establish dominance. This method has been achieved repeatedly throughout history, and complete takeovers have often occurred.

Ezekiel describes how this type of community disorganization can be utilized to degrade culture to whatever extent necessary to establish a sanctuary. The process can be facilitated first through demoralization of the targeted population, and once that has been accomplished, it becomes easier to begin the takeover. Part of the process involves choosing individuals or institutions to become Statist operatives, which then create a sanctuary from which to expand their agenda. For this purpose, Ezekiel is chosen. He has popularity and fame as a prophet, so he already has credibility.

> **Ezekiel 1:3 The word of the Lord came expressly unto Ezekiel the priest, the son of Buzi, in the land of the Chaldeans by the river Chebar; and the hand of the Lord was there upon him.**

Having now been chosen, Ezekiel meets with the Cherubim, who we know are bureaucracies or influential institutions created to instill awe and fear as an obstacle. If you will recall, we have met them before.

> **Ezekiel 1:10 As for the likeness of their faces, they four had the face of a man, and the face of a lion, on the right side: and they four had the face of an ox on the left side; they four also had the face of an eagle.**

If the purpose is to instill fear and confusion, then having lots of faces is a huge asset. The whole purpose of Cherubim is to produce a sense of helplessness, and usually does so through both intimidation and through the confusion of presenting a different face for each situation. They have been with The Powers That Be from the beginning and were instrumental in ejecting man from Eden.

> **Ezekiel 1:17 When they went, they went upon their four sides: and they turned not when they went. 18. As for their rings, they were so high that they were dreadful; and their rings were full of eyes round about them four. 19. And when the living creatures went, the**

wheels went by them: and when the living creatures were lifted up from the earth, the wheels were lifted up. 20. Whithersoever the spirit was to go, they went, thither was their spirit to go; and the wheels were lifted up over against them: for the spirit of the living creature was in the wheels. 21. When those went, these went; and when those stood, these stood; and when those were lifted up from the earth, the wheels were lifted up over against them: for the spirit of the living creature was in the wheels.

Running confusing circles around someone through deceptive institutions or bureaucracies is nothing new, and it is often impossible to know where they are coming from or where they are going. The more layers of confusing bureaucracy you can create, then the more job security there is for insider Statists who have a vested interest in self-perpetuation. Many have fallen victim to the subversive Cherubim because of their menacing displays of wealth and power and their close association with the God of Statism. These Cherubim often present their human face in the beginning. Meanwhile, after having been dazzled and intimated by the Cherubim...

Ezekiel 1:28 As the appearance of the bow that is in the cloud in the day of rain, so was the appearance of the likeness of the glory of the Lord. And when I saw it, I fell upon my face, and I heard a voice of one that spake.

Ezekiel 2:1 And he said unto me, Son of man, stand upon thy feet, and I will speak unto thee. 2. And the spirit entered into me when he spake unto me, and set me upon my feet, that I heard him that spake unto me. 3. And he said unto me, Son of man, I send thee to the children of Israel, to a rebellious nation that hath rebelled against me: they and their fathers have transgressed against me, even unto this very day. 4. For they are impudent children and stiffhearted. I do send thee unto them; and thou shalt say unto them,

Thus saith the Lord God. 5. And they, whether they will hear, or whether they will forbear, (for they are a rebellious house,) yet shall know that there hath been a prophet among them.

Using admired and popularly accepted personalities and giving them false validity is common among Statists. Today they often groom entertainers, TV hosts, or attractive news broadcasters to spread their propaganda to promote a Statist agenda. Before the popularity of Ezekiel can be made useful, he must be indoctrinated and provided with the narrative.

Ezekiel 2:8 But thou, son of man, hear what I say unto thee; Be not thou rebellious like that rebellious house: open thy mouth, and eat that I give thee. 9. And when I looked, behold, an hand was sent unto me; and, lo, a roll of a book was therein; 10. And he spread it before me; and it was written within and without: and there was written therein lamentations, and mourning, and woe. Ezekiel 3:1 Moreover he said unto me, Son of man, eat that thou findest; eat this roll, and go speak unto the house of Israel. 2. So I opened my mouth, and he caused me to eat that roll. 3. And he said unto me, Son of man, cause thy belly to eat, and fill thy bowels with this roll that I give thee. Then did I eat it; and it was in my mouth as honey for sweetness. 4. And he said unto me, Son of man, go, get thee unto the house of Israel, and speak with my words unto them.

The phrase "drink the kool-aid" {[41]} had not yet been invented, but you get the idea. The narrative of Statism always consists of "lamentations, and mourning, and woe", to recruit those who are already inclined to believe they are victims. Those who achieve happiness and prosperity "by thine own right hand" have the unpleasant characteristic of thinking they don't need to be saved. Once the narrative has been established, and Ezekiel has accepted

---

[41] https://en.wikipedia.org/wiki/Drinking_the_Kool-Aid

his mission, God then lets him know his intentions toward the stiff-hearted nation.

Ezekiel 5:7 Therefore thus saith the Lord God; Because ye multiplied more than the nations that are round about you, and have not walked in my statutes, neither have kept my judgments, neither have done according to the judgments of the (Statist) **nations that are round about you; 8. Therefore thus saith the Lord God; Behold, I, even I, am against thee, and will execute judgments in the midst of thee in the sight of the nations. 9. And I will do in thee that which I have not done, and whereunto I will not do any more the like, because of all thine abominations.**

Since the people of Judah have refused to capitulate, and instead have prospered without him just as in Babel, God will use multiple methods of attack simultaneously. These methods have since become popular to subversive institutions around the world to create a need for authority and a return to Statism. The effects on the people would still be familiar in some regions.

Ezekiel 6:12 A third part of thee shall die with the pestilence, and with famine shall they be consumed in the midst of thee: and a third part shall fall by the sword round about thee; and I will scatter a third part into all the winds, and I will draw out a sword after them. 13. Thus shall mine anger be accomplished, and I will cause my fury to rest upon them, and I will be comforted: and they shall know that I the Lord have spoken it in my zeal, when I have accomplished my fury in them. 14. Moreover I will make thee waste, and a reproach among the nations that are round about thee, in the sight of all that pass by. 15. So it shall be a reproach and a taunt, an instruction and an astonishment unto the nations that are round about thee, when I shall execute judgments in thee in anger and in fury and in furious rebukes. I the Lord have spoken it.

Still today pestilence, famine, and war are all prevalent wherever a nation has suffered the wrath of God with the intention of imposing Statism through internal strife. God convinces Ezekiel that whatever they do to the people of Judah, it is perfectly justified because they are rebellious, an abomination, and are vile and disloyal. Since insiders are being used instead of an invading army, first they will have to separate out those who are loyal followers and determine who are among the "chosen". Once a sanctuary is established, the terrorism from within can begin.

> **Ezekiel 9:4 And the Lord said unto him, Go through the midst of the city, through the midst of Jerusalem, and set a mark upon the foreheads of the men that sigh and that cry for all the abominations that be done in the midst thereof. 5. And to the others he said in mine hearing, Go ye after him through the city, and smite: let not your eye spare, neither have ye pity: 6. Slay utterly old and young, both maids, and little children, and women: but come not near any man upon whom is the mark; and begin at my sanctuary. Then they began at the ancient men which were before the house. 7. And he said unto them, Defile the house, and fill the courts with the slain: go ye forth. And they went forth, and slew in the city. 8. And it came to pass, while they were slaying them, and I was left, that I fell upon my face, and cried, and said, Ah Lord God! Wilt thou destroy all the residue of Israel in thy pouring out of thy fury upon Jerusalem? 9. Then he said unto me, The iniquity of the house of Israel and Judah is exceeding great, and the land is full of blood, and the city is full of perverseness: for they say, The Lord hath forsaken the earth, and the Lord seeth not. 10. And as for me also, mine eye shall not spare, neither will I have pity, but I will recompense their way upon their head.**

Ezekiel had been indoctrinated into thinking he was doing the right thing and identifies those who "sigh and cry" against their neighbors to determine loyalty. This is a God that cares nothing of the innocence of the citizens, even the women and children. The only consideration is loyalty and inflicts death and suffering on all without his mark. Without loyalty, you are an abomination that must be purged through terrorism. This still takes place today in many countries where the God of Statism is still in the early stages within a nation. These tactics can also occur where power is being reestablished in peaceful societies and as we have seen before, innocent women and children are sometimes specifically targeted to further demoralize the population.

What the writers are saying through these stories is that our own actions determine who will be our God. If you like the plan to keep your God of Statism, you can keep your plan. If you want your Statist God, you can have your Statist God. On the other hand, you might want to consider the possibility it may be based on lies before it gains a sanctuary within your culture, and before the strife and turmoil of terrorism begins.

The justification for the terrorism becomes clear in the next part of the story. There is one thing in that really annoys the God of Statism, and that is the idea of self-rule. This concept had apparently been invented in Greece, and to a great degree adopted by the Yahwists and then promoted in Israel. The idea of a culture of self-determination then began to spread into other areas such as in Canaan, Egypt, and among the Philistines and Assyrians. The culture of stiff-necked resistance to Statism by the Israelites was beginning to gain favor among other civilizations. This cannot be tolerated, and as always Judah would be punished.

> **Ezekiel 16:29 Thou hast moreover multiplied thy fornication in the land of Canaan unto Chaldea; and yet thou wast not satisfied herewith. 30. How weak is thine heart, saith the Lord God, seeing thou doest all these things, the work of an imperious whorish woman; 31. In that thou buildest thine eminent place in the head of every way, and makest thine high place in every street; and hast not been as an harlot, in that thou scornest hire; 32. But as a wife that committeth**

adultery, which taketh strangers instead of her husband! 33. They give gifts to all whores: but thou givest thy gifts to all thy lovers, and hirest them, that they may come unto thee on every side for thy whoredom. 34. And the contrary is in thee from other women in thy whoredom, whereas none followeth thee to commit whoredoms: and in that thou givest a reward, and no reward is given unto thee, therefore thou art contrary.

You spread your contrarian message of self-rule, you participate in free trade among the Canaanites, you create jobs and share ideas not only among yourselves, but also among those around you. Then it is they who receive the reward! You are worse than a whore! At least a self-respecting whore charges for their services, but you hire your lovers! You are an abomination! "Thou givest a reward, and no reward is given unto thee" is not acceptable. Have you forgotten my covenant to take you to the promised land some day? You ungrateful wretches, therefore I will again turn these people against you for punishment until I fundamentally transform your nation and your culture!

Ezekiel 16:38 And I will judge thee, as women that break wedlock and shed blood are judged; and I will give thee blood in fury and jealousy. 39. And I will also give thee into their hand, and they shall throw down thine eminent place, and shall break down thy high places: they shall strip thee also of thy clothes, and shall take thy fair jewels, and leave thee naked and bare.

After there has been a transfer of wealth through economic chaos and social engineering to benefit those that are more "chosen" God will now have sufficient powers and numbers and will give "thee into their hand" and will mold a Statist nation as he sees fit. Once a sufficient number of followers have been acquired, the minions will not be kind.

Ezekiel 16:40 They shall also bring up a company against thee, and they shall stone thee with stones, and

thrust thee through with their swords. 41. And they shall burn thine houses with fire, and execute judgments upon thee in the sight of many women: and I will cause thee to cease from playing the harlot, and thou also shalt give no hire any more. 42. So will I make my fury toward thee to rest, and my jealousy shall depart from thee, and I will be quiet, and will be no more angry.

The fury and jealousy of the Powers That Be will continue until Israel's "whoredom" comes to a stop, and a more Statist society has been created. Stop spreading your message of freedom and self-rule and letting others also receive the benefits, or else the attacks will continue until you stop. The punishment continues today, and so the parable is still very relevant. In response, God will turn the people against each other from within. The ability to turn people against each other provides God with the opportunity to participate in his favorite activities, which are war and engaging in the purging process.

Ezekiel 20:36 Like as I pleaded with your fathers in the wilderness of the land of Egypt, so will I plead with you, saith the Lord God. 37. And I will cause you to pass under the rod, and I will bring you into the bond of the covenant: 38. And I will purge out from among you the rebels, and them that transgress against me: I will bring them forth out of the country where they sojourn, and they shall know that I am the Lord.

The end game, as always, is the same.

Ezekiel 20:40 For in mine holy mountain, in the mountain of the height of Israel, saith the Lord God, there shall all the house of Israel, all of them in the land, serve me: there will I accept them, and there will I require your offerings, and the firstfruits of your oblations, with all your holy things.

Then, admitting his needs for "your offerings and first fruits of your oblations" the God of Statism then explains to Ezekiel the justification of the subterfuge.

> **Ezekiel 22:7 In thee have they set light by father and mother: in the midst of thee have they dealt by oppression with the stranger: in thee have they vexed the fatherless and the widow. 8. Thou hast despised mine holy things, and hast profaned my sabbaths. 9. In thee are men that carry tales to shed blood: and in thee they eat upon the mountains: in the midst of thee they commit lewdness. 10. In thee have they discovered their fathers' nakedness: in thee have they humbled her that was set apart for pollution. 11. And one hath committed abomination with his neighbor's wife; and another hath lewdly defiled his daughter in law; and another in thee hast taken usury and increase, and thou hast greedily gained of thy neighbours by extortion, and hast forgotten me, saith the Lord God.**

God explains to Ezekiel his assistance is justified because the evil Israelites don't respect older people, have been mean to immigrants, they don't care about orphans, are haters waging a war on women, have no respect for Statist authority and rules, are conspiracy theorists, are sexually immoral and depraved, and worst of all, they participate in free market capitalistic whoredom. It is no wonder the Israelites need the God of Statism so badly. Without him they are nothing more than a basket full of irredeemable deplorables {[42]}.

This God has a solution though, which is to make everyone the same through a method called the melting pot. This will not be done through assimilation but forced through fire and fury.

> **Ezekiel 22:18 Son of man, the house of Israel is to me become dross: all they are brass, and tin, and iron, and lead, in the midst of the furnace; they are even the dross of silver. 19. Therefore thus saith the Lord God;**

---

[42] https://en.wikipedia.org/wiki/Basket_of_deplorables

Because ye are all become dross, behold, therefore I will gather you into the midst of Jerusalem. 20. As they gather silver, and brass, and iron, and lead, and tin, into the midst of the furnace, to blow the fire upon it, to melt it; so will I gather you in mine anger and in my fury, and I will leave you there, and melt you. 21. Yea, I will gather you, and blow upon you in the fire of my wrath, and ye shall be melted in the midst thereof. 22. As silver is melted in the midst of the furnace, so shall ye be melted in the midst thereof; and ye shall know that I the Lord have poured out my fury upon you.

Once everyone is mixed equally, except of course for the elitists and insiders, the people are much easier to control. This God doesn't like individuality. Once God has established the solution to the deplorability of the Israelites by imposing a system making everyone the same and equal, and thoroughly intertwined with other cultures to again begin the process of identity politics, he returns to set up house. You must give this God credit for never giving up. Basically, this God never gives up because he has nowhere else to go. While the people can exist quite well and prosper culturally without Statism, Statism cannot exist without the people.

As someone indoctrinated into becoming a subversive working from within, Ezekiel has been successful, and now watches God's minions measure out each room of the area where his elaborate and imposing temple will be built, presumably with brand new drapes. "The Powers That Be" get to work and once again determines the chosen that will be allowed into the inner circle, imposes many laws, demands taxes and tribute and creates a bureaucracy for their collection and begins once again to rule over the Israelites—for their own good. Political borders are set to divide up each group, and a large area is set up in the city for the collection of taxes and other offerings from each tribe.

Ezekiel 48:19 And they that serve the city shall serve it out of all the tribes of Israel. 20. All the oblation shall be five and twenty thousand by five and twenty

thousand: ye shall offer the holy oblation foursquare, with the possession of the city. 21. And the residue shall be for the prince, on the one side and on the other of the holy oblation, and of the possession of the city, over against the five and twenty thousand toward the east border, and westward over against the five and twenty thousand toward the west border, over against the portions for the prince: and it shall be the holy oblation; and the sanctuary of the house shall be in the midst of thereof. 22. Moreover from the possession of the Levites, and from the possession of the city, being in the midst of that which is the princes', between the border of Judah and the border of Benjamin, shall be for the prince.

...and so on, and so forth. The writers show how easy it is for history to repeat itself, and for Statism to become reestablished. These cycles will continue until they are stopped by We The People.

Daniel—The Despised Outsider

The story of Daniel has some very different and interesting parables, because rather than accepting the narrative by swallowing the scroll of "lamentations, mourning, and woes", as does Ezekiel, he refuses to do so. This parable shows what happens when an outsider is introduced into a firmly established Statist culture. As a Jew, he has been taken into exile because God has sold Judah out to the larger State of Babylon as slaves. Of course, we know they are speaking of the God of Statism. For those who have ever justified slavery by saying God approves, they are correct and this is the God they are referring to. Speaking of Nebuchadnezzar, the king of Babylon, their story goes...

Daniel 1:2 And the Lord gave Jehoiakim king of Judah into his hand, with part of the vessels of the house of God: which he carried into the land of Shinar to the house of his God; and he brought the vessels into the treasure house of his God. And the king spake unto Ashpenaz the master of his eunuchs, that he should bring certain of the children of Israel, and of the king's seed, and of the princes; 4. Children in whom was no blemish, but well favoured, and skillful in all wisdom, and cunning in knowledge, and understanding science, and such as had ability in them to stand in the king's palace, and whom they might teach the learning and the tongue of the Chaldeans.

Daniel and a few of his friends were among the young people brought into the king's court. Many leaders favor foreigners who are already trained to be elitists, so long as they promise to be of service and are attractive. They are often given pardons or special favors. This may have been an acceptable idea from some nations but choosing some from within Judea would cause problems. What we will see is that Daniel and his friends were even more cunning in knowledge than their new owners would guess. By choosing a few that are "cunning in knowledge, and understanding science", they may have unknowingly included a group of Jewish Yahwists, so there would be trouble.

The writers point out that leaders often prefer palace eunuchs to be their servants. This is still true today, especially among those whose authority is not to be questioned. There are now huge numbers of palace eunuchs leading departments and agencies and high courts everywhere in nations with centralized government institutions. Their efforts are still overwhelmingly devoted to the preservation of their own jobs, which makes them extremely loyal to the State.

Daniel and his friends were offered fattening provisions by the king, such as meat and wine. Instead, he requested they be allowed to eat food consumed by the common people, such as vegetables. Daniel was already wise enough to be a dietary guru, but in addition, and just as the writers had already pointed out in Proverbs, Daniel was also wise enough to know accepting free stuff from the State never goes well.

Proverbs 23:1 When thou sittest to eat with a ruler, consider diligently what is before thee: 2. And put a knife to thy throat, if thou be a man given to appetite. 3. Be not desirous of his dainties: for they are deceitful meat.

In other words, the State never offers free stuff unless they want something in return, which is usually political loyalty and the accompanying loss of your birthright of independence. Because of their refusal to accept the dainties the king offered, and because of their store of knowledge, Daniel and his buddies earned grudging admiration for their wisdom and were soon included into the king's collection of wise men. These were largely made up of magicians, astrologers, and soothsayers. His privileged position gave Daniel an opportunity to interpret a dream for king Nebuchadnezzar.

The king called the wise men together and told them to interpret his dream but couldn't tell them what the dream was because he had forgotten. He informed them that if they couldn't remind him of the dream, and then also interpret the dream, then they were all frauds and would be put to death. Threats of violence have always been a popular pass time for Statists at the top.

Of course, the others failed to interpret the dream but Daniel stepped in with a combination of flattery and predictions of a bright future for the king with his own interpretation. This is a good tactic to use with rulers. Daniel described the king as being the golden head of a large figure representing his own kingdom, and then also predicted the fate of future inferior kingdoms in ways that were even more flattering to Nebuchadnezzar, such that he was unable to deny that had been his dream all along. Daniel described the kingdoms following Nebuchadnezzar as being inferior, but that the king is currently the golden head and hence far superior because future kingdoms will fail. There is, of course, an underlying message in the interpretation.

> **Daniel 2:31 Thou, O king, sawest, and behold a great image. This great image, whose brightness was excellent, stood before thee; and the form thereof was terrible. 32. This image's head was of fine gold, his breast and his arms of silver, his belly and his thighs of brass, 33. His legs of iron, his feet part of iron and part of clay. 34. Thou sawest till that a stone was cut without hands, which smote the image upon his feet that were of iron and clay, and brake them to pieces. 35. Then was the iron, the clay, the brass, the silver, and the gold, broken to pieces together, and became like the chaff of the summer threshingfloors; and the wind carried them away, that no place was found for them: and the stone that smote the image became a great mountain, and filled the whole earth.**

Being experts at parables, the writers use a story that shows Daniel flattering the king, but also cleverly predicts the end of the times of being led by all-powerful leaders chosen by God. The stone "cut without hands, which smote the image upon his feet" represents the potential of We the People, who are the foundation of society and when they "smote the image upon his feet" there is an end to the hierarchies of Statism and the Power of the People can become "a great mountain". The self-formed stone is powerful enough to strike and destroy the giant figure, which will be reduced and decentralized "and the wind carried them away".

> **Daniel 2:37 Thou, O King, art a king of kings: for the God of heaven hath given thee a kingdom, power, and strength, and glory. 38. And wheresoever the children of men dwell, the beasts of the field and the fowls of the heaven hath he given into thine hand, and hath made thee a ruler over them all. Thou art this head of gold. 39. And after thee shall arise another kingdom inferior to thee, and another kingdom of brass, which shall bear rule over all the earth. 40. And the fourth kingdom shall be strong as iron: forasmuch as iron breaketh in pieces and subdueth all things: and as iron that breaketh all these, shall it break in pieces and bruise. 41. And whereas thou sawest the feet and toes, part of potters' clay, and part of iron, the kingdom shall be divided; but there shall be in it the strength of the iron, forasmuch as thou sawest the iron mixed with miry clay. 42. And as the toes of the feet were part of iron, and part of clay, so the kingdom shall be partly strong, and partly broken. 43. And whereas thou sawest iron mixed with miry clay, they shall mingle themselves with the seed of men: but they shall not cleave one to another, even as iron is not mixed with clay. 44. And in the days of these kings shall the God of heaven set up a kingdom, which shall never be destroyed: and the kingdom shall not be left to other people, but it shall break in pieces and consume all these kingdoms, and it shall stand for ever.**

Through this amazing and well thought out parable the Jewish writers are predicting, or at least advocating for, the eventual destruction of cultures dominated by Statism. It will be replaced by a progressively more decentralized system led by lesser figures, that finally do not "cleave to one another, even as iron is not mixed with clay". The "miry clay" in the feet of the figure becomes the usual reference to the people making up the foundation of society, with the advantage of such a society being "'partly strong, and partly broken". The iron strength of decentralization would result in breaking up the other progressively weaker and "exalted" metals generally thought of as superior, but not as tough as iron, which would in turn be mixed in clay and therefore "not cleave one to another". This could be the first Yahwist conception of a decentralized society that gets its strength through the power of The People that shall "stand forever", and "consume all these kingdoms", as they try to imagine a solution to Statism. Eventually this idea would lead to a revelation, but in the meantime, before the Leviathan figure can be shattered, the stiff-necked Jews still have kings to deal with. For now, it is only a dream. For most of the world today it is still only a dream.

True to form, king Nebuchadnezzar chooses only to heed the flattering part of the story about himself as the golden "king of kings" and builds a golden statue in his own likeness in self-congratulation. Also, in kingly fashion he then calls a meeting among the eunuchs and bureaucrats, so he can be properly exalted.

Daniel 3:2 Then Nebuchadnezzar the king sent to gather together the princes, the governors, and the captains, the judges, the treasurers, the counsellors, the sheriffs, and all the rulers of the provinces, to come to the dedication of the image which Nebuchadnezzar the king had set up. 4. Then an herald cried aloud, To you it is commanded, O people, nations, and languages, 5. That at what time ye hear the sound of the coronet, flute, harp, sackbut, psaltery, dulcimer, and all kinds of music, ye fall down and worship the golden image that Nebuchadnezzar the king hath set up: 6. And whoso falleth not down and worshippeth shall the same hour be cast into the midst of a burning fiery furnace.

Daniel and his buddies Shadrack, Meshach, and Abednego failed to heed either the harp or the sackbut. At this point, Daniel's flattering story of the king wasn't going to help him or his fellow Yahwists because of their lack of proper reverence.

> **Daniel 3:21 Then these men were bound in their coats, their hosen, and their hats, and their other garments, and were cast into the midst of the burning fiery furnace.**

Daniel and his buddies ignored the flames. The collection of bureaucrat insiders was a little surprised and disappointed when Daniel and his associates didn't burn the way they were supposed to. Trying to burn those who are a threat to the insiders today is much the same but now is generally done through slander, false accusations, carefully crafted opposition narrative, using State resources as political weapons, etc. and can even include the use of corrupt judges and prosecutors which force the victim to defend to themselves publicly against false witnesses, which can often ruin the reputation of those who are innocent. Using all these tools for "burning" political rivals are common in Statist cultures.

> **Daniel 3:27 And the princes, governors, and captains, and the king's counsellors, being gathered together, saw these men, upon whose bodies the fire had no power, nor was an hair of their head singed, neither were their coats changed, nor the smell of the fire had passed on them.**

When bureaucrats and palace eunuch insiders gang up and try to publicly burn you it isn't expected for you to just ignore the fire. You are supposed to remain burned and disappear from public life. We still see these methods being used on an almost daily basis in Washington, which is an indication we now are being ruled once again by The God of Statism and his palace eunuchs. At this point, king Nebuchadnezzar should have left well enough alone and stopped asking anyone to interpret his dreams—but he didn't.

Having been publicly humiliated for trying to burn someone that wouldn't stay burned, the bureaucrats and eunuchs are forced, at least publicly, to again show grudging respect for the courage of the outsiders. Daniel and his group are then rewarded for surviving.

But now the king has another dream about a giant tree that gets chopped off at ground level and only the roots are left, and which also incidentally predicts the king living in poverty as a beast, just as many of his subjects have been living. This is another parable of the people winning again.

> **Daniel 4:30 The king spake, and said, Is not this great Babylon, that I have built for the house of the kingdom by the might of my power, and for the honour of my majesty? 31. While the word was in the king's mouth, there fell a voice from heaven, saying, O king Nebuchadnezzar, to thee it is spoken; The kingdom is departed from thee. 32. And they shall drive thee from men, and thy dwelling shall be with beasts of the field: they shall make thee to eat grass as oxen, and seven times shall pass over thee, until thou know that the most High ruleth in the kingdom of men, and giveth it to whomsoever he will. 33. The same hour was the thing fulfilled upon Nebuchadnezzar: and he was driven from men, and did eat grass as oxen, and his body was wet with the dew of heaven, till his hairs were grown like eagles' feathers, and his nails like birds' claws.**

This dream is basically the same theme as before, but the writers want to make sure you get the point that Statist power can always be reduced, and true justice would be if kings were to live the same way they force others to live. They include the seemingly random statement "and seven times shall pass over thee, until thou know that the most High ruleth in the kingdom of men". Again, we see the hoped-for completion of the cycle represented by the number seven, which is the Sabbath. King Nebuchadnezzar will receive the "pass over" by coming to recognize the truth and will now recognize the "kingdom of men", rather than having the kingdom for himself, so we can see cultural evolution taking place. Unfortunately for Nebuchadnezzar, living in the kingdom of men just isn't the same as having a kingdom created just for yourself, so after living in the real world and eating grass for a while, he repents.

Daniel 4:37 Now I Nebuchadnezzar praise and extol and honour the King of heaven, all whose works are truth, and his ways judgment: and those that walk in pride he is able to abase.

The writers want you to recognize that any semblance of a heavenly culture in "the kingdom of men" has no place for those who exalt themselves and "walk in pride". The next parable in Daniel comes straight to the point and is the source of the expression "I see the writing on the wall". This is the story of the next king of Babylon, Belshazzar, who is having a party with his princes, his wives, and his concubines.

Daniel 5:4 They drank wine, and praised the gods of gold, and of silver, of brass, of iron, of wood, and of stone. 5. In the same hour came forth fingers of a man's hand, and wrote over against the candlestick upon the plaster of the wall of the king's palace: and the king saw the part of the hand that wrote. 6. Then the king's countenance was changed, and his thoughts troubled him, so that the joints of his loins were loosed, and his knees smote one another.

It seems they had forgotten the gods of clay but would soon be reminded.

Daniel 5:25 And this is the writing that was written MeNe, MENE, Tekel, Upharsin.

As his knees smote one another because of his loose loin joints, Belshazzar also summoned Daniel, just as had the hapless king Nebuchadnezzar before him. Daniel and his friends are still being forced to hang around in Babylon because of their exile from their own land by God. Having prophesied the fall of king Nebuchadnezzar, he then interpreted the writing on the wall for king Belshazzar.

Daniel 5:26 This is the interpretation of the thing: Mene; God hath numbered thy kingdom, and finished

it. 27. Tekel, Thou art weighed in the balances, and art found wanting. 28. Peres; Thy kingdom is divided, and given to the Medes and Persians. 29. Then commanded Belshazzar, and they clothed Daniel with scarlet, and put a chain of gold about his neck, and made a proclamation concerning him, that he should be the third ruler in the kingdom. 30. In that night was Belshazzar the king of the Chaldeans slain.

It seems a little far-fetched that the king would reward Daniel for saying, in effect, "your kingdom sucks and you're going down", but the writers are making the usual point that all kingdoms fall into inequity and eventually die. It would be a very long time before the idea of making "nobility" figureheads only, so the authors of this story were way ahead of their time. Belshazzar would fall and would be the last king of Babylon. Daniel's prophecy of progressively weaker Statism in Babylon had come to pass.

We can't leave the story of Daniel the Yahwist without mentioning another story that makes him notable, and that is being thrown to the lions during the rule of king Darius. This is another demonstration of the purging process within a bureaucracy. Daniel had achieved a high level of influence, but he still didn't fit in well. As an honest and wise person, he made the other bureaucratic palace eunuchs uncomfortable, and so was not accepted as a legitimate insider.

Daniel 6:3 Then this Daniel was preferred above the presidents and princes, because an excellent spirit was in him; and the king thought to set him over the whole realm. 4. Then the presidents and princes sought to find occasion against Daniel concerning the kingdom; but they could find none occasion nor fault; forasmuch as he was faithful, neither was there any error or fault found in him.

People like Daniel always make other bureaucrats feel they need to scurry to their safe spaces, so they came up with a plan to purge him by setting him up to be condemned.

Daniel 6:6 Then these presidents and princes assembled together to the king, and said thus unto him, King Darius, live forever. 7. All the presidents of the kingdom, the governors, and the princes, the counsellors, and the captains, have consulted together to establish a royal statute, and to make a firm decree, that whosoever shall ask a petition of any God or man for thirty days, save of thee, O king, he shall be cast into the den of lions. 8. Now, O king, establish the decree, and sign the writing, that it not be changed, according to the law of the Medes and Persians, which altereth not. 9. Wherefore king Darius signed the writing and the decree.

The plot worked, because they knew Daniel had his own version of a God within him, to which he often consulted as did Job, and he continued to do so despite the threat he knew existed from the palace eunuchs and other insiders. Those jealous of his position and reputation promptly attempted to condemn him by using the laws they had made specifically for that purpose. We still often see modern judges and other insiders making up laws and rulings that have no other purpose but to persecute unwanted but successful political opponents. We see this tactic is also nothing new in politics.

Daniel 6:13 Then answered they and said before the king, That Daniel, which is of the children of the captivity of Judah, regardeth not thee, O king, nor the decree that thou hast signed, but maketh his petition three times a day.

The king, although partial to Daniel because of his popularity, reluctantly found himself trapped by his own law and agreed to allow the insider bureaucrats to throw Daniel to the lions just as he been thrown into the furnace. As mentioned before, in the bible a lion almost always represents the collective population of a nation. As a lion, the people have a certain amount of power, but of course not the same power as the Behemoth or Leviathan created by the God of Statism. So, when Daniel is "thrown to the lions" it means

209

he is being thrown onto the judgment of public opinion. Since the bureaucrats had gone to a lot of trouble discrediting and condemning Daniel through their false witnessing and the public vilification process, they assumed he would be devoured. But just as Daniel had chosen to ignore the fire, the "lions" now chose to ignore the false narrative and did not devour Daniel. The plan backfired, the accusers themselves were thrown to the lions, and were promptly eaten. This parable is one to which we would be well advised to pay heed, because it also is still very relevant. The moral here is that sometimes the people can see through the lies and deceit. The people are often not as gullible as the elitists and palace eunuchs believe they are.

The story of Daniel then continues with predictions of the standard issue cycles of the rise and fall of kings and empires, which by now have become as certain as the boom and bust financial cycles inflicted upon modern people by their own Statist leaders through economic manipulation. There is, however, one other story that stands out in the book of Daniel.

The book ends with a discourse between Daniel, whose name means "judge of god", and another character who appears called Michael, whose name means "who is god?" Through these characters, the authors appear to be suggesting it is time to make a judgment regarding God (The Powers that Be) and who God should be. They describe the rise of yet another kingdom and the inevitable warfare and eventual downfall because of Statism:

> **Daniel 11:42 He shall stretch forth his hand also upon the countries: and the land of Egypt shall not escape. 43. But he shall have power over the treasures of gold and silver, and over all the precious things of Egypt: and the Libyans and the Ethiopians shall be at his steps. 44. But tidings out of the east and out of the north shall trouble him: therefore he shall go forth with great fury to destroy, and utterly to make away many. 45. And he shall plant the tabernacles of his palace between the seas in the glorious holy mountain; yet he shall come to his end, and none shall help him.**

By now we are now all familiar with the Powers That Be and how the nations always end with war and chaos, but then something strange happens after the predictable failure of the most recent kingdom. A representative appears, suggesting who God could be if the people were to demand it for themselves.

Daniel 12:1 And at that time shall Michael stand up, the great prince which standeth for the children of thy people: and there shall be a time of trouble, such as never was since there was a nation even to that same time: and at that time thy people shall be delivered, every one that shall be found written in the book. And many of them that sleep in the dust of the earth shall awake, some to everlasting life, and some to shame and everlasting contempt. 3. And they that be wise shall shine as the brightness of the firmament; and they that turn many to righteousness as the stars for ever and ever. 4. But thou, O Daniel, shut up the words, and seal the book, even to the time of the end: many shall run to and fro, and knowledge shall be increased.

The writers seem to be suggesting that the books of the bible should be closed until "knowledge shall be increased" for their understanding. The "prince which standeth for the children of thy people" is predicting again that there will be much cultural turmoil before the books can be understood and appreciated enough for the Power of the People to make an entrance. When it does, at that time the characters in the books of the bible will be remembered and judged according to their reputation. Some will be remembered for their wisdom, and some for their shame. Some shall awake "to everlasting life, and some to shame and everlasting contempt". This will not happen until understanding is increased and the message of the bible and the characters are understood. They knew that could be far in the future, and until then history would continue to repeat itself like watching reruns of a movie that always ends with the rise and fall of an empire led by the God of Statism. As history shows, they would be correct in the prophecy.

Daniel 12:8 And I heard, but I understood not: then said I, O my Lord, what shall be the end of these things? 9. And he said, Go thy way, Daniel: for the words are closed up and sealed till the time of the end. 10. Many shall be purified, and made white, and tried; but the wicked shall do wickedly: and none of the wicked shall understand; but the wise shall understand.

Wisdom and understanding would in fact be a long time coming but, fortunately for us, more books would be written. There were still more lessons to be learned—and relearned.

Hosea—The God of Statism vs Free Market

There are few activities more feared by the God of Statism than free markets and private ownership, and those writing the bible did not fail to address this phenomenon. The stronger this God in any society, the less of these two things you have. The attacks on the Canaanites (merchants and traders) was only the beginning. The writers again demonstrate this through their story of Hosea. Once again, God is disgusted because of the whoredom of the deplorables in Judah and Israel. Hosea {43}, (which means salvation) is told by God to marry a whore called Gomer {44} (which really means complete, or perfect). Gomer not only represents Israel in the parable, but also God's contempt of the inhabitants, who continue to stray into the whoredom of free trade. God has yet another plan to bring them back within his fold. Remember, character names are often used in place of cities or nations.

Hosea 1:2 The beginning of the word of the Lord by Hosea. And the Lord said to Hosea, Go, take unto thee a wife of whoredoms and children of whoredoms: for the land hath committed great whoredom, departing from the Lord. 3. So he went and took Gomer the daughter of Diblaim; which conceived, and bare him a son. 4. And the Lord said unto him, Call his name Jezreel {45} (which means God sewing a seed); **for yet a little while, and I will avenge the blood of Jezreel upon the house of Jehu, and will cause to cease the kingdom of Israel. 5. And it shall come to pass at that day, that I will break the bow of Israel in the valley of Jezreel. 6. And she conceived again, and bare a daughter. And God said unto him, Call her name Loruhamah** {46} (which means without love or affection):

[43] https://en.wikipedia.org/wiki/Hosea

[44] http://www.abarim-publications.com/Meaning/Gomer.html#.XaJ6cEZKjIU

[45] http://www.abarim-publications.com/Meaning/Jezreel.html#.XaJ7E0ZKjIU

[46] http://www.abarim-publications.com/Meaning/Lo-

for I will no more have mercy upon the house of Israel; but I will utterly take them away. 7. But I will have mercy upon the house of Judah, and will save them by the Lord their God, and will not save them by bow, nor by sword, nor by battle, by horses, nor by horsemen. 8. Now when she had weaned Loruhamah, she conceived, and bare a son. 9. Then said God, Call his name Loammi {[47]} (which means not my people)**: for ye are not my people, and I will not be your God. 10. Yet the number of the children of Israel shall be as the sand of the sea, which cannot be measured nor numbered; and it shall come to pass, that in the place where it was said unto them, Ye are not my people, there it shall be said unto them, Ye are the sons of the living God. 11. Then shall the children of Israel be gathered together, and appoint themselves one head, and they shall come up out of the land: for great shall be the day of Jezreel.**

God's plan is to bring Judah and Israel together by sowing the seeds (Jezreel) that will convince the people who are "without his love" and "not his people" to form a new nation with new cities. That will be accomplished, not by war and sword as before, but by making nice through deception long enough to create a new nation state so they can "appoint themselves one head", who, no doubt, will be chosen by God. But why does this God show contempt for the people of Israel through his description of Gomer as a prostitute? We can see in the next verse. Speaking of Israel God says...

Hosea 2:2 Plead with your mother, plead: for she is not my wife, neither am I her husband: let her therefore put away her whoredoms out of her sight, and her adulteries from between her breasts; 3. Lest I strip her naked, and set her as in the day that she was born, and make her as a wilderness, and set her like a dry land, and slay her with thirst. 4. And I will not

ruhamah.html#.XaJ8EEZKjIU
[47] http://www.abarim-publications.com/Meaning/Lo-ammi.html#.XaJ8zUZKjIU

have mercy upon her children; for they be the children of whoredoms. 5. For their mother hath played the harlot: she that conceived them hath done shamefully: for she said, I will go after my lovers, that give me my bread and my water, my wool and my flax, mine oil and my drink. 6. Therefore, behold, I will hedge up thy way with thorns, and make a wall, that she shall not find her paths.

Those who supply their needs through free market activities (her lovers) makes Gomer a whore. If you supply yourself with bread, water, wool, flax, oil, and drink through free trade without first going through the God of Statism to provide those for you, or at least allow control through taxation and regulation to create dependency, then you need to be punished by God, who will "hedge up thy way with thorns, and make a wall, that she shall not find her paths".

There is still a lot of this going on today, even in relatively free market societies, as Statism continues to grow in power once again. This God has contempt for those who independently provide for themselves. This God considers free trade to be comparable to whoredom because free trade causes happiness, prosperity, and worst of all, free thinking. Free thinking leads to little need for the God of Statism. This God must defeat this whoredom to rein people in and, once again, render them dependent on the State. This is a God that believes that all should be owned or controlled by him, therefore he must receive the credit for its existence, and distribution of wealth and commodities must be through him.

Hosea 2:8 For she did not know that I gave her corn (corn is an ancient word for grain) **and wine, and oil, and multiplied her silver and gold, which they prepared for Baal** (other gods, such as free market capitalism).

Since God feels all resources must be owned, regulated, and distributed by the State, he will reach his goals first through creating economic chaos. This will create a need for the people to return to Statism for help, so that a centralized system under "one head" can again be created.

Hosea 2:9 Therefore will I return, and take away my corn in the time thereof, and my wine in the season thereof, and will recover my wool and my flax given to cover her nakedness. 10. And now will I discover her lewdness in the sight of her lovers, and none shall deliver her out of mine hand. 11. I will also cause all her mirth to cease, her feast days, her new moons, and her sabbaths, and all her solemn feasts. 12. And I will destroy her vines and her fig trees, whereof she hath said, These are my rewards that my lovers have given me and I will make them a forest, and the beasts of the field shall eat them. 13. And I will visit upon her the days of Baalim, wherein she burned incense to them, and she decked herself with her earrings and her jewels, and she went after her lovers, and forgat me, saith the Lord.

Economic chaos to defeat prosperity and free thinking is easily achieved by a Statist God, and almost all Nation States do this at some point to reduce the threat of unregulated free market activities and unbridled prosperity. It becomes incredibly tempting for any centralized State to manipulate and redistribute money to further its own political agenda. At the very least, taxes can always be raised. Also, money can be printed and distributed in such amounts that it can render the script worthless "and wormy" through inflation. Then the supply of money and credit can be restricted through regulation, or outright cronyism within the banking industry. National debt can be increased to the point that the entire economy can suffer and jobs which allow independence will disappear. Trade restrictions may also come into play, etc. Once this has been accomplished, then God knows the people will return if comfort is offered.

Hosea 2:14 Therefore, behold, I will allure her, and bring her into the wilderness, and speak comfortably unto her. 15. And I will give her her vineyards from thence, and the valley of Achor {48} (which means

trouble) **for a door of hope: and she shall sing there, as in the days of her youth, and as in the day when she came up out of the land of Egypt. 16. And it shall be at that day, saith the Lord, that thou shalt call me Ishi** (which means husband)**; and shall no more call me Baali {[49]}** (which means possessor).

The ploy is that once the economy and the "whoredom" of free trade has been reduced to shambles by the God of Statism, then he will "speak comfortably to her" and "free" things will now be provided through the benevolence of God. The people will once again be married to the God of Statism, just as they were under Moses in the search for the "promised land". If there is enough economic chaos, then it becomes acceptable to nationalize the source of the "whoredom", and natural resources (such as the Nile river in Egypt) and other sources of wealth can be confiscated, and the wealth will be redistributed by the State as sees fit to purchase loyalty. Speaking of the whore that is Israel, God predicts the results of the economic chaos...

> **Hosea 3:2 So I bought her to me for fifteen pieces of silver, and for an homer of barley, and an half home of barley: 3. And I said unto her, Thou shalt abide for me many days; thou shalt not play the harlot, and thou shalt not be for another man: so will I also be for thee. 4. For the children of Israel shall abide many days without a king, and without a prince, and without a sacrifice, and without an image, and without an ephod, and without teraphim: 5. Afterward shall the children of Israel return, and seek the Lord their God, and David their king; and shall fear the Lord and his goodness in the latter days.**

---

[48] http://www.abarim-publications.com/Meaning/Achor.html#.XaJ-wkZKjIU

[49] http://www.abarim-publications.com/Meaning/Achor.html#.XaJ_KEZKjIV

Given enough hardship and economic uncertainty, most will accept welfare, or government jobs and programs, which in turn strengthens the "The Powers That Be". The Israelites may go for a long time without kings and princes and priests in funny costumes, but for a small price, along with a large dose of economic chaos at the right time, Israel can once again be expected to surrender their birthright of freedom. God knows they will return to the dependency of bureaucratic "comfort", and surrender their independence, private ownership, and self-reliance. Ordinarily this would work every time, but the Israelites are still just too stubborn. That the writers have so clearly made their point in a way that it is still very relevant to our own modern world is yet another testament to their Yahwist wisdom.

Joel—Never Waste a Good Crisis

The phrase "never let a good crisis go to waste" has been attributed to Machiavelli, who wrote political satire aimed at those who are opportunistic and cunning, especially in politics. Deserved or not, Machiavellianism became synonymous for political deceitfulness {[50]}. The story of Joel exemplifies one way this takes place. A horrible locust infestation plagued Israel. The invasion greatly reduced the oblations (taxes) offered to God by the people. Of course, this was of great concern to the God of Statism.

> **Joel 1:13 Gird yourselves, and lament, ye priests: howl, ye ministers of my God: for the meat offering and the drink offering is withholden from the house of your God.**

The invasion of locusts was so bad they left total devastation in their wake. The fires used to stop the infestation caused even more destruction, because the locusts had been preceded by a drought.

> **Joel 2:2 A day of darkness and of gloominess, a day of clouds and of thick darkness, as the morning spread upon the mountains: a great people and a strong; there hath not been ever the like, neither shall be any more after it, even to the years of many generations. 3. A fire devoureth before them; and behind them a flame burneth: the land is as the garden of Eden before them, and behind them a desolate wilderness; yea, and nothing shall escape them. 4. The appearance of them is as the appearance of horses; and as horsemen so shall they run.**

But not to worry, God will save and serve and protect you, if only you turn to him for assistance in return for loyalty and dependency.

> **Joel 2:11 And the Lord shall utter his voice before his army: for his camp is very great: for he is strong that executeth his word: for the day of the Lord is great**

---

[50] https://www.merriam-webster.com/dictionary/Machiavellian

and very terrible; and who can abide by it? 12. Therefore also now, saith the Lord, turn ye even to me with all your heart, and with fasting, and with weeping, and with mourning: 13. And rend your heart, and not your garments, and turn unto the Lord your God: for he is gracious and merciful, slow to anger, and of great kindness, and repenteth him of the evil.

God is repentant of the economic chaos he has caused, but has the resources to help, so if the people show faith through "fasting and weeping and mourning" and demonstrate groveling loyalty he will say in effect, "We're from the government and we're here to help you" [51].

Let the priests, the ministers of the Lord, weep between the porch and the altar, and let them say, Spare thy people, O Lord, and give not thine heritage to reproach, that the heathen should rule over them: wherefore should they say among the people, Where is their God?

God can't be accused of not having the power to save the people, because in addition to being humiliating to the State, the priests and the ministers, that would cause the people to call their God into question.

Joel 2:21 Fear not, O land; be glad and rejoice: for the Lord will do great things. 22. Be not afraid, ye beasts of the field: for the pastures of the wilderness do spring, for the tree beareth her fruit, the fig tree and the vine do yield their strength. 23. Be glad then, ye children of Zion, and rejoice in the Lord your God: for he hath given you the former rain moderately, and he will cause to come down for you the rain, the former rain, and the latter rain in the first month. 24. And the floors shall be full of wheat, and the vats shall overflow with wine and oil. 25. And I will restore to you the years that the locust hath eaten, and cankerworm, and

---

[51] https://www.brainyquote.com/quotes/ronald_reagan_128358

the caterpillar, and the palmerworm, my great army which I sent among you. 26. And ye shall eat in plenty, and be satisfied, and praise the name of the Lord your God, that hath dealt wondrously with you: and my people shall never be ashamed. 27. And ye shall know that I am in the midst of Israel, and that I am the Lord your God, and none else: and my people shall never be ashamed.

Be grateful and give credit to the Powers That Be when things return to normal. Sometimes you need to get a handle on things as such weather variations and other natural disasters and bring back the rain to save God from being mocked by the heathens. God will then save and serve and protect you and will "cause to come down for you the former rain moderately" and eventually the rain will return to normal—once God fixes the climate. In fact, not only will God eventually get a handle on weather deviations and bring back the rain but, because of new-found faith in God in their lamenting and pleading, he will even repent selling his people into slavery to make a comeback as he regains strength.

Joel 3:1 For, behold, in those days, and in that time, when I shall bring again the captivity of Judah and Jerusalem, 2. I will also gather all nations, and will bring them down into the valley of Jehoshaphat, and will plead with them there for my people and for my heritage Israel, whom they have scattered among the nations, and parted my land. 3. And they have cast lots for my people; and have given a boy for an harlot, and sold a girl for wine, that they might drink. 4. Yea, and what have ye to do with me, O Tyre, and Zidon, and all the coasts of Palestine? Will ye render me a recompense? And if ye recompense me, swiftly and speedily will I return your recompense upon your own head; 5. Because ye have taken my silver and my gold, and have carried into your temples my goodly pleasant things: 6. The children also of Judah and the children

of Jerusalem have ye sold unto the Grecians, that ye might remove them far from their border.

If you want to get along with this God, you should never take his gold and silver and pleasant things. His complaint is that he has not been properly recompensed after selling his people into slavery. Natural disasters have weakened other kingdoms also, and now provide an opportunity to seek compensation through war. The original intention was to punish the people for their lack of loyalty, but the resulting loss of gold and silver and the dispersal of the people will now require another war to regain wealth and power. Hopefully rebuilding the kingdom will also result in a more loyal constituency. Besides, we now have someone else to blame for God's slavery, child trafficking, economic chaos, and climate change.

> **Joel 3:9 Proclaim ye this among the Gentiles; Prepare war, wake up the mighty men, let all the men of war draw near; let them come up: 10. Beat your plowshares into swords, and your pruning hooks into spears: let the weak say, I am strong. 11. Assemble yourselves, and come, all ye heathen, and gather yourselves round about: thither cause thy mighty one to come down, O Lord. 12. Let the heathen be awakened, and come up to the valley of Jehoshaphat: for there will I sit to judge all the heathen round about. 13. Put ye in the sickle, for harvest is ripe: come, get you down; for the press is full, the vats overflow; for their wickedness is great. 14. Multitudes, multitudes in the valley of decision: for the day of the Lord is near in the valley of decision.**

Once again, it is time to reap the harvest of war. It is time to beat your plowshares back into swords, and your pruning hooks back into spears. Taking advantage of natural disasters, and then promising comfort, gains enough loyalty for another opportunity to gather for war. As usual, warfare can in turn be a cause for the regathering of the rebellious together under one strong centralized State. Once that has been accomplished, the people of Zion will finally return to God once again, despite the fact he has been the source most of their problems.

> **Joel 3:15 The sun and the moon shall be darkened, and the stars shall withdraw their shining. 16. The Lord also shall roar out of Zion, and utter his voice from Jerusalem; and the heavens and the earth shall shake: but the Lord will be the hope of his people, and the strength of the children of Israel. 17. So shall ye know that I am the Lord your God dwelling in Zion, my holy mountain: then shall Jerusalem be holy, and there shall no strangers pass through her any more.**

God will repent his former punitive actions, and Zion will once again be gathered back together from their slavery and all will be well, providing there is adequate loyalty. Any strangers with strange ideas will be purged.

> **Joel 3:18 And it shall come to pass in that day, that the mountains shall drop down new wine, and the hills shall flow with milk, and all the rivers of Judah shall flow with waters, and a fountain shall come forth of the house of the Lord, and shall water the valley of Shittim. 19. Egypt shall be a desolation, and Edom shall be a desolate wilderness, for the violence against the children of Judah, because they have shed innocent blood in their land. 20. But Judah shall dwell for ever, and Jerusalem from generations to generation. 21. For I will cleanse their blood that I have not cleansed: for the Lord dwelleth in Zion.**

According to The Powers That Be, Judah just needs to have their blood cleansed again through the purging process to get them back on track through warfare and dependency so the hills can once again flow with milk. Failing that, the nations can always be divided and turned against each other again. Just as with the starving Esau, natural disasters can help to deprive the people of their birthright of freedom and self-reliance if they rely on God's assistance.

Amos—The Beatings Will Continue Until You Love Me

Despite all God's effort, the stiff-necked Israelites continue to be defiant as they have all through history. God's conniving just never seems to pay off with these stubborn people. They will continue to be subjected to ever more threats, and the writers will use more parables demonstrating how and why the God of Statism continues to strive for control. If left frustrated, this God's efforts can become psychotic in nature. The natural disasters and wars have not had the desired effect of bringing the people to "weep and moan" for their god to return.

Amos 4:9 I have smitten you with blasting and mildew: when your gardens and your vineyards and your fig trees and your olive trees increased, the palmerworm devoured them: yet have ye not returned unto me saith the Lord. 10. I have sent among you the pestilence after the manner of Egypt: your young men have I slain with the sword, and have taken away your horses; and I have made the stink of your camps to come up unto your nostrils: yet have ye not returned unto me, saith the Lord. 11. I have overthrown some of you, as God overthrew Sodom and Gomorrah, and ye were as a firebrand plucked out of the burning: yet have ye not returned unto me, saith the Lord.

I wonder why the refusal to return? Talk about negative reinforcement! The torment will continue until morale improves! This is a sarcastic joke with no real traceable origins, but it can used very appropriately to describe God's actions against the Jewish people. Little wonder, because as we have seen before, there's only one way you can deal with people this stubborn, and that's to once again punish them harshly and deal out more torment, because otherwise they could end up with "nothing being restrained from them".

Amos 7:17 Therefore thus saith the Lord; Thy wife shall be an harlot in the city, and thy sons and thy daughters shall fall by the sword, and thy land shall be divided by line; and thou shalt die in a polluted land: and Israel shall surely go into captivity forth of his land.

But again, not to worry because as always, once you have been punished adequately through division, purging, economic chaos, warfare, pestilence, and slavery then again God will return to care for you.

Amos 9:14 And I will bring again the captivity of my people of Israel, and they shall build the waste cities, and inhabit them; and they shall plant vineyards, and drink the wine thereof; they shall also make gardens, and eat the fruit of them. 15. And I will plant them upon their land which I have given them, saith the Lord thy God.

Wherever Statism prevails, the Powers That Be spends most of its efforts in solving problems caused by itself, which ironically increases job security for the loyal Statists. Also, to avoid punishment you just need to remember that whatever you have, and however you gained, and whatever you own, is because the God of Statism allowed it to happen or has given it directly to you. Whatever you accomplish on your own—you didn't do that.

Jonah—The Statist Hypocrite

Having shown the ways the God of Statism works its way into society, the writers demonstrate again the hazards that arise when you are willing to accept benefits from the Powers That Be. The benefits of Statism are always temporary, and this is emphasized again through the story of Jonah. Through this parable they show the hypocrisy of accepting those benefits, whether it be for power, wealth, or security. By accepting benefits, it is hypocritical to think you are not an enabler for the Powers That Be.

God gives instructions to Jonah to warn Ninevah they are about to be destroyed for a lack of loyalty unless they surrender to Statist control.

> **Jonah 1:2 Arise, go to Ninevah, that great city, and cry against it; for their wickedness is come up before me. 3. But Jonah rose up to flee unto Tarshish from the presence of the Lord, and went down to Joppa; and he found a ship going to Tarshish: so he paid the fare thereof, and went down into it, to go with them unto Tarshish from the presence of the Lord.**

Clearly not wanting to accept his assignment to spread Statist influence, Jonah had decided to escape the task he was given. To bring him back into line, God brings his Powers to bear. A great tempest surrounded Jonah on his escape boat and it was on the verge of sinking. He was not alone, so the other men feared for their lives also.

> **Jonah 1:11 Then they said unto him, What shall we do unto thee, that the sea may be calm unto us? For the sea wrought, and was tempestuous. 12. And he said unto them, Take me up, and cast me forth into the sea; so shall the sea be calm unto you: for I know that for my sake this great tempest is upon you. 13. Nevertheless the men rowed hard to bring it to the land; but they could not: for the sea wrought, and was tempestuous against them. 14. Wherefore they cried unto the Lord and said, We beseech thee, O Lord, we**

beseech thee, let us not perish for this man's life, and lay not upon us innocent blood; for thou, O Lord, hast done as it pleased thee. 15. So they took up Jonah, and cast him forth into the sea: and the sea ceased from her raging.

This is a parable demonstrating what is quite common in any oppressed society. If you have been targeted by The Powers That Be, those around you often find it necessary to abandon you to escape the tempest. Others will fear for their own lives and reputations and will shun you to avoid bringing harm to themselves. This is accomplished when they toss Jonah overboard, but God isn't through with Jonah, because he must accept his role in enabling Statism despite his desire to escape accountability.

Jonah 1:15 So they took up Jonah, and cast him forth into the sea: and the sea ceased from her raging. 16. Then the men feared the Lord exceedingly, and offered a sacrifice unto the Lord, and made vows. 17. Now the Lord had prepared a great fish to swallow up Jonah. And Jonah was in the belly of the fish three days and three nights. Jonah 2:1 Then Jonah prayed unto the Lord his God out of the fishs' belly, 2. And said, I cried by reason of mine affliction unto the Lord, and he heard me; out of the belly of hell cried I, and thou heardest my voice. 2. For thou hadst cast me into the deep, in the midst of the seas; and the floods compassed me about: all thy billows and thy waves passed over me. Then said I, I am cast out of thy sight; yet I will look again toward thy holy temple. …7. When my soul fainted within me I remembered the Lord: and my prayer came in unto thee, into thine holy temple. 8. They that observe lying vanities forsake their own mercy. 9. But I will sacrifice unto thee with the voice of thanksgiving; I will pay that I have vowed. Salvation is to the Lord. 10. And the Lord spake unto the fish, and it vomited out Jonah upon the dry land.

When an insider attempts to betray the vow of loyalty which has brought him benefits he will become an outcast and will be tossed into the "belly of hell" by God. Once you have been swallowed up and been isolated to the point you are willing to cave, you will be vomited back up and returned into the culture you were trying to escape. For most us, eventually our soul will "faint within" us when we are ostracized and isolated and will eventually repent and beg forgiveness. However, Jonah still did not want to accept accountability for spreading Statism to others, even though he hypocritically had been willing to accept benefits for himself.

Just as Jonah had feared, God's instructions resulted in Ninevah becoming Statist, and God quickly accepted them into his fold. This made Jonah both sad and angry. The point they are making is that Jonah had been willing to accept the benefits of Statism for himself, but he did not want to accept responsibility for encouraging others to do the same.

They then drive the point home by having God create a plant that shelters Jonah as he sits remorsefully on a hillside. The gourd plant provided comfort from the sun, which he was glad to accept, but that very night God planted a worm that destroyed the plant and followed that up with a hot wind that made Jonah faint. The point being that if you have chosen this God in exchange for benefits for yourself, then you cannot escape the fact you are spreading the influence of this Statist God to others. You must accept accountability for spreading an ideology that, despite benefits in the short term, will in the end result in more suffering and social and economic chaos.

Jonah 4:6 And the Lord God prepared a gourd, and made it to come up over Jonah, that it might be a shadow over his head, to deliver him from his grief. So Jonah was exceeding glad of the gourd. 7. But God prepared a worm when the morning rose the next day, and it smote the gourd that it withered. 8. And it came to pass, when the sun did arise, that God prepared a vehement east wind; and the sun beat upon the head of Jonah, that he fainted, and wished in himself to die,

and said it is better for me to die than to live. 9. And God said to Jonah, Doeth thou well to be angry for the gourd? And he said, I do well to be angry, even unto death. 10. Then said the Lord, Thou hast had pity on the gourd, for the which thou hast not laboured, neither madest it grow; which came up in a night, and perished in a night: 11. And should not I spare Ninevah, that great city, wherein are more than sixscore thousand persons that cannot discern between their right hand and their left hand; and also much cattle?

Jonah had no choice but to accept the hypocrisy of his willingness to welcome short-term benefits and security for himself, knowing someone else would have to pay the price. He had accepted the benefits without considering it would ultimately lead to cultural degradation and suffering for others in the future. We might keep this in mind when we accept the king's dainties such as jobs, welfare, and other benefits "for the which thou hast not laboured, neither madest it grow". If we accept the benefits, then ultimately, we must accept accountability for spreading that ideology. This is especially true for those who don't know their left hand from their right hand, who are the perfect victims.

The stories will continue with ever more punishment against the Jewish ancestors for being stubborn and rebellious against this God. Accepting the temptations and fearing God will continue to wreak cultural havoc, economic chaos, social division, etc. in the stories of the "lesser prophets". It is clear the writers are fearful of the God of Statism, which they know is their own cultural creation. They have laid out all the reasons why it is so difficult to rid themselves of this God, and through the parables of the prophets make it clear they are fearful that despite resistance, the people will always be seduced into returning to Statism. While the long-term threats are recognized, there is always the tempting promise that God will bestow great blessings upon the people in the short term, just as the temporary shade of the gourd. The benefits will always be temporary, but the consequences continue into the next generations.

This Time It Will Be Different!

We now have even more "lesser prophets" in Micah, Nahum, Habakkuk, Zephaniah, Haggai, Zechariah and Malachi all predicting the endless cycles of warfare, and the continuing rise and fall of kingdoms. After having been exiled and sold into slavery by God for years, some Jews can return to their homeland, but God would return to watch over and judge them. More chaos would be inflicted upon them right up to the end of the Old Testament. The writers have God, once again, admitting it is he who creates the chaos, and just in case you missed the point...

Zechariah 8:10 For before these days there was no hire for man, nor any hire for beast; neither was there any peace to him that went out or came in because of the affliction: for I set all men every one against his neighbor. 11. But now I will not be unto the residue of this people as in the former days, saith the Lord of hosts. 12. For the seed shall be prosperous; the vine shall give her fruit, and the ground shall give her increase, and the heavens shall give their dew; and I will cause the remnant of this people to possess all these things. 13. And it shall come to pass, that as ye were a curse among the heathen, O house of Judah, and the house of Israel; so will I save you, and ye shall be a blessing: fear not, but let your hands be strong. 14. For thus saith the Lord of hosts; As I thought to punish you, when your fathers provoked me to wrath, saith the Lord of hosts, and I repented not: 15. So again have I thought in these days to do well unto Jerusalem and to the house of Judah: fear ye not.

The authors of the Bible show God confessing he has caused the chaos and division and war but "fear ye not", this time it will be different, and he will once again "repent" and make a great nation using whatever is left of the Jewish population he has relentlessly punished over the ages. There are more predictions of success, but as we have seen, this god usually does not deliver as promised. In response to their stiff-necked resistance, God will tantalize them with a new king that he will choose to rule over them that will arrive humbly.

Zechariah 9:9 Rejoice greatly, O daughter of Zion; shout, O daughter of Jerusalem: behold, thy King cometh unto thee: he is just, and having salvation; lowly, and riding upon an ass, and upon a colt the foal of an ass.

To placate the stubborn Jewish tribes that continue to complain of his interference, there would be a different kind of king to offer salvation. A radical rebel in the future would try to emulate this idea to fulfill the prophecies. For now, the God of Statism would still prevail. God admits he has punished the Judahites due to the disloyalty of their elites, and admits it is the people who always pay the price. This would not change because he needs the participation of the people.

Zechariah 10:3 Mine anger was kindled against the shepherds, and I punished the goats: for the Lord of hosts hath visited his flock the house of Judah, and hath made them as his goodly horse in the battle. 4. Out of him came forth the corner, out of him the nail, out of him the battle bow, out of him every oppressor together.

God needs the "goats" to provide him with warriors and oppressors against other tribes. A culture of warfare always produces those most loyal to Statism. Those most loyal become the new elites of society.

5. And they shall be as mighty men, which tread down their enemies in the mire of the streets in the battle: and they shall fight, because the Lord is with them, and the riders on horses shall be confounded. 6. And I will strengthen the house of Judah, and I will save the house of Joseph, and I will bring them again to place

them; for I have mercy upon them: and they shall be as though I had not cast them off: for I am the Lord their God, and will hear them.

God again has great plans for the Judahites, once they have been gathered from all the places to which he has scattered them. Once they have been gathered again into a nation, he will encourage them to war against other tribes, and it will be "as though I had not cast them off". Good times will return, and great battles will be fought.

Zechariah 12:5 And the governors of Judah shall say in their heart, The inhabitants of Jerusalem shall be my strength in the Lord of hosts their God. 6. In that day I will make the governors of Judah like an hearth of fire among the wood, and like a torch of fire in a sheaf; and they shall devour all the people round about, on the right hand and on the left: and Jerusalem shall be inhabited again in her own place, even in Jerusalem. 7. The Lord also shall save the tents of Judah first, that the glory of the house of David and the glory of the inhabitants of Jerusalem do not magnify themselves against Judah. 8. In that day shall the Lord defend the inhabitants of Jerusalem; and he that is feeble among them at that day shall be as David; and the house of David shall be as God, as the angel of the Lord before them. 9. And it shall come to pass in that day, that I will seek to destroy all the nations that come against Jerusalem.

When it comes to creating war, rebuilding a nation you have destroyed is just as good as creating new ones, and maybe even better because now you have scores to settle. The new governors will be "like a torch of fire in a sheaf". This God will continue with war and chaos until a New World Order is achieved where everyone can live happily under the one God. The "feeble" among the inhabitants of Jerusalem will return to a love of bureaucracy, just as king David. Judah and Jerusalem will become a single nation and everything will be different this time.

233

Zechariah 14:8 And it shall be in that day, that living waters shall go out from Jerusalem; half of them toward the former sea, and half of them toward the hinder sea: in summer and in winter shall it be. 9. And the Lord shall be king over all the earth: in that day shall there be one Lord, and his name one.

The chaos of war, and having scores to settle against the neighbors, always presents another opportunity for The Powers That Be to become "king over all the earth" in one global entity, which will make everything bigger and better.

Zechariah 14:12 And this shall be the plague wherewith the Lord will smite all the people that have fought against Jerusalem; Their flesh shall consume away while they stand upon their feet, and their eyes shall consume away in their holes, and their tongue shall consume away in their mouth. 13. And it shall come to pass in that day, that a great tumult from the Lord shall be among them; and they shall lay hold every one on the hand of his neighbor, and his hand shall rise up against the hand of his neighbor. 14. And Judah also shall fight at Jerusalem; and the wealth of all the heathen round about shall be gathered together, gold, and silver, and apparel, in great abundance. 15. And so shall be the plague of the horse, of the mule, of the camel, and of the ass, and of all the beasts that shall be in these tents, as this plague. 16. And it shall come to pass, that every one that is left of all the nations which came up against Jerusalem shall even go up from year to year to worship the King, the Lord of hosts, and to keep the feast of tabernacles. 17. And it shall be, that whoso will not come up of all the families of the earth unto Jerusalem to worship the King, the Lord of hosts, even upon them shall be no rain. 18. And if the family of Egypt go not up, and come not, that have no rain; there shall be the plague, wherewith the Lord will smite the heathen that come not up to

keep the feast of tabernacles. 19. This shall be the punishment of Egypt, and the punishment of all nations that come not up to keep the feast of tabernacles.

Then, just to make it clear where this New Power is going, plagues against the neighbors of Jerusalem will encourage them to bring the "gold, and silver, and apparel in great abundance", for the privilege of worshiping God...

Zechariah 14:21 Yea, every pot in Jerusalem and in Judah shall be holiness unto the Lord of hosts: and all they that sacrifice shall come and take of them, and seethe therein: and in that day there shall be no more the Canaanite in the house of the Lord of hosts.

Once all the families of earth worship a single God, there will be no more need for merchantmen (Canaanites) and hence no more free market capitalism. This would have been a great plan for the God of Statism, but once again he would not be successful because of the stiff-necked Judahites. The Judahites still would not willingly allow this God to become The Powers That Be in their culture. The people of Israel are still today struggling against this God, while most of the world still welcomes him in return for dependency and the promise of benefits for the elites and a new "promised land".

One of the last conversations God would have in the Old Testament would be through Malachi and would be regarding taxes and the stinginess of "his" people in their offerings to The Powers That Be and their continued stubborn resistance.

Malachi 3:7 Even from the days of your fathers ye are gone away from mine ordinances, and have not kept them. Return unto me, and I will return unto you, saith the Lord of hosts. But ye said, Wherein shall we return? 8. Will a man rob God? Yet ye have robbed me? But ye say, Wherein have we robbed thee? In tithes and offerings. 9. Ye are cursed with a curse: for ye have robbed me, even this whole nation. 10. Bring

ye all the tithes into the storehouse, that there may be meat in mine house, and prove me now herewith, saith the Lord of hosts, if I will not open you the windows of heaven, and pour out a blessing, that there shall not be room enough to receive it.

Provided the people pay well enough there is always lots of saving, serving, and protecting to be done, and there will be many blessings—but the people aren't sure they're getting what they pay for.

Malachi 3:13 Your words have been stout against me, saith the Lord. Yet ye say, What have we spoken so much against thee? 14. Ye have said, It is vain to serve God: and what profit is it that we have kept his ordinance, and that we have walked mournfully before the Lord of hosts? 15. And now we call the proud happy; yea, they that work wickedness are set up; yea, they that tempt God are even the delivered.

As usual, the promises don't match the reality. The only benefactors of following the God of Statism are the proud and the wicked. The Yahwists that wrote the Old Testament instinctively understood their savior will be a cultural savior that is of We The People, and not The Powers That Be. An attempt to present a solution will be through new books that will come to be called the New Testament. But does the New Testament really present a solution to a culture of dependency and submission, or is Jesus just another God of Statism?

Christianity—A Good Idea Gone Bad?

To those who are now comfortably ensconced in Protestant churches in freedom-loving nations, it may seem Christianity has always provided comfort and salvation to those of faith. That is several stonings from the truth. For most of the history of Christianity, simply doing what you now take for granted would have resulted in you being pulled from your pew, dragged before a tribunal, tortured, then taken out into the courtyard and burned to death at the stake simply for taking your family into a Protestant church. Before that, people were even being hung for translating the bible into English or other languages.

Until recently, Christianity was that of a Statist terrorist organization that would wage war against any who presented a threat. This would have included anyone having the gall to attend any of the Protestant churches of today and there would have been a great slaughter as in the Old Testament for anyone "evil in the sight of the Lord".

The Christian monarchy that eventually came to power, maintained bureaucracies and armies, collected taxes, persecuted the competitors (mostly Jews), and basically did everything any Statist organization such as a kingdom would do, just as did the god in the Old Testament. For those that have taken the time to study the history of Christianity, it is not a question of whether Christianity went bad, but simply how and when. Christian religious freedom is a recent phenomenon and is a result of relatively non-Statist societies and contrarians who rejected Statism to adopt Protestantism, both politically and spiritually. To a great extent, Protestantism is simply a return to the same contrarian Judaic Yahwism espoused by the resistance demonstrated by the Jewish ancestors.

We now know the god in the Old Testament was the God of Statism, and was a cultural system created by the corruption and selfishness of those who benefit from that system. As we have seen, the bible is not a story of the wonderful experience we would have if only we would love God without question. Rather, the purpose of their books was to identify and illustrate the problems of Statist oppression that prevent us from creating our own Eden. We can assume that if the New Testament was written under the same philosophy, then they would have created the character Jesus to be the opposite of the God of Statism and be a champion of We The People if he was meant to be an actual solution.

As a reminder, it is no secret that Jews still reject the notion of Jesus-as-God as promoted by Christianity, because for Jesus to be just another centralized God figure around which to be subservient and fearful would defeat the purpose of their Judaic stories of resistance in the Old Testament. Therefore, it is small wonder they would reject the idea of Jesus-as-God. Since they wrote the books, maybe we should keep this in mind as we go through the New Testaments to determine if Jesus was meant to be a god figure, and if so, to determine what that means.

In opposition to the original authors, the consensus among today's Christians is that Jesus was the Messiah, which means anointed to rule over us in a new kingdom. The word messiah is the same as the word christ, which means the "anointed one". There were many anointed ones in ancient Hebrew times, and it was a title or job description bestowed on anyone considered to be the highest authority in a chosen field of endeavor, particularly as a ruler {52}. This title was most often bestowed on kings or high priests. Since Jesus was considered by many to have that job description, we should ask ourselves who he is, and if anointed then by whom, because it was not a premise accepted by the Jewish ancestors who wrote the books and happened much later.

To get to know Jesus and what he represents we can start with his birth because we have some information. We immediately run into some contradictions with the concept of Jesus-as-God. For one thing, there is no reference to a virgin birth in the original Jewish scriptures. In modern translations they have Matthew quoting Isaiah as saying:

---

52 http://www.bibleinfo.com/en/questions/what-does-christ-mean

Matthew 1:23 Behold a virgin shall be with child and shall bear a son and they shall call his name Immanuel.

However, in the original Jewish version the closest reference says...

Isaiah 7:14 Behold the young woman is with a child and shall bear a son and she will call His name Immanuel.

So, we have a couple of problems already since the original doesn't agree. The suggestion of a supernatural birth doesn't seem to be consistent either with the original Old Testament or with the purpose of their books. To be consistent, the original writers would have understood no virgin birth had been suggested in the Old Testament, so why would they put a deliberate spin on the story? This suggests there may have been some monkey business going on after the fact to change the narrative. Of course, it could be there was an honest misunderstanding when different languages were used to translate, but that seems unlikely. We have much better translations today but there is still a perpetuation of the virgin birth story. Or you could make the argument that in the New Testament they were simply using a virgin birth as a parable to represent a complete break with the past, and to create an entirely new narrative. Either way, we know for sure Jesus-as-God is contrary to Jewish tradition, so why would they contradict themselves? They didn't, it was done later.

Also, it seems if the original intent had been to create Jesus-as-God he would have been called Immanuel to emulate the Old Testament in Isaiah, but that never happens. Even their meanings are different. Immanuel means "God is With Us" {[53]} and could mean a warning if written in the same spirit as the rest of the Old Testament. If it was a warning, then we should give them credit because it was they who had the correct prophecy when you consider the failure of Christianity. On the other hand, Jesus

---

[53] https://en.wikipedia.org/wiki/Immanuel

means "rescue, or deliver" {54}. As we have seen, there is a big difference between being "with us" and "rescuing" us.

As another curiosity to consider, it seems Jesus-as-God would invite the use of a special and reverent name to make him exclusive, but instead they used the name Jesus, which was so common it would have been the equivalent of Average Joe in our times. Since this is the case, maybe his name could be an effort to present Jesus as one of We the People rather than a god, which is consistent with both Judaism and Yahwism. Since he came from a nowhere place like Nazareth his name would essentially mean "an average Joe from nowhere has the power to save". That doesn't seem like someone the authors were setting up as a king. Again, since they are the ones that wrote the bible, we should consider these inconsistencies. So far, Jesus-as-God doesn't add up, but we can keep an open mind. We can delve further in the New Testaments to see if we can find the original intent.

---

54 http://www.abarim-
publications.com/Meaning/Jesus.html#.XaMCWUZKjIU

Wise Guys—The Instigators

As we would expect from books whose purpose is to examine the culture of politics, the story of Jesus begins with political turmoil that begins at his birth, and Statism does not appear to be his friend. There are "wise men" from the East who were there around the time of his birth, whose purpose appears to create paranoia and resentment in the kingdom of Herod against the Jewish people. They had been in the area for a couple of years publicly claiming that there would be a new King of the Jews that would be born and grow up to be a risk to the authorities. We don't know if there were only two or if there were two hundred, because the bible doesn't say. We do know that the bible doesn't say three, as commonly accepted.

> **Now when Jesus was born in Bethlehem of Judea in the days of Herod the king, behold, there came wise men from the east to Jerusalem, 2. Saying, Where is he that is born King of the Jews? For we have seen his star in the east, and are come to worship him.**

The "wise men" would have known perfectly well that making this announcement publicly would have put the Jewish people at risk of reprisal, so we must assume it was a deliberate attempt by the writers to once again demonstrate the risks of Statism to the people. If the purpose of the wise men in the story had been solely to search for someone to worship, they wouldn't have gone around publicly asking for the location of a newborn "King of the Jews" for two years. After all, they apparently had their own version of GPS in the form of a star that pointed directly to his address. Once found, if their intent was not deliberate trouble making, then they simply had to keep their mouth shut and worship to their hearts content. Instead, they goaded king Herod into responding in a way that to most would seem devious and psychotic, which is consistent with how Statist rulers are commonly portrayed in the bible.

> **Matthew 2:3 When Herod the king had heard these things, he was troubled, and all Jerusalem with him. 4. And when he had gathered all the chief priests and**

scribes of the people together, he demanded of them where Christ should be born. 5. And they said unto him, In Bethlehem of Judaea: for thus it is written by the prophet, 6. And thou Bethlehem, in the land of Juda, art not the least among the princes of Juda: for out of thee shall come a Governor, that shall rule my people Israel. 7. Then Herod, when he had privily called the wise men, inquired of them diligently what time the star appeared. 8. And he sent them to Bethlehem, and said, Go and search diligently for the young child; and when ye have found him, bring me word again, that I may come and worship him also.

The wise men, knowing they had served their purpose, which was for some reason to either instigate resentment against Jews, or simply to make a fool of Herod, picked out a newborn based on their star GPS. After giving him gifts, they immediately high-tailed it back to the east where they came from without returning to tell the king. If their purpose was turning Herod against the Jewish people then they were successful, because he realized they had just been mocking him all along.

Matthew 3:16 Then Herod, when he saw that he was mocked of the wise men, was exceeding wroth, and sent forth, and slew all the children that were in Bethlehem, and in all the coasts thereof, from two years old and under, according to the time which he had diligently inquired of the wise men.

Whatever their real purpose, the subversives were successful in both making a fool of Herod and creating political resentment against the Jews. We know they had been in the area for a couple of years before this event, because Herod had felt compelled to slay all children "from two years old and under; according to the time which he had diligently inquired of the wise men". At this point he had no interest in anyone called Jesus, and was just concerned with a Christ, which means anointed as a "chosen leader", which would have been in violation of Roman law. The wise men never referred to the child they had chosen either as Jesus or Christ, but simply referred to him as "the young child", and there was apparently never any attempt at anointing him. The intent of the story seems to be to demonstrate the political dangers of introducing new ideas into an established Statist culture, because as we will see, Jesus would in fact represent a new idea.

While all this was going on, Jesus' father Joseph was doing a lot of dreaming. First, he dreamed it was OK to marry a pregnant woman because she was pregnant by the Holy Ghost, then he dreamed he should leave Bethlehem and go to Egypt before Herod killed all the children in Jerusalem. Then after Herod died, he dreamed he should return to Israel, but then had another dream he should instead go somewhere else. Joseph must have been a fitful sleeper. Nevertheless, avoiding the authorities of the Powers That Be seemed to be the main issue. He finally ended up in the Galilee area. Nazareth was an insignificant little town in Galilee.

Matthew 2:23 And he came and dwelt in a city called Nazareth: that it might be fulfilled which was spoken by the prophets, He shall be called a Nazarene.

This presents another problem because at no point in the Old Testament is this prophecy ever mentioned. It seems whoever was writing (or rewriting) the New Testament was obsessed with meeting all the supposed prophecies in the Old Testament for validation, even if they had to make them up. To Jewish scholars this leads to another reason to question the validity of Jesus-as-God. They don't question the validity of the New Testament. They just object to the notion that the New Testament presents Jesus as a king, a messiah, a god, or any other centralized authority figure. There are many suspicious inaccuracies and contradictions, but for our purposes we are still only concerned with the same issue—and that is intent. Was Jesus meant to suggest a solution as hoped, or was he just intended to rule over us as another Statist God in a new kingdom? Our purpose does not require picking out words and phrases to determine contradictions or literal correctness, but simply an implied purpose. So far, Jesus-as-God still doesn't seem to be the original intent of the writers, but that could change, so we can keep our options open as we continue.

Jesus disappeared for several years as his father Joseph waited for the murderous Herod to die, but in chapter three of Matthew, Jesus reappeared and came up from Galilee where he was living with his family. There he met the contrarian river guy, John the Baptist. As we recall, John placed little value on State or religious leaders, and pretty much held them both in contempt. It seems he would have been suspicious if Jesus had presented himself as a god, but instead they hit it off right away. We see in the next passage John's attitude toward religious elites.

Matthew 3:7 But when he saw many of the Pharisees and Sadducees come to his baptism, he said unto them, O generation of vipers, who hath warned you to flee from the wrath to come? 8. Bring forth therefore fruits meet for repentance: 9. And think not to say within yourselves, We have Abraham to our father: for I say unto you, that God is able of these stones to raise up children unto Abraham.

He didn't seem to think it was worth wasting much time with what would have been, at least outwardly, the most pious among the people of the time. He also didn't seem to think much of heritage or lineage claims.

Matthew 3:11 I indeed baptize you with water unto repentance: but he that cometh after me is mightier than I, whose shoes I am not worthy to bear: he shall baptize you with the Holy Ghost, and with fire: 12 Whose fan is in his hand, and he will thoroughly purge his floor, and gather his wheat into the garner; but he will burn up the chaff with unquenchable fire.

We already know from Isaiah and other entries that the definition of the Holy Ghost, (or the Holy Spirit, which for some reason the KJV uses interchangeably, unlike other translations) is the spirit of wisdom and understanding. Those who choose not to receive his message will be separated from those who do and will receive the fire of perdition of their own making.

244

Isaiah 11:2 And the spirit of the Lord shall rest upon him, the spirit of wisdom and understanding, the spirit of counsel and might, the spirit of knowledge and of the fear of the Lord;

John seems to be presenting Jesus as someone very culturally wise, with the "spirit of knowledge", which doesn't require being a God. Jesus agreed to be baptized in the living and flowing water by John just as everyone else, and this is where the authors show him having an epiphany.

Matthew 3:16 And Jesus, when he was baptized, went up straightway out of the water: and, lo, the heavens were opened unto him, and he saw the Spirit of God descending upon him: like a dove, and lighting upon him. 17. And lo a voice from heaven, saying, This is my beloved Son, in whom I am well pleased.

In addition to receiving the "spirit of wisdom and understanding" Jesus also got a voice of reference from heaven, which are signs the writers were not representing him as a God. If they were, he would have been the source of understanding and wisdom, instead of receiving it himself. Also, he would not have required a reference. He did, however, receive the Spirit of God, which was "descending lightly like a dove, and lighting upon him". So far Jesus seems far more Yahwist than godlike, but the next incident seems to confirm this even further because he was yanked directly from his epiphany and dumped in the wilderness by the writers to be tested with the temptations of Statism. Once again, God would use his assistant the devil (or Satan) as a tool for purposes of torment, just as in the story of Job.

Matthew 4:1 Then was Jesus led up of the Spirit into the wilderness to be tempted of the devil. 2. And when the tempter came to him, he said, If thou be the Son of God, command that these stones be made bread. 4. But he answered and said, It is written, Man shall not live by bread alone, but by every word that proceedeth out of the mouth of God.

Jesus seemed to believe he thought wealth, comfort, security and all the things bread represents would still not be as important as the word of God, which is our chosen culture, and suggests he did not think of himself as "anointed", which would have been a real selling point with the devil. This resistance to temptation is consistent with Yahwism.

> **Matthew 4:5 Then the devil taketh him up into the holy city, and setteth him on a pinnacle of the temple, 6. And saith unto him, If thou be the Son of God, cast thyself down: for it is written, He shall give his angels charge concerning thee: and in their hands they shall bear thee up, lest at any time thou dash thy foot against a stone. 7. Jesus said unto him, It is written again, Thou shalt not tempt the Lord thy God.**

This indicates Jesus believed he was responsible for his own actions and should not expect to be cared for by others higher up, especially by a Statist god. This too is consistent with Yahwism. Now the biggest test of all.

> **Matthew 4:8 Again, the devil taketh him up into an exceeding high mountain, and sheweth him all the kingdoms of the world, and the glory of them; 9. And saith unto him, All these things will I give thee, if thou wilt fall down and worship me. 10. Then saith Jesus unto him, Get thee hence, Satan: for it is written, Thou shalt worship the Lord thy God, and him only shalt thou serve. 11. Then the devil leaveth him, and, behold, angels came and administered to him.**

The writers portray Jesus as successfully passing all tests, showing he was not tempted by man's cultural adversary (the devil), which are the temptations of Statism. That Jesus, unlike all others before him, would turn down having his own kingdom with which to oppress the population and enrich himself is definitely "a new thing" which they suggested in the Old Testament. Just as Job and Daniel, he apparently believes only in the God within him, which is his own culture, rather than a culture imposed upon him.

But there is an even more important issues that dispute the Jesus-as-God notion.

First, how is it that you can go about tempting a deity? Why would Satan waste his time? And why would God tempt his own Son? So far, these contradictions are very good news for those of who believe the bible is teaching us it is up to We The People to determine the nature of God, rather than having a Statist God determine the nature of We The People. Happily, it could very well be that Jesus was originally meant to be a champion of the people rather than the next God of Statism. That would mean the teachings of Jesus didn't start out bad; the concept just fell victim to Statism, just as had Judaism under the Pharisees. This is what the prophets had warned us about.

We next have Jesus doing something else not very godlike. Jesus had hardly finished high-fiving the angels in celebration of passing the Statist tests, when he heard John had been thrown into prison. In the Old Testament he would have acquired an army starting with victim groups, inflicted a great smiting and slaughter upon the enemy, and been rewarded by God for the slaughter by being made king if he were successful. Instead, he used common sense and ran from the State. In fact, he would spend most of his life avoiding the Statist authorities and any type of open conflict, unlike the god in the Old Testament. So far, he doesn't sound even remotely like any "god" we have met in the earlier books.

Once he had placed a safe distance between himself and his enemies, he began to form a gang of like-minded people to help with his cause. The gang would not be warriors, and he would not become a warlord. Unlike king David and others like him, he would become a teacher and his followers would become students, who would then go on to teach others. This also seems to be consistent with Yahwism. The God of Statism and his kings in the Old Testament never had any interest in students or teachers, and instead specialized in war and oppression.

Matthew 4:18 And Jesus, walking by the sea of Galilee, saw two brethren, Simon called Peter, and Andrew his brother, casting a net into the sea: for they

were fishers. 19. And he saith unto them, Follow me, and I will make you fishers of men. 20. And they straightway left their nets, and followed them. 21. And going on from thence, he saw other two brethren, James the son of Zebedee, and John his brother, in a ship with Zebedee their father, mending their nets; and he called them. 22. And they immediately left the ship and their father, and followed him.

Again, unlike king David, who we recall gained followers from victim groups as we saw in this passage...

Samuel 22:2 And every one that was in distress, and every one that was in debt, and every one that was discontented, gathered themselves unto him; and he became a captain over them:

This would not be a tactic that would be used by Jesus. Instead, Jesus acquired his first followers from working-class people that were self-reliant and did not identify as victims. There also does not appear to be any hint of dividing spoils of war or any girding of swords, which is yet another break from the past. There are even more breaks from tradition, with many accounts of teaching and healing of diseases from Jesus in his travels. These were not activities taken up by the Powers That Be in the Old Testament.

Matthew 4:23 And Jesus went about all Galilee, teaching in their synagogues, and preaching the gospel of the kingdom, and healing all manner of sickness and all manner of disease among the people.

Jesus does heal some in the New Testament. Does this make Jesus a God? Just as John the Baptist and Job, Jesus had the power to heal from what he had learned from observing nature and asking questions of knowledgeable people. Even in his youth Jesus apparently spent a lot of time hanging out with doctors, and one point his family even lost track of him during a trip as he sought his own education.

Luke 2:46 And it came to pass, that after three days they found him in the temple, sitting in the midst of the

doctors, both hearing them, and asking them questions.

I don't recall any previous gods feeling the need to learn anything, especially about how to heal others. This could be because the Powers That Be spent most of their time smiting, so didn't have time for healing. It is now not uncommon for healers to bring some back from the dead, to heal leprosy, defeat afflictions of all sorts, and with proper treatment to even cast out the occasional evil spirit. It is unlikely that those who do these things consider themselves to be gods. It stands to reason he was simply implying what people could accomplish on their own if allowed to do so, provided they had faith in themselves. Both teaching and the knowledge of healing would be consistent with Yahwism, and his predictions of our ability to learn to heal have come to pass. There are no accounts of king Solomon, the wisest of them all, ever using his wisdom to directly benefit the people or heal anyone. Not surprisingly, before he died he concluded all was vanity, and wisdom was not worth having. For him, knowledge did not translate into cultural virtue as it seems to for Jesus.

Statism does not encourage virtue through learning or understanding, and we can find examples demonstrating this everywhere today. Not many people want to go to North Korea or Africa to seek medical treatment because of their great advances in medicine. North Korea and most countries in Africa are ruled by corrupt Statists, and rely on outside countries to provide them with education, medicines, food, cash, and other forms of aid. Both Russia and China are also Statist societies that have advanced technologically only recently, and often because the technology is stolen. As Jesus seemed to predict, most of the diseases mentioned in the bible have since been defeated in non-Statist cultures that place emphasis on education, self-accountability, and self-determination.

It appears the Jewish philosophy of Yahwism is still winning in the Jesus-as-God debate. At this point Jesus is still simply following the wisdom and optimism of Yahwism, and rather than being represented as a god, is simply promoting the capabilities of We The People.

The next part of Matthew deals with the sermon on the mount. Just as with Proverbs in the Old Testament, it deals entirely with the main theme of the bible, which is the importance of a virtuous culture. It offers many suggestions as to how ordinary citizens can achieve a heavenly culture through healthy interaction. Again, we don't need to address each bit of wisdom individually, because they are readily available. Most people would simply regard them as common sense, but a few stand out that provide an insight to Jesus' thoughts on Statism.

Matthew 5:25 Agree with thine adversary quickly, whiles thou art in the way with him; lest at any time the adversary deliver thee to the judge, and the judge deliver thee to the officer, and thou be cast into prison.

Unlike Moses the Statist, it doesn't sound like he was a big fan of turning to the State justice system to solve disputes. Instead, in the next passage he acknowledges cultural interactions among the people themselves were of far more importance.

Matthew 5:25 And if thy right eye offend thee, pluck it out, and cast it from thee: for it is profitable for thee that one of thy members should perish, and not that thy whole body should be cast into hell. 30. And if thy right hand offend thee, cut it off, and cast it from thee: for it is profitable for thee that one of thy members should perish, and not that thy whole body should be cast into hell.

Of course, he is speaking not of the physical body, but of the cultural body. It seems he had a dim view of one small section of society being allowed to destroy the culture of the larger group. Those bent on disrupting or destroying culture needed to be either healed, cast out, or cut off, which translates to no tolerance for the offenders. Those who would destroy a successful culture need to be restricted in such a way that would preserve the good of the larger culture, while still maintaining tolerance to new ideas.

Today it seems we expend far too much effort catering to any minority culture instead of preserving whatever larger success that has been achieved. This is all done in the name of "political correctness", and "multiculturalism", which results in all culture being brought down to the lowest common denominator.

He never claims to have the ability to teach all, but only those who believe in virtue and wisdom. In fact, he often avoids skeptical unbelievers rather than attempt to convert anyone to his way of thinking and advises his apostles to do likewise. Surprisingly, and in contradiction to those who follow Jesus-as-God teachings, Jesus specifically requests that good deeds or miracles should never be done in his name.

> **Matthew 7:21 Not every one that saith unto me, Lord, Lord, shall enter into the kingdom of heaven; but he that doeth the will of my Father which is in heaven. 22. Many will say to me in that day, Lord, Lord, have we not prophesied in thy name? And in thy name have cast out devils? And in thy name done many wonderful works? 23. And then will I profess unto them, I never knew you: depart from me, ye that work inequity.**

This sort of gives a whole new twist on all that healing and saving done in the name of Jesus doesn't it? Instead, he taught that any real healing and saving will be because of the creation of a successful culture because of learning from our history (Father) and using the spirit of truth and wisdom. He did not teach this wisdom would come from a god, but only through cultural virtue. It seems if Jesus had thought of himself as a god he would have actively encouraged doing miracles in his name.

One of the most promising aspects of the New Testament that still agrees with the Old is there still appears to be no concept of ""us against them", so long as others show a willingness to fit into a successful culture by ridding themselves of God's evil spirit. Matthew is a perfect example. He was a Statist working as a tax collector when Jesus asked for his help. He was used as an example of how culture can evolve quickly, especially within a single individual.

> **Matthew 9:9 And as Jesus passed forth from thence, he saw a man, named Matthew, sitting at the receipt of custom: and he saith unto him, Follow me. And he rose, and followed him. 10. And it came to pass, as Jesus sat at meat in the house, behold, many publicans** (government workers) **and sinners came and sat down with him and his disciples. 11. And when the Pharisees saw it, they said unto his disciples, Why eateth your Master with publicans and sinners? 12. But when Jesus heard that, he said unto them, They that be whole need not a physician, but they that are sick. 13. But go ye and learn what that meaneth, I will have mercy, and not sacrifice: for I am not come to call the righteous, but sinners to repentance.**

He made it clear he was not there to preach to the choir. Helping to pull the willing into a successful culture, regardless of their history or even their current employment situation, would be consistent with Yahwist wisdom. Even government workers actively participating in Statism were considered valuable to Jesus as potential allies, provided they followed his path instead. Despite all the harm they do, Statists were thought of as victims and not condemned as perpetrators.

There are more passages that on first inspection might appear to be equating Jesus to an all-powerful God, and one example is through the ability to feed the multitudes. In fact, this would not be out of line with Yahwist thinking. Relatively non-statist societies have always had the magical ability to feed the multitudes. On the other hand, Statist societies have often had the magical ability to starve the multitudes. I would refer you to the agricultural history of our favorite bad examples such as Stalinist Russia, Maoist China, and the family cartel that runs North Korea. They have since necessarily refined their methods of control in these regions to prevent further wholesale starvation, but that was not always the case when Statism was first being imposed upon the citizens. Statist social engineering resulted in the starvation of millions.

Jesus seems to simply be representative of the capabilities of We the People in the ability to heal and feed the multitudes, so long as there is no Statist interference. Those powers would not be considered abnormal in any healthy society, which these parables demonstrate. His abilities would be representative of the miraculous powers of We The People, and again do not require Jesus-as-God.

As we would expect from those who understand the importance of cultural evolution, sinning does not seem to be a huge issue with Jesus either, so long as it is a learning experience.

> **Matthew 12:31 Wherefore I say to you, All manner of sin and blasphemy shall be forgiven unto men: but the blasphemy against the Holy Ghost shall not be forgiven unto men. 32. And whosoever speaketh a word against the Son of man, it shall be forgiven him: but whosoever speaketh against the Holy Ghost, it shall not be forgiven him, neither in this world, neither in the world to come. 33. Either make the tree good, and his fruit good; or else make the tree corrupt, and his fruit corrupt: for the tree is known by his fruit.**

Unlike the god in the Old Testament, where criticism of the God of Statism would be followed by stoning, he apparently couldn't care less about anyone being critical of himself, but you can't be truly successful in life or learn from sin by avoiding the spirit of truth and wisdom (Holy Ghost).

Anyone who has even a passing interest in culture understands that we need our sins and our sinfulness for culture to evolve. Without sin, (sins mean "missing the mark" culturally), we would simply evolve as mindless automatons with no wisdom, understanding, or immunity. He never suggests we should be without sin, but only that we should forgive and learn from sin. We need our sins culturally just as much as our bodies need viruses and bacteria physically, even though they are sometimes harmful.

Just as with sinning, evolving without the little bugs that test us constantly would mean our bodies would have no recognition or understanding, and therefore no immunity. This is the principle behind vaccinations, which are essentially used to educate our physiology to existing threats. The same is true of cultural sins, without which we would be left vulnerable, and minus the immunity of virtue. Jesus had no problem with learning from sin but had a huge problem with ignoring the Holy Ghost, which is the spirit of truth and understanding of cultural sin, and the learning that should follow. Without learning, sinning is simply corruption of culture, and leads to no good fruit produced for future generations. He furthered the point by comparing this understanding to the foolishness of rejecting some foods over others in deference to tradition, and of the necessity of both good and bad pathogens in our natural world that test us and strengthen our immunity.

> **Matthew 15:1 Then came to Jesus scribes and Pharisees, which were of Jerusalem, saying, 2. Why do the disciples transgress the tradition of the elders? For they wash not their hands when they eat bread.**

Also:

> **Matthew 15:10 And he called the multitude, and said unto them, Hear and understand: 11. Not that which goeth into the mouth defileth a man; but that which cometh out of the mouth, this defileth a man. 12. Then came his disciples, and said unto him, Knowest thou that the Pharisees were offended, after they heard this saying? 13. But he answered and said, Every plant, which my heavenly Father hath not planted, shall be rooted up. 14. Let them alone: they be blind. And if the blind lead the blind, both shall fall into the ditch.**

In contrast to the Old Testament god, Jesus never attempts to force his beliefs and teachings on others through persecution, but simply points out foolishness where it exists. It seems that blindness toward not only culture, but also physical health is still very common. It is only recently that the importance of building and maintaining a healthy immune system through avoiding overly sterile environments and antibiotics, especially for infants, has regained favor. We are learning that defying the natural order of things leads to national health epidemics caused by "purified" foods that are highly processed and sterilized, and of poor nutritional quality. This in turn leads to such things as allergies, obesity, and diabetes. Most of our health problems today would best be solved through a better understanding of nature, and not of counterproductive regulations that encourage even more sterilization and overly processed foods. The same is true of sinning and the attempts to solve cultural problems through more laws.

Moving on to new lessons, there are some references in the New Testament that refer directly to why the God of Statism began punishing the Jewish ancestors in the first place, which was to prevent them from achieving self-confidence and self-determination. At one point a guy brings his son to Jesus "for he is a lunatic" to be healed, and the disciples asked why they had not been able to do it themselves.

> **Matthew 17:20 And Jesus said unto them, Because of your unbelief: for verily I say unto you, If ye have faith as a grain of mustard seed, ye shall say unto this mountain, Remove hence to yonder place, and it shall remove;** *and nothing shall be impossible unto you.*

This call to have faith in yourself and that "nothing shall be impossible unto you" is clearly a call for the people to have faith in their own abilities. He does not say, "Hey, stand back and watch me move this mountain, because I'm a god and you should have faith in me!" As you will recall, the god in the Old Testament did not want the people to have faith in themselves, and divided and punished them stop that from happening. That executive order to rely on a god rather than relying on oneself has now clearly been reversed.

> **Genesis 11:6 And the Lord said, and behold, the people is one, and they have all one language; and this they do: and now nothing will be restrained from**

them, which they have imagined to do. 7. Go to, let us go down, and there confound their language, that they may not understand one another's speech.

In order to prevent self-reliance, the Old Testament God of Statism imposed cultural division and identity politics, just as any modern-day Statist does. Again, Jesus does not seem to have much in common with that god.

Even though Jesus never ran for any political office, he did begin to gain a following, which is always interpreted as a threat by Statists. On several occasions he was subjected to "gotcha" questions designed to have him make comments to be used to suggest foolishness or unlawfulness. On one occasion he was asked about something they felt sure would implicate him as lawbreaker, which was taxation. Tax laws are still often used to bring down political opponents to Statism.

Matthew 22:17 Tell us therefore, What thinkest thou? Is it lawful to give tribute unto Caesar, or not? 18. But Jesus perceived their wickedness, and said, Why tempt ye me, ye hypocrites? 19. Show me the the tribute money. And they brought unto him a penny. 20. And he saith unto them, Whose is this image and superscription? 21. They say unto him, Caesar's. Then he saith he unto them, Render therefore unto Caesar the things which are Caesar's; and unto God the things that are God's.

According to Jesus, you can go ahead and use government minted script when it is useful, but don't think for one moment it belongs to you. It will always belong to the State, and it can be taxed and manipulated to control culture and to determine winners and losers almost at will. The implication is that we need a reliable exchange currency, but that using government printed script is anything but reliable. Among other things, using it creates depressions, recessions, and market bubbles followed by financial crashes. As a result, we have the endless economic chaos of Statism. Allowing the State to create, and then tax and manipulate our currency, must be some form of cultural insanity. However, it is a valuable tool to impose Statist control, so the use of it is still widely promoted.

Because of his contrarian teachings, Jesus finally gets arrested by the State. The bible makes it clear who are the real culprits.

> **Matthew 26:3 Then assembled together the chief priests, and the scribes, and the elders of the people, unto the palace of the high priest, who was Caiaphas. 4. and consulted that they might take Jesus by subtilty, and kill him. 5. But they said, Not on the feast day, lest there be an uproar among the people.**

As usual, the greatest threat to the palace insiders was the people. To maintain control and divert the narrative away from Jesus' success at teaching a message of self-determination, it became necessary to use manipulation tactics. First, to discredit Jesus sufficiently, a mob (probably paid, just as they are today) was formed.

> **Matthew 26:55 In that same hour said Jesus to the multitudes, Are ye come out as against a thief with swords and staves for to take me? I sat daily with you teaching in the temple, and ye laid no hold on me. 56. But all this was done, that the scriptures of the prophets might be fulfilled. Then all the disciples forsook him, and fled.**

Despite all the miracles, the gang Jesus brought together apparently still did not regard him as a god. Hiking their skirts and running to the hills at the first sign of trouble doesn't sound like something they would do if they thought their BFF was a god. Unlike those chosen by the Powers That Be before him, his purpose wasn't to start war or to hurt others. Instead, he seemed to have a good grasp on his goal and the purpose of his actions. During one inquisition he was again asked many gotcha questions, still in the hope he would implicate himself...

> **Matthew 26:63 But Jesus held his peace. And the high priest answered and said unto him, I adjure thee by the living God, that thou tell us whether thou be the**

257

Christ, the Son of God. 64. Jesus saith unto him, Thou hast said: nevertheless I say unto you, Hereafter shall ye see the Son of man sitting on the right hand of power, and coming in the clouds of heaven.

He didn't take the bait, and certainly never claimed to be a god, even though this would have been the perfect opportunity. That "ye shall see the Son of man sitting on the right hand of power; and coming in the clouds of heaven" sounds exactly like the meaning is that The People will be the "right hand of power" in the creation a heavenly culture. This is almost exactly what God was saying to Job when he said you will be saved by "thine own right hand". At this point, Jesus still has never presented himself as a god or encouraged others to do so.

Jesus—The Cure is Already in Our Blood

Needless to say, Jesus was eventually murdered by the political and religious authorities that feared the effects his message would have on the people. As he hung from the poles dying, he asked a question, not of himself we assume, but of the Old Testament God of Statism.

> **Matthew 27:46 And about the ninth hour Jesus cried with a loud voice, saying Eli, Eli, lama sabach-thani? That is to say, My God, my God why has thou forsaken me?**

This presents another clear contradiction to the Jesus-as-God issue. It doesn't seem fitting for a god to be questioning himself, or for that matter his father either, if they are on equal terms and know the same things. We, however, know exactly to which god he was referring, and so we know the answer to his question. The God of Statism always forsakes We The People, and the writers want to emphasize this fact. This is a god that will always require suffering and sacrifice. We saw this with Abraham receiving instructions to murder his son at God's direction. In addition, this exact same inquiry was made by another of God's victims, in Psalm 22 by king David. He also was forsaken on many occasions despite being loved by God. However, this story is significantly different in one respect because, even though God forsakes and sacrifices his son, Jesus would return to be resurrected. By one account his death even resulted in a zombie apocalypse.

> **Matthew 27:50 Jesus, when he had cried again with a loud voice, yielded up the ghost. 51. And, behold, the veil of the temple was rent in twain from the top to the bottom; and the earth did quake, and the rocks rent; 52. And the graves were opened; and many bodies of the saints which slept arose, 53. And came out of the graves after his resurrection, and went into the holy city, and appeared unto many.**

This concept has given rise to a whole genre of horror movies, but in this case, it appears the zombies were the good guys. I suppose you could even make the case these zombies had an appetite for brains, because those escaping from the graves were prophets that had been inclined to learn by devouring everything other brains had to offer, and then spreading that knowledge through infecting whomever would be willing to listen through teaching. To Statists who needing to maintain a firm grip on centralized cultural indoctrination that would have been very horrifying. The point is, this time We The People would see a way to be resurrected from being forsaken and sacrificed.

The disciples, who had scattered like chickens during the trials of Jesus, now returned and met with him in Galilee per instructions sent by two women after the resurrection. Both women were named Mary, one of whom was apparently his mother. And there was Mary Magdalene, whose relationship with Jesus is still mysterious and has led to much conjecture. There were only eleven disciples now because Judas, who had identified Jesus to the morality police for money, had committed suicide in shame.

> **Matthew 28:16 Then the eleven disciples went away into Galilee, into a mountain where Jesus had appointed them. 17. And when they saw him, they worshiped him: but some doubted. 18. And Jesus came and spake unto them, saying, All power is given unto me in heaven and in earth. 19. Go ye therefore, and teach all nations, baptizing them in the name of the Father, and of the Son, and of the Holy Ghost: 20. Teaching them to observe all things whatsoever I have commanded you: and, lo, I am with you always, even unto the end of the world. Amen.**

And so ends the first of the New Testaments. Notice he did not request that baptisms be done in the name of Jesus, but of the Father, Son, and Holy Ghost. So, what are we to take from this? Jesus never had an army, but instead he formed a gang of teachers, so clearly his superpower was knowledge, truth, understanding, and virtue, which is another way of saying Father, Son, and Holy

Ghost. He does not claim to be to be a god that will return as our messiah to be our salvation. Instead, he says "I am with you always" which means he does not need to return, because he is the cultural potential that is always within us. Jesus-as-god still does not appear to be the case at this point, unless you want to take the view that We The People, who he represents, are all gods. This may be an acceptable position to take because the authors of the bible even say we are.

> **Psalm 82:5 They know not, neither will they understand; they walk on in darkness: all the foundations of the earth are out of course. 6.** *I have said, Ye are gods; and all of you are children of the most High.*

For us to be gods does not mean we walk around on clouds. It simply means there is no one above us who is responsible for us because the Power is within us. This would mean we are the ultimate authority (anointed) over ourselves and our culture. This also seems to be a main point in the message that is being taught through the story of Jesus. In fact, it seems if we remove the name Jesus in the New Testament and replace that name with the phrase, We The People, then we have a very good representation of his message, which now makes sense and confirms the lessons of the Old Testament.

It is We The People who are responsible for ourselves and our well-being and helping and teaching others. It is We The People who can replicate every miracle ascribed to Jesus. It is We who are always crucified and persecuted by authorities who fear us because of our desire for self-determination. It is We who are responsible for our own resurrection every time freedom is defeated.

The conclusion seems to be that it was never Jesus who is our savior, and he was never meant to be a God. Our savior is his *message* that our culture should be determined by We The People, and freedom can only be resurrected through a virtuous culture so that we can avoid Statism. His message seems to be that a virtuous culture created by ourselves will be our Messiah and Savior. To live up to the promise of his message we cannot escape the responsibility for creating the conditions that would allow our own Eden. That would mean Jesus would have to be virtually the exact opposite of Moses the Statist.

As a test to the idea, we can do a comparison. We now know that Moses is the story of how Statism takes root to control the people and culture. Therefore, if Jesus represents We The People then we would expect a reversal to occur in his story as opposed to the Moses story—so let's check it out.

Moses   Learned benefits of Statism at early age

Jesus   Learned a trade at an early age

Moses   Grew up in privilege and wealth as an elite

Jesus   Grew up in working class

Moses   Gained followers through plagues and division

Jesus   Gained followers through healing and teaching

Moses   Created and participated in viscous tribal warfare

Jesus   Avoided conflict and taught tolerance

Moses   Created laws and bureaucracies

Jesus   Pointed out flaws in laws and bureaucracies

Moses   Used laws to enforce loyalty under penalty of death

Jesus   Simply allowed others to follow their own beliefs

Moses   Used bureaucracy to create dependency

Jesus   Encouraged faith in oneself and self-reliance

Moses   Created and enforced tax laws to redistribute wealth

Jesus   Encouraged charity directly to the poor and discouraged use of State money

Moses   Required sacrifices for every service rendered, and assigned tax collectors

Jesus   Never charged for any service and converted tax collectors to his cause

Moses   Created endless rituals and rules

Jesus   Despised meaningless rituals and rules

Moses   Believed in mob rule and collective persecution

Jesus   Believed in collective forgiveness

Moses   Promoted and led people to a "promised land" acquired through genocide, theft, and confiscation

Jesus   Promoted salvation which would be acquired through a virtuous culture

Moses   Brutally attacked merchants (Canaanites)

Jesus   Recruited merchants as allies and teachers

Moses	Appointed a surrogate to rule over the people

Jesus	Anointed the people to rule over themselves

There doesn't seem to be much doubt Jesus was meant to be an antidote to Moses-style Statism. If Jesus were to be reintroduced today, what kind of person would he be? From what we have seen, he has characteristics most of us would recognize. For example, Jesus didn't care about the religious costumes and pointless rituals that were popular at the time among the "pious" so we could assume he still wouldn't today. In showing his contempt for religious authorities and their traditions, it seemed to be his purpose to convince people the message of the bible had been distorted to promote a Statist God.

The Old Testament God represented a central authority figure, which the bible teaches us to avoid. Still showing their defiance, the writers presented Jesus as a person who thought there was a solution, if only we heeded the public warning announcements in the Old Testament as they were intended. Jesus knew the religious leadership of his time were not teaching the original meaning of the bible, just as most still are not today, and criticized them for sending the wrong message. They were not teaching a culture of virtue that would be immune to Statism.

> **Mathew 23:1 Then Jesus said to the crowds and to his disciples, 2. "The teachers of religious law and the Pharisees are the official interpreters of the law of Moses. 3. So practice and obey whatever they tell you, but don't follow their example. For they don't practice what they teach. 4. They crush people with unbearable religious demands and never lift a finger to ease the burden. 5. "Everything they do is for show. On their arms they wear extra wide prayer boxes with Scripture verses inside, and they wear robes with extra long tassels. 6. And they love to sit at the head table at banquets and in the seats of honor in the synagogues.**

7. They love to receive respectful greetings as they walk in the marketplaces, and to be called 'Rabbi.' **8.** "Don't let anyone call you 'Rabbi,' for you have only one teacher, and all of you are equal as brothers and sisters. **9.** And don't address anyone here on earth as 'Father', for only God in heaven is your father. **10.** And don't let anyone call you 'Teacher', for you have only one teacher, the Messiah. **11.** The greatest among you must be servant. **12.** But those who exalt themselves will be humbled, and those who humble themselves will be exalted. **13.** "What sorrow awaits you teachers of religious law and you Pharisees. Hypocrites! For you shut the door of the Kingdom of Heaven in people's faces. You won't go in yourselves, and you don't let others enter either. **14.** "Woe unto you, scribes and Pharisees, hypocrites! For ye devour widows' houses, and for a pretence make long prayer: therefore ye shall receive the greater damnation. **15.** What sorrow awaits you teachers of religious law and you Pharisees. Hypocrites! For you cross land and sea to make one convert, and then you turn that person into twice the child of hell you yourselves are!

The statements he made are very strong coming from a book we are falsely taught has the specific purpose of promoting biblical law. That's because that isn't the purpose of the books at all. The purpose of the book is to warn us of those who make the laws, and then carve them into stone as a witness against the people.

To say the Jewish construction worker portrayed by the writers was politically incorrect is an understatement, and for that he was killed. It is irrelevant whether you believe he was an actual person, or simply a character created by the authors to make their point, because regardless the message is still valid. He thought the people should learn from the lessons in the Old Testament, and not from the leaders or clergy who interpreted them to serve their own interests. He also made it clear that an important part of the message of the bible was that the "exalted" should be representatives and servants—not leaders. The Messiah will appear when We The People create a virtuous culture that rejects Statism, because it is We The People who are the Messiah.

Despite the clear warnings in the bible, this non-Statist concept was mostly unheard of even at the time of Jesus, because the true message was not being taught. Culture was not being determined by the people, and he wanted to bring back the original purpose of the bible, which is to teach us how to avoid oppressive Statism through self-determination and cooperation. He did that by pointing out the humble among the people should be the real leaders, and not the powerful or charismatic, which are often nothing more than bullies who exalt themselves, or those who would profit from supporting them. Most of the population of the world today still live with some form of oppression, so the message is still very relevant.

The writers emphasize Jesus was We The People, and not a God. He only cared about the people and their ability to create their own culture, which was the non-Statist culture he and John had agreed on at the river. That effort cost him, his buddy John, and most of his gang their lives, just as that same message continues to cost many lives around the world.

From what we know now, if Jesus were to be introduced today he would probably be known as Mr. Everybody Man. Christ means the "anointed one", but Jesus was never anointed as a king, a leader, or a god, but simply a teacher. Pointedly, the name Jesus, or a version of it, is used about a thousand times throughout the biblical books. Many names, such as Elisha, Joshua, Isaiah, Hosea, etc. were just different versions of the same name. (For an excellent treatise on this subject go to abarim-publications.com, then look up Jesus) It wasn't until the bible was translated that different names were given to the characters. A more common name could not have been chosen and was used repeatedly.

The writers wanted to emphasize the importance of their message, and not a specific character to create a cult of personality. For the most part, the message of the Jewish authors is still being buried under Christian doctrine propagated by a corrupted narrative, which in turn is a tool of Statism. Just as the Pharisees in his day, church leadership would eventually pervert the message to once again impose Statism to benefit themselves by promoting Jesus-as-God.

Since Jesus clearly represents We The People, we should share his optimism and have a little fun. Maybe today he would be introduced as Jesus Six-pack, who would become renowned for his mysterious ability to go into his garage and turn water into beer, to be shared at weddings and other festivities. Maybe he would be happy to sit and have a few beers with you and help rid your mind of whatever demons that might plague you. He might even share his knowledge of how to catch more fish, or an idea he had to create enough bread to feed a lot of people much more efficiently. He would probably be happy to give you a ride to the doctor for medical treatment, or tell you about some of his home remedies, but complain about how much better health care could be around the world if the doctors were allowed to have faith in their own abilities to learn, instead of placing such importance in lawyers, counter-productive regulations that increase costs, bureaucracies that prevent medical progress, or in promoting the use of dangerous but very profitable drugs. If you were tempted to lavish praise for his wisdom on Jesus Six-pack he would wonder why, because all his knowledge had been passed down through what he and his Father and other ancestors had learned from nature, to which he would be quick to attribute credit. If you were to create a church in his name and hang a statue of his dead body on the wall he would be embarrassed and disgusted and might be tempted to ask you to get away from him, because it would be clear you never really knew him. He would think you were most likely attempting to fraudulently promote his image to provoke sadness and guilt for gain under false pretenses.

He would place a lot of trust in his fellow man so long as they had a virtuous culture and believed in self-reliance rather than dependency and victimhood. He would have an instinctive distrust of those who would claim authority over others, so using a State-built torture device in the form of a cross, and then claiming it was represented his beliefs, would be the ultimate insult. He would warn that the cross does not represent salvation. Instead, he would point out the cross is a warning against the horrors of Statism. On the other hand, he might get a kick out of the fish image. In short, the writers of the bible wanted us to understand that Jesus Six-pack is Us, he is We The People. And yes, given the freedom to do so, we can perform miracles. The Messiah will arrive when we allow him to, through creating a virtuous culture that rejects the temptations of Statism.

More Radicalism

Often today much is made of "radical" religious zealots that use terrorism to promote their beliefs. As we can see from history, they are not radical at all. In fact, they are being quite ordinary and old fashioned. What is new and radical is not using terrorism. This is true whether the subject is politics or religion, which have historically been the same entity. It wasn't Jesus that used violence and terrorism, but it was used against him. Yet he was considered quite a radical threat to the authorities, which made his murder necessary by the religious and political authorities who were the true terrorists.

Another characteristic of the radical Jesus character was that he had little concern for large synagogues and other houses of worship, because he knew the true temple was the people themselves. They didn't understand when he said he could rebuild his temple in three days he was talking about the Temple of the People. As he predicted, the temple of stone would not last. Hopefully the Jews still waiting for their temple to be rebuilt will someday realize they are the Temple that matters, and not the opulent temple built with stolen wealth long in the past.

Most Jewish people understand instinctively, but maybe not outwardly because of self-imposed political correctness, that the temple itself is not something that needs to be rebuilt. They could take over the former temple construction site in Jerusalem and rebuild the temple whenever they want. That they do not, and are willing to share the area with other cultures hostile to them, demonstrate the temple has already been rebuilt. This is true because, just as Jesus pointed out—they are the temple. The Jewish people are still the same stiff-necked temple of non-Statist defiance, just as they were all through the Old Testament. Besides, according to the authors of the bible, Solomon himself would eventually admit it was for pure vanity he had built the original temple, and that doesn't sound like something anyone would want to rebuild. True cultural freedom will only exist when there are no temples of any kind, other than the people themselves.

The God of Statism still exists in the Middle East and the Ark of the Covenant has been transferred into the hands of different victims. The new owners of the Ark now have the plagues that go with it, just as when the Ark had been captured by the Philistines in times past. It did not serve them any better than the current Palestinians and brings constant plagues into their midst.

However, people should not be judged by their religious or political leaders, but by their own potential to determine their own culture. The non-Statist behavior by the Jews for thousands of years for which they have paid such a high price is the Holy Grail of society, and a temple built of stone and filled with stolen treasure is not necessary. If the Yahwist message of non-Statism in the bible could be spread, surely world peace would prevail, and we could rebuild Eden. As we learned from the Old Testament, wars do not originate from people—wars originate from Statist elites and crony institutions who profit from division and conflict. A culture capable of resisting Statism should be our goal.

As We the People, it is for our own incredible abilities which we should be praying and seeking salvation. According to the authors, the act of prayer is supposed to be an act of introspection for the purposes of evaluating our own culture, and not a petition to a higher Being. Prayer is supposed to express the desire to achieve a higher level of culture through self-examination. Quotes in the bible make this point.

> **Mathew 6:5 And when thou prayest, thou shalt not be as the hypocrites are: for they love to pray standing in the synagogues and in the corners of the streets, that they may be seen of men. Verily I say unto you, They have their reward. 6. But thou, when thou prayest, enter into thy closet, and when thou hast shut thy door, pray to thy Father which is in secret; and thy Father which seeth in secret shall reward thee openly. 7. But when ye pray, use not vain repetitions, as the heathen do: for they think that they shall be heard for**

their much speaking. 8. Be not ye therefore like unto them: for your Father knoweth what things ye have need of, before ye ask him.

In short, prayer is something to be done for and within oneself. You already know beforehand what you need to think about, and your prayers are not meant to be impressive to others or to Gods. The first thing that must happen is to have faith in ourselves before Eden can be built, and according to Everybody Man we can find that faith through the creation of a virtuous culture because of our own efforts. The word "church" is derived from a Greek word for a location to discuss politics among the people, and not a place to beg for salvation from an exalted God figure. Jesus knew the Yahwist culture of wisdom had been lost, and only through reeducating the people could it be resurrected.

Now we know why Christianity failed to be the promised solution. What would come to be known as Christianity would also fall victim to Statism and they would become the new owners of the Ark. The same had happened to Judaism through the Pharisee clergy and others like them. But remember, the temple of We the People can be rebuilt in the proverbial three days whenever we want to have another resurrection. We just need to have faith in ourselves and want it bad enough to give up on the dependency of Statism. No doubt there will be much cultural turmoil before that resurrection can occur, but the price of cultural turmoil is far better than the endless cycles of war, famine, disease, favoritism, cronyism, poverty, and the division of identity politics which are all symptoms of Statism.

The price citizens anywhere have paid for their politically incorrect insolence of placing more importance in their own culture than in the power of elitist leaders has been horrific for people under all political systems, but the Jewish people win all awards in that department. Politicians often despise them for their non-Statist tendencies. If they had only volunteered to be the best of the goose-steppers for Hitler, millions of them may not have been slaughtered, at least not by their own government. The holocaust was just one more in a long line of crucifixions the Jewish people have endured.

The persecution they have experienced all over the world is a direct result of stiff-necked defiance to oppression by powerful leadership and has cost the Jewish people dearly wherever Statism prevails. They have been vilified by every Statist institution and continue to pay the price just as they did all through the bible. Even today, in the small country of Israel, the Statist societies surrounding them want to eradicate them from the face of the Earth. Their existence is still seen as a risk to The Powers That Be. These are only some recent examples of the persecution they continue to face, and their history covers most of civilization. These kinds of people probably exist in almost every culture, but all too often are ignored or persecuted.

So What Now?

Now that we have determined Christianity has failed because of the introduction of Statism, just as it did for Judaism under the Pharisees, is it possible to bring back the real message of Jesus as We The People? Transforming Jesus into a God in defiance of the Jewish tradition and beliefs of those who wrote the stories has obstructed the process. It is simply a way of once again transferring the Power of We The People into the hands of another central authority system by those who benefit from Statism. Christianity probably fell completely victim to Statism right around the time Constantine decided to incorporate that religion into his newly conquered empire and although there has since been progress through the Reformation, it has never fully recovered. In the approximately three hundred years before Constantine, Jesus was not universally considered to be a god, and never by the Jewish people who wrote the stories.

Maybe some did consider him a supernatural deity, but most did not. This argument is not useful for our purposes. What made him a perfect representative was that he himself never claimed to be a god, but instead said "ye are the gods". The bible also stated, "All who are led by the Spirit of God are *sons of God*." Therefore, he was a son of God, just as are the rest of us who understand the message. His point was that we are the highest authority over ourselves. To exalt a centralized authority as a deity is a Statist concept.

Constantine was a successful warlord who made himself an emperor, which means he felt a strong desire to centralize and control religion along with the rest of his new empire. Also, it was a long-standing tradition to claim to be anointed by a god and as a result of this he and those among the Christians who capitulated created another Statist empire under Constantine, which would include the Roman Catholic Church. It was decided to make Jesus a "God", who was then credited for having chosen Constantine as his representative on earth. As though by magic the church then became very rich and powerful, which to many is an indication of success.

However, there were Christian sects other than the Roman Catholics, such as the Cathars, that probably came much closer to getting the original message of the bible by rejecting oppressive Statism and its powerful central figures {55}. Their priests even had regular day jobs. They were wiped out by the Catholic armies with the help of the emperor, and the persecution continued through the Inquisition over centuries. Combining Statist religion with Statist politics is double jeopardy, and always leads to oppressive control over the culture of the citizens. For more information on this subject I would refer you to the Islamic nations.

If Jesus-the-Message can be corrupted into Jesus-the-God, then transformation into Statism can happen anywhere, so the best solution would be in learning prevention. As we have seen in the Old Testament, the temptations of Statism are very strong. There are many ways to manipulate the people into compliance and dependency, so it will never be easy to stop or reverse the process. There are still more stories we haven't covered in the New Testament so hopefully they will provide additional insight as to how this cultural manipulation can be avoided.

The message of Jesus is the opposite of the division of identity politics. There are writings in the next book of Mark which seem to confirm again that he does not consider himself a central figure around which people should gather to receive salvation.

Mark 9:36 And he took a child, and set him in the midst of them: and when he had taken him in his arms, he said unto them, 37. Whosoever shall receive one of such children in my name, receiveth me: *and whosoever shall receive me, receiveth not me, but him that sent me.*

55 https://en.wikipedia.org/wiki/Catharism

This doesn't sound like someone who would exalt himself as a god, but simply someone who recognizes the necessity of virtue and innocence regarding culture.

> **Mark 10:17 And when he was gone forth into the way, there came one running, and kneeled to him, and asked him, Good Master, what shall I do that I may inherit eternal life? 18. And Jesus said unto him, *Why callest thou me good? There is none good but one, that is, God.***

He clearly did not consider himself as separate from the whole culture of society. Good can only come from the Power of the individual. He makes the point repeatedly that no individual should be exalted as a leader of culture but should only be a student and a participant. Comparing power and authority, he uses the Gentiles (Romans) as an example of Statist dysfunction as a warning to his disciples.

> **Mark 10:42 But Jesus called them to him, and saith unto them, Ye know that they which are accounted to rule over the Gentiles exercise lordship over them; and their great ones exercise authority upon them. 43. *But so shall it not be among you: but whosoever will be great among you, shall be your minister: 44. And whosoever of you will be the chiefest, shall be servant of all.* 45. For even the Son of man came not to be ministered unto, but to minister, and to give his life a ransom for many.**

Jesus believed that the mere absence of Statism works to increase freedom, creativity, and virtue, and would devote his life to that message. He was not there to rule, but to serve. He was promoting the idea of a truly representative society. However, he also recognized once Statism is entrenched, then the fruits of salvation cannot be achieved before virtue is reestablished. You cannot defeat Statism through rebellion, but only through teaching the wisdom of a virtuous culture. Cultural freedom and social evolution cannot be achieved before virtue and self-determination. There is another parable that demonstrates this. One evening, Jesus and his gang decided to enter Jerusalem, so he sent a couple of his guys to get a donkey's colt for him to ride into the city. The idea was to fulfill one of the prophecies in the Old Testament, which Jesus often used for inspiration.

Mark 11:4 And they went their way, and found the colt tied by the door without in a place where two ways met; and they loose him. 5. And certain of them that stood there said unto them, What do ye, loosening the colt? 6. And they said unto them even as Jesus had commanded: and they let them go. 7. And they brought the colt to Jesus, and cast their garments on him; and he sat upon him. 8. And many spread their garments in the way: and others cut down branches off the trees, and strawed them in the way. 9. And they that went before, and they that followed, cried, saying, Hosanna; Blessed is he that cometh in the name of the Lord: 10. Blessed be the kingdom of our father David, that cometh in the name of the Lord: Hosanna in the highest. 11. And Jesus entered into Jerusalem, and into the temple: and when he had looked around about upon all things, and now the eventide was come, he went out unto Bethany with the twelve.

This story seems anticlimactic, because it appears he doesn't do anything until you read the very next parables to see how the writers were setting up a very critical point. The very next paragraph is the parable of the fig tree.

Mark 11:12 And on the morrow, when they were come from Bethany, he was hungry: 13. And seeing a fig tree afar off having leaves, he came, if haply he might find anything thereon: and when he came to it, he found nothing but leaves; for the time of figs was not yet. 14. And Jesus answered and said unto it, No man eat fruit of thee hereafter forever. And his disciples heard it.

Keeping this in mind, in the following passage we see his reaction to the reception he received the previous day, and his actions would make the fig tree relevant. Jesus made himself a leather whip...

Mark 11:15 And they come to Jerusalem: and Jesus went into the temple, and began to cast out them that sold and bought in the temple, and overthrew the tables of the moneychangers, and the seats of them that sold doves; 16. And would not suffer that any man should carry any vessel through the temple. 17. And he taught, saying unto them, Is it not written, My house shall be called of all nations the house of prayer? But ye have made it a den of thieves. 18. And the scribes and chief priests heard it, and sought how they might destroy him: for the people were astonished at his doctrine.

The writers use these parables to demonstrate what is never supposed to happen among freedom loving people. First, the colt used the day before was found "without in a place where two ways met", which meant there were two different paths that could be taken. The path they had chosen was shown by the reaction of the people upon his arrival.

The word Hosanna {⁵⁶} means "Save us Please!", which they repeated as they exalted Jesus and begged to be saved. Jesus then walked into the temple and looked around in disgust before leaving to return the next day. The people had chosen the path of looking to someone else to save them instead of turning to their own abilities to save themselves. The fig tree was the people, and "he found nothing but leaves; for the time of figs was not yet". He knew the people were not yet ready to trust themselves and would instead turn to "exalted" figures to beg for salvation, and as a result would surrender their birthright of freedom and self-determination.

His reaction is what we would expect as he returned to the temple the next day and threw out those who sold animals to sacrifice to the God of Statism, and the moneychangers of State minted script who worked hand in hand with the priests. They next show the importance of confidence and self-determination, which

---

he was trying to teach when Peter noticed the fig tree had withered as they were leaving Jerusalem. It bears repeating.

Mark 12:23 For verily I say unto you, this mountain, Be thou removed, and be thou cast into the sea; and shall not doubt in his heart, but shall believe that those thing which he saith shall come to pass; he shall have whatsoever he saith. 24. Therefore I say unto you, What things soever ye desire, when ye pray, believe that ye receive them, and ye shall have them.

The moral to the story being the miraculous abilities of the people would not come from sacrificing to a God in a temple, or pleading to exalted leaders for salvation, but only through the confidence and faith the people should have in themselves. That they could be their own savior was in them all along, but they chose a different path and produced no fruit themselves because just as the fig tree, they were still not ready and therefore their culture withered. The people crying out to be saved were proof to Jesus they were not ready.

At one point, Peter asked Jesus if he would be the one to create a new kingdom on earth, and what would be the signs it was imminent. He would warn them that was not going to happen, but there would be many pretenders saying it would.

Mark 13:5 And Jesus answering them began to say, Take heed lest any man deceive you: 6. For many shall come in my name, saying, I am Christ; and shall deceive many.

Simply put, now we know anyone representing Jesus as a single individual or a god is a fraud, which makes perfect sense since we know he doesn't represent a single exalted figure but is We The People. Most clergy still promote a cult of personality, and so our culture continues to wither. This continues the cycles of failure. He warned his people to be careful of those who would expose themselves as their real adversary. Those would present him as being a king or a god, rather a teacher. He also warned Statists respond quickly to perceived threats from We The People.

278

Mark 13:9 But take heed to yourselves; for they shall deliver you up to councils; and in the synagogues ye shall be beaten: and ye shall be brought before rulers and kings for my sake, for a testimony against them.

Also:

Mark 13:13 And ye shall be hated of all men for my name's sake: but he that shall endure unto the end, the same shall be saved. 14. But when ye shall see the abomination of of desolation, spoken of by Daniel the prophet, standing where it ought not, (let him that readeth understand,) then let them that be in Judea flee to the mountains.

In the end, We The People will have to be saved in our own name. To have an exalted figurehead would always lead to the crucifixion of culture, especially if it were done in his name. As predicted, that is exactly what has happened which is why we continue to see the decay of Western culture despite the feeble and misguided efforts of Christianity. The other testaments are similar to Matthew's, and Jesus was mocked while he was dying.

Mark 15:29 And they that passed by railed on him, wagging their heads, and saying, Ah, thou that destroyest the temple, and buildest it in three days, 30. Save thyself, and come down from the cross. 31. Likewise also the chief priests mocking said among themselves with the scribes, He saved others; himself he cannot save. 32. Let Christ the King of Israel descend now from the cross, that we may see and believe. And they that were crucified with him reviled him.

The people still did not get the message of Jesus, which is they *are* the gods. They didn't understand that salvation would never come from Gods or Kings. They didn't understand salvation would be received only when they realized We The People are the anointed, and they were in fact crucifying themselves. Jesus would not hang around either as a God or a King. He would only leave behind the message of cultural virtue as the path to salvation as he defied the Statists.

On another occasion he was asked when the kingdom of God would appear. He brushed off the question with a response indicating they themselves were the kings and each individual the temple.

> **Luke 18:20 And when he was demanded of the Pharisees, when the kingdom of God should come, he answered them and said, The kingdom of God cometh not with observation: 21. Neither shall they say, Lo here! Or, lo there!** *For, behold, the kingdom of God is within you.*

When the kingdom of heaven arrives, it will not be a physical manifestation that can be observed, or even occur at a particular time or place or through a single individual. It will have to come from within We The People, and not through the arrival of a king/god. There is another story in Luke that demonstrates that when the kingdom does appear, it will be within the people as they realize they are their own king. As he was speaking to his disciples, he used a parable to explain why he would not be advocating for, or creating any kind of earthly kingdom, which is what in their ignorance the disciples expected to happen. This parable is so important it is necessary to examine it in its entirety.

> **Luke 19:10 For the Son of man is come to seek and to save that which was lost. 11. And as they heard these things, he added and spake a parable, because he was nigh to Jerusalem, and because they thought that the kingdom of God should immediately appear. 12. He said therefore, A certain nobleman went into a far country to receive for himself a kingdom, and to return. 13. And he called his ten servants, and delivered them ten pounds, and said unto them, Occupy till I come. 14. But his citizens hated him, and sent a message after him, saying, We will not have this man to reign over us. 15. And it came to pass, that when he was returned, having received the kingdom,**

then he commanded these servants to be called unto him, to whom he had given the money, that he might know how much every man had gained by trading. 16. Then came the first, saying, Lord, thy pound hath gained ten pounds. 17. And he said unto him, Well, thou good servant: because thou hast been faithful in a very little, have thou authority over ten cities. 18. And the second came, saying, Lord thy pound hath gained five pounds. 19. And he said likewise to him, Be thou also over five cities. 20. And another came, saying, Lord, behold, here is thy pound, which I have kept laid up in a napkin: 21. For I feared thee, because thou art an austere man: thou takest up that thou layest not down, and reapest that thou didst not sow. 22. And he saith unto him, Out of thine own mouth will I judge thee, thou wicked servant. Thou knewest that I was an austere man, taking up that I laid not down, and reaping that I did not sow: 23. Wherefore then gavest not thou my money into the bank, that at my coming I might have required mine own with usury? 24. And he said unto them that stood by, Take from him the pound, and give it to him that hath ten pounds. 25. (And they said unto him, Lord, he hath ten pounds.) 26. For I say unto you, That every one which hath shall be given; and from that hath not, even that he hath shall be taken away from him. 27. But those mine enemies, which would not that I should reign over them, bring hither, and slay them before me.

It is astounding some interpret this hated and greedy nobleman as being Jesus. This parable demonstrates very clearly that Jesus knew perfectly well how Statism works, and exactly why he would never create a kingdom as his apostles expected. Instead, his story explains how Statism enriches the ruling elite that "reign over them" and their cronies who become ever wealthier, while the poor who recognize the iniquities of their leaders become ever poorer, and even what little they have is taken from them. Those who do not enrich the corrupt leadership are brought before the State and are economically, culturally, and often even physically slain. The emphasis for Jesus is always that the kingdom of heaven has no leader but We The People, and this parable explains why. Those who attempt to promote the nobleman as being Jesus are teaching false doctrine.

The authors would never have compared himself to a nobleman that would give favoritism to the cronies that enriched him as do Statists, whereby the rich become richer through the efforts of subordinates, and the poor are persecuted and punished.

So back to the story of his grand entry into Jerusalem in Luke's testament. Did Jesus celebrate with his worshippers as he rode into Jerusalem on the colt with arms raised to receive admiration and praise with a triumphant entry to the giant and beautiful temple? No, he wept at the reception he received because of the things the people were saying and predicted the destruction of the temple.

Luke 19:41 And when he was come near, he beheld the city, and wept over it, 42. Saying if thou hadst known, even thou, at least in this thy day, the things which belong unto thy peace! But now they are hid from thine eyes. 43. For the days shall come upon thee, that thine enemies shall cast a trench about thee, and compass thee round, and keep thee in on every side, 44. And shall lay thee even with the ground, and thy children within thee; and they shall not leave in thee one stone upon another; because thou knewest not the time of the visitation.

It made Jesus both sad and furious the people still looked to an exalted leader to save them from themselves. It also made him especially disturbed that it was directed towards him, because he was there to point out salvation would never come from an exalted leader or be found in a temple. He was angry enough to return and break bad on the money changers and the priests that, rather than being teachers promoting the faith the people should have in themselves, had created just another Statist enterprise. As a result, the people were still a tree with no fruit, and therefore he predicted they would bring destruction upon themselves and their precious temple. They still did not accept their own potential, and this is pointed out in John's testament. They had missed their opportunity because they "knewest not the time of the visitation".

John 1:4 *In him was life; and the life was the light of men.* 5. And the light shineth in darkness; and the darkness comprehended it not.

John 1:11 He came unto *his own*, and *his own* received him not.

I think we can be sure that "his own" were We The People, and not other gods. The people still did not receive his message to believe in themselves, and instead looked to leaders for salvation.

John 4:36 He that believeth on the Son hath everlasting life: and he that believeth not the Son shall not see life; but the *wrath of God abideth on him.*

The "wrath of God" would still "abideth" among those who do not believe they are the gods and are themselves responsible for creating a heavenly culture that could have everlasting life, rather than being subjected to cycles of failure. He even refers to the manna from Moses the Statist as he gave bread to his disciples.

John 6:58 This is that bread which came down from heaven: *not as your fathers did eat manna, and are dead:* he that eateth of this bread shall live for ever.

The bread in this case would represent his message of knowledge, freedom, and a virtuous culture. Manna, on the other hand, represented Statist dependency and should be avoided. If you want a culture that is not dead and has everlasting life, his message is the bread you want to be eating. On another occasion Moses was again mentioned when the Pharisees brought a woman before him that had been caught in the act of adultery. This provided another opportunity for the clergy to set Jesus up for public failure.

John 8:5 Now Moses in the law commanded us, that such should be stoned: but what sayest thou? 6. This they said, tempting him, that they might have to accuse him. But Jesus stooped down, and with his

finger wrote on the ground, as though he heard them not. 7. So when they continued asking him, he lifted up himself, and said unto them, He that is without sin among you, let him first cast a stone at her.

The accusers then left one by one without casting a stone. Unlike with Moses, mob rule and mandatory group participation in the persecution and purging process would no longer be a thing if you followed the teachings of Jesus. I think the writers are having a good time with contradicting everything perpetrated by the God of Statism and his cronies in the Old Testament. We have yet another executive order reversal, and even more deregulation. The message continues along this vein.

John 10:7 Then said Jesus unto them again, Verily, verily, I say unto you, I am the door of the sheep. 8. *All that ever came before me are thieves and robbers: but the sheep did not hear them.* 9. I am the door: by me if any man enter in, he shall be saved, and shall go in and out, and find pasture. 10. The thief cometh not, but for to steal, and to kill, and to destroy: I am come that they might have life, and that they might have it more abundantly.

He makes his point clear again when he points out the people themselves must be the source for a living and flowing culture that "they might have life, and that they might have it more abundantly". As usual, this does not make the authorities happy.

John 10:31 Then the Jews took up stones again to stone him. 32. Jesus answered them, Many good works have I shewed you from my Father; for which of those works do ye stone me? 33. The Jews answered him, saying, For a good work we stone thee not; but for blasphemy; and because that thou, being a man, makest thyself God. 34. *Jesus answered them, Is it not written in your law, I said, Ye are gods?* 35. If he called them gods, unto whom the word of God came, and the scripture cannot be broken; 36. Say ye of him, whom the Father hath sanctified, and sent into the world,

Thou blasphemist; because I said, I am the Son of God?

He knew his accusers weren't making any sense because we are all the sons of God, which is our culture and our history. The only real question to him was what god we wanted for our future, and he didn't believe it was the one created by the Pharisees. Then Jesus demonstrates what should be the goal of the disciples.

John 13:4 He riseth from supper, and laid aside his garments; and took a towel, and girded himself. 5. After that he poureth water into a basin, and began to wash the disciples' feet, and to wipe them with the towel wherewith he was girded.

Just as in Daniel's interpretation of the king's dream, the feet always represent the foundation of society. The purpose of the disciples was to teach a culture of virtue and to cleanse society of cultural dysfunction so that the people, as the foundation of society, could be their own rulers. His purpose was not to show humility as we are taught today, because there is nothing humiliating about cleansing cultural dysfunction. Teaching virtue and learning from land forgiving sin would be their true purpose. Again, he points out that the Holy Spirit is simply wisdom and understanding and lives within the people who have a culture of virtue.

John 15:17 Even the Spirit of truth, whom the world cannot receive, because it seeth him not, neither knoweth him: but ye know him; *for he dwelleth with you, and shall be in you.*

He makes the point again that the Spirit of truth is not something tangible you can see but is something that should exist within us all. He intention, therefore, is to send a Comforter which helps that Spirit to grow and become strong enough to provide us with inner strength and understanding, just as it did for Job and Daniel.

John 15:26 But when the Comforter is come, whom I will send unto you from the Father, *even the Spirit of* *truth*, which proceedeth from the Father, he shall testify of me.

The Comforter, of course, is always the "Spirit of truth" and the understanding of the message. The last paragraph in John also provides confirmation of who Jesus really is.

John 21:25 And there are also many other things which Jesus did, the which, if they should be written every one, I suppose that even the world itself could not contain the books that should be written. Amen.

This isn't the sort of thing you would say about a single individual who only lived a short life. However, it would be very accurate for the writers to say this about mankind in general. It is a statement that would be made if the reference was to We The People, who Jesus represented.

A Mistrial

We have gone through some of the testaments, but it is necessary to point out all the debate that has taken place over the centuries concerning the New Testaments, especially the crucifixion and resurrection. There were books written concerning the crucifixion that were rejected and not included in the bible. In addition, among the books and testaments that have been included, there are many contradictions, especially as to how and when Jesus was crucified. Some researchers have spent their whole lives trying to prove it did or did not take place, and if so, how it took place.

Even the original disciples could not get their story straight. Some said before the crucifixion he carried the cross, some say not. Some say a cross was used and others say a pole or even a tree. Some say an earthquake occurred upon his death, but some never noticed if there was. Some say graves were opened and saints rose from them, but some never noticed that either. There is little agreement on the time, place, or method. There are so many contradictions, and no doubt mistranslations and misunderstandings regarding these events that if the same circumstances were a modern crime scene all concerned with trying to get to the real story would throw up their hands in frustration and despair. If a trial took place the only thing ultimately agreed on would be that someone may have been crucified somehow, but no crime could be determined beyond a reasonable doubt. If it were adjudicated, it would no doubt end in a mistrial. They couldn't even find a body to determine if there was an actual death, because it kept moving around until it finally disappeared. Any junior level attorney could poke holes in the crucifixion and resurrection story.

None of this is important for determining the purpose of the bible. To us, one basic question should be—why is it so critical that everything in the New Testament, especially this story, be determined as absolute literal truth? As with the rest of the Bible books, which openly admit to being parables based on actual events, the New Testament should also be used as a cultural instruction manual. The only thing that matters is the message. It sounds like a double standard that we can easily overlook such things as burning bushes and donkeys that can talk to people {57} {58} , but that the crucifixion and resurrection are subjected to intense scrutiny and must be literally true and factual.

The answer is simple. If you are *in christ*, it doesn't matter. It is the wisdom and intent of the bible that matters. But if you are a *Christian* it matters a great deal that Jesus must be a God, and he must be proven without question to be a God. Those teaching Christianity as a Statist institution in which Jesus is a god are missing the point entirely. The point being made is that unlike the Statist God in the Old Testament, which makes man in his image, Jesus is created in the image of We The People. Either way we are necessarily in god's image, and it is just a question of who oversees culture. We The People are not required to be exalted as gods and therefore neither is Jesus. We instead should have a natural desire to take his advice and pursue having a culture of virtue and wisdom, and to become our own salvation free of manipulation. It is We The People who should be anointed as The Powers That Be. The problem is that Christianity, just as Judaism, fell victim to Statism.

For the return of the God of Statism, there had to be a central authority figure around which to gather based on a cult of personality, just as with Leninism or Maoism. Therefore, Jesus must be exalted as an individual, and shown to be a perfect and superior authority figure over all the rest. *Hosanna! Save us Please!* If this persists, the Bible will never be the savior it was intended by the Yahwists who wrote the books. This is the very

---

57

https://www.biblegateway.com/quicksearch/?quicksearch=balaam & 0

58

https://www.biblegateway.com/passage/?search=Exodus%203&version=NIV

thing Jesus railed against at the temple. Recognizing this, we can now pursue the successes and failures of the apostles in the same spirit of truth and understanding.

The Apostles on Solomon's Porch

In the first part of the New Testament, it was pointed out by the writers that the disciples of Jesus were often corrupt, cowardly, faithless, and greedy. In other words, they were ordinary people with ordinary weaknesses. Yet despite their own imperfections, the apostles seemed determined to continue the message of Jesus after his crucifixion. The disciples (students) are now apostles (teachers) which means their purpose was to spread the message. They knew only through their teachings could the people become their own messiah. This was an ambitious undertaking, and we can follow some of their successes and failures through Acts. First, they are told by Jesus they will be receiving the spirit of truth and wisdom, which they must have before they can teach others. At this point, still not having completely understood the message, they are expecting something like a kingdom because they have never known any other way.

> **Acts 1:6 When they therefore were come together, they asked of him, saying, Lord, wilt thou at this time restore again the kingdom to Israel? 7. And he said unto them, It is not for you to know the times or the seasons, which the Father hath put in his own power. 8. *But ye shall receive power, after that the Holy Ghost is come upon you:* and ye shall be witnesses unto me both in Jerusalem, and in all Judea, and in Samaria, and unto the uttermost part of the earth.**

After saying this, Jesus soon disappeared, leaving the disciples to their own devices to continue their learning process. There would be no restoration of the kingdom of Israel. Instead, it would be the opposite. He would reappear when there existed a cultural heaven in which the people realized they are their own kings and when they understood "ye shall receive power" among themselves. This would only happen when the "Holy Ghost is come upon them" which is truth and the understanding of a self-determined culture. That would not happen until the apostles understood their own purpose and could convey the message effectively to the people.

There is another event in Acts that provides yet another reversal of an executive order committed by the God of Statism in Genesis. This event is something that occurred during an agricultural celebration called Pentecost {[59]}, where there was a large gathering of people.

> **Act 2:2 And suddenly there came a sound from heaven as of a rushing mighty wind, and it filled all the house where they were sitting. 3. And there appeared unto them cloven tongues like as of fire, and it sat upon each of them. 4. And they were all filled with the Holy Ghost, and began to speak with other tongues, as the spirit gave them utterance. 5. And there were dwelling at Jerusalem Jews, devout men, out of every nation under heaven. 6. Now when this was noised abroad, the multitude came together, and were confounded, because that every man heard them speak in his own language. 7. And they were all amazed and marvelled, saying one to another, Behold are not all these which speak Galilaeans? 8. And how hear we every man in our own tongue, wherein we were born?**

This story is a reversal of the story of Babylon. It should be noted that to speak in tongues does not mean speaking in the unintelligible gibberish that is popular among evangelists to impress their audience. It meant that all understood what was said to them, because they would once again have the all-important common language and cultural values they had before God divided the people at Babel. This reverses the parable in Genesis when The Powers That Be said "let us go down, and there confound their language, that they may not understand one another's speech". This is a reversal that would represent another success story. Once the people have again achieved a common language, it is predicted a new phenomenon would take place.

---

[59] https://www.biblestudytools.com/dictionary/pentecost/

Acts 2:17 And it shall come to pass in the last days, saith God, I will pour out of my Spirit upon all flesh: and your sons and your daughters shall prophesy, and your young men shall see visions, and your old men shall dream dreams: 18. And on my servants and on my handmaidens I will pour out in those days of my Spirit; and they shall prophesy.

It seems that becoming successful prophets or dreamers first requires a common language and culture. After the truth (Spirit) is received at the Pentecost, there is the following passage concerning welfare, which is commonly used by Statists to create dependency and loyalty.

Acts 3:2 And a certain man lame from his mother's womb was carried, whom they laid daily at the gate of the temple which is called Beautiful, to ask alms of them that entered into the temple. 3. Who seeing Peter and John about to go into the temple asked an alms. 4. And Peter, fastening his eyes upon him with John, said, Look on us. 5. And he gave heed unto them, expecting to receive something of them. 6. Then Peter said, Silver and gold have I none; but such as I have to give I thee: In the name of Jesus Christ of Nazareth rise up and walk. 7. And he took him by the right hand, and lifted him up: and immediately his feet and ankle bones received strength.

They gave a guy that had been dependent on others all his life a hand up instead of a hand out. They did not give him money. Instead, he was given independence and could now care for himself. That is the difference between charity and welfare. However, when the people began to exalt and praise the apostles for this act of charity, they set the record straight.

Acts 3:12 And when Peter saw it, he answered unto the people, Ye men of Israel, why marvel ye at this? Or why look ye so earnestly on us, as though by our own power or holiness we had made this man to walk?

The healing, of course, had been in the spirit of wisdom, knowledge, and charity characterized by Jesus. Even this act brought suspicion from the authorities.

> **Act 4:5 And it came to pass on the morrow, that their rulers, and elders, and scribes, 6. And Annas the high priest and Caiaphas, and John, and Alexander, and as many as were of the kindred of the high priest were gathered together at Jerusalem. 7. And when they had set them in the midst, they asked, By what power, or by what name, have ye done this? 8. Then Peter, filled with the Holy Ghost, said unto them; Ye rulers of the people, and elders of Israel, 9. If we this day be examined of the good deed done to the impotent man, by what means he is made whole; 10. Be it known unto you all, and to all the people of Israel, that by the name of Jesus Christ of Nazareth, whom ye crucified, whom God raised from the dead, even by him doth this man stand here before you whole. 11. This is the stone which was set at naught of you builders, which is become the head of the corner.**

Upon being badgered by the authorities, Peter had forgotten his instructions. Since Jesus had specifically forbade doing any miracles in his name, we can assume that when Peter healed the lame person he did it in the holy spirit of Jesus and not in his name. Still, by using the opportunity to speak of his resentment at the crucifixion, his statement set off alarm bells that attracted the usual attention from the authorities. Jesus had warned them not to proclaim miracles in his name, but Peter had ignored the warning. Peter may have had good intentions, but nevertheless they would all pay a heavy price for his mistake in using Jesus' name against his advice. There would be more mistakes from the apostles.

Peter the Wobbly Stone

Since the apostles are depicted as imperfect, we would expect there to be more errors made and teachable moments from which to learn, and we are not disappointed in that regard. Peter is a case in point. He began as the apostle Simon, which means "hearing", but Jesus would change his name to Peter which is the translation of Petros and means small wobbly stone and denotes instability {[60]}. There are several examples of that instability.

Simon/Peter is the one who metaphorically decided to walk to meet Jesus from a boat across water, and promptly sank for his lack of understanding of the message and a lack of faith in himself. Also, as Jesus was being arrested and taken to trial, Simon/Peter is the one who denied three times he ever knew him. There are other examples of the apostles straying from the message of Jesus, as we can see from the following:

Acts 4:32 And the multitude of them that believed were of one heart and of one soul: neither said any of them that aught of the things which he possessed was his own, but they had all things common. 33. And with great power gave the apostles witness of the resurrection of the Lord Jesus: and great grace was upon them all. 34. Neither was there any among them that lacked: for as many as were possessors of lands or houses sold them, and brought the prices of the things that were sold, 35. And laid them down at the apostle's feet: and distribution was made unto every man according as he had need.

We have had this system of socialist communism reintroduced exactly as had the Statists in the Old Testament many times and is still prevalent in many parts of the world. Productivity and wealth must once again be collected and redistributed by central authority figures. Whatever you possess as an individual must be laid at the

---

[60] http://www.abarim-publications.com/Meaning/Peter.html#.XaMOpkZKjIU

feet of the apostles. This is always a horrible mistake, and the effects of this mistake were learned in antiquity.

Acts 5:1 But a certain man named Ananias, with Sapphira his wife, sold a possession, 2. And kept back a part of the price, his wife also being privy to it, and brought a certain part, and laid it at the apostle's feet. 3. But Peter said, Ananias, why hath Satan filled thine heart to lie to the Holy Ghost, and to keep back part of the price of the land? 4. Whiles it remained, was it not thine own? And after it was sold, was it not in thine own power? Why hast thou conceived this thing in thine heart? Thou hast not lied unto men, but unto God. 5. And Ananias hearing these words fell down, and gave up the ghost: and great fear came on all them that heard these things. 6. And the young men arose, wound him up, and carried him out, and buried him. 7. And it was about the space of three hours after, when his wife, not knowing what was done, came in. 8. And Peter answered unto her, Tell me whether ye sold the land for so much? And she said, Yea, for so much. 9. Then Peter said unto her, How is it that ye have agreed together to tempt the Spirit of the Lord? Behold, the feet of them which have buried thy husband are at the door, and shall carry thee out. 10. Then fell she down straightway at his feet, and yielded up the ghost: and the young men came in, and found her dead, and, carrying her forth, buried her by her husband. 11. And great fear came upon all the church, and upon as many as heard these things. 12. And by the hands of the apostles were many signs and wonders wrought among the people; (and they were all with one accord in Solomons' porch. 13. And of the rest durst no man join himself to them: but the people magnified them. 14. And believers were the more added to the Lord, multitudes both of men and women).

This terrible story presents yet another lesson from which to gain wisdom and understanding. Had Jesus still been in his grave he would certainly have been rolling over in a frenzy. Under the direction of Peter, religion is once again the source of death and destruction, and mandatory taxation is reintroduced as they sat on Solomon's porch, which in itself is a clue from the writers. As a result, the people would once again fear the apostles as authority figures and exalt them as their ticket to heaven rather than themselves. This went against everything about Jesus' teachings. Jesus had already warned about those who would do "many signs and wonders" in his name. He must have been referring to his own apostles, who were being used as more examples of what not to do, just as the characters in the Old Testament.

The damage caused by their foolishness is exemplified in the statement "And of the rest durst no man join himself to them: but the people magnified them." Their whole purpose was to create more teachers that would join them to spread understanding, and not to "magnify" themselves before the people. In this story, they were doing the opposite of being "in christ", and there would be more consequences. Peter's mistakes provide more lessons for the reader.

Did Jesus ever demand that his followers sell off their worldly goods and deliver the spoils to his feet? No, in fact he once told a wealthy State official he could redeem himself, not by delivering the money to him after selling his property, but that the man should distribute the money himself to the poor as he saw fit (Matthew 19:21). This was not a punishment or a tax, it was just Jesus pointing out the nobleman's greed for State money prevented him from the salvation of freedom. Anything he himself distributed, such as food, he had not taken from others but had created himself. Any money used by the apostles when he was in charge was through voluntary donations or their own efforts, and not mandatory tithes.

However, Jesus had no problem with prosperity—just prosperity earned through Statism or cronyism that prevented freedom, which is why he said it would be difficult, but not impossible, for a rich man to enter heaven {[61]} because of the temptations they would face. He would never have seen fit to witness the deaths of a couple for not giving all their wealth to him, as did Peter. Peter is claimed by the Roman Catholics as their first Pope, so perhaps there is something prophetic in his behavior. Some sources say Simon/ Peter was eventually crucified upside down to show the difference between him and Jesus at his own request, which would have been appropriate and provides yet another clue for the reader. He had turned the teachings of Jesus upside down.

That the apostles now saw fit to exalt themselves instead of the people is demonstrated again when they received complaints of their behavior from the Grecians and other groups.

Acts 6:1 And in those days, when the number of the disciples was multiplied, there arose a murmuring of the Grecians against the Hebrews, because their widows were neglected in the daily ministration. 2. Then the twelve called the multitude of the disciples unto them, and said, It is not reason that we should leave the word of God, and serve tables. 3. Wherefore, brethren, look ye out among you seven men of honest report, full of the Holy Ghost and wisdom, whom we may appoint over this business. 4. But we will give ourselves continually to prayer, and to the ministry of the word.

Again, this is against the teachings of Jesus. By bowing to pressure to create a welfare program, they had shown it was more important for them to create the appearance of compassion rather than expressing true charity coming from themselves or between others. Cultural charity comes from giving others the ability to care for themselves, which creates a strong and virtuous culture. Welfare is redistributing funds taken from others and does not show charity. Instead, it creates dependency and a degradation of culture. For Statists, welfare provides an opportunity to exalt

---

[61] https://en.wikipedia.org/wiki/Eye_of_a_needle

themselves and produce more loyal subjects, rather than more teachers. Jesus, even though capable of performing miracles, never did anything that would encourage dependency.

Unlike Moses, Jesus never provided free and dependable manna. I don't recall anywhere in the Scriptures that he distributed baskets of money among the poor. Not only were the apostles ignoring those not capable of feeding themselves, which caused complaints, but were also ignoring an opportunity to show true compassion. Were the widows themselves not capable of serving a table, which would have provided the perfect opportunity to instill a sense of responsibility, self-determination, dignity, and self-respect and therefore true salvation?

Again ignoring the advice of Jesus, the bureaucracy created by the apostles had the predictable result of being perceived as a threat to the authorities. Stephen {[62]} (whose name means wreath, or crown), who had been put in charge of the welfare department, became a victim of his own Statism by giving reason for persecution from the self-serving authorities. He became powerful and influential by offering free benefits in competition with the State, which left him open to attack.

Act 6:12 And they stirred up the people, and the elders, and the scribes, and came upon him, and caught him, and brought him to the council, (just as Jesus had warned) **13. And set up false witnesses, which said, This man ceaseth not to speak blasphemous words against this holy place, and the law: 14. For we have heard him say Jesus of Nazareth shall destroy this place, and shall change the customs which Moses delivered us.**

Stephen responded with public criticism rather than forgiveness and explanation, so once again we have the predictable result.

---

[62] https://en.wikipedia.org/wiki/Stephen

Acts 7:57 Then they cried out with a loud voice, and stopped their ears, and ran upon him with one accord, 58. And cast him out of the city, and stoned him: and the witnesses laid down their clothes at a young man's feet, whose name was Saul (who later would become Paul, an apostle himself). **59. And they stoned Stephen, calling upon God, and saying, Lord Jesus, receive my spirit.**

At this point, Stephen was no longer of use either to the people or himself—because he was dead. Saul/Paul at this point was still under the employment of the State and would use Stephen's behavior as an excuse to continue his reign of terror upon the apostles and their followers for some time, putting many of them in prison. The apostles, who eventually escaped, would now be scattered into other parts of the world. Their sojourns into other lands do not appear to be voluntary as is commonly taught. Fortunately, for the most part they do appear to have learned valuable lessons about hanging out on Solomon's porch and collecting tithes and would now change their methods.

By showing us their mistakes, there are some great lessons taught in Acts through the stories of the apostles, and of course as always, they are all concerned with culture. But they also had some great success stories. One is the story of Simon in the city of Samaria, to where one of the apostles called Philip had escaped.

Acts 8:8 And there was great joy in that city. 9. But there was a certain man, called Simon (supposedly a different Simon, but which could very well have represented another aspect of Simon/Peter)**, which beforetime in the same city used sorcery, and bewitched the people of Samaria, giving out that himself was some great one: 10. To whom they all gave heed, from the least to the greatest, saying, This man is the great power of God. 11. And to him they had regard because that of long time he had bewitched them with sorceries.**

After talking to Philip, one of the more intelligent apostles, Simon discovered there are miracles and magic of a different kind that didn't involve sorcery or pretending to be a "great one" at all. It involved offering the spirit of wisdom and knowledge to the people, but he didn't have a good understanding of how that happened.

Acts 8:13 And when Simon saw that through laying on of the apostle's hands the Holy Ghost was given, he offered them money, 19. Saying, Give me also this power, that on whomsoever I lay hands, he may receive the Holy Ghost. 20. But Peter said unto him, Thy money perish with thee, because thou hast thought that the gift of God may be purchased with money.

The value of the message, as compared to the pursuit of State-minted money, could not be made clearer.

Another tale is the story of a palace eunuch, which are still common in the upper echelons of bureaucracies. What isn't as common is the open mindedness of this particular eunuch visiting from a foreign land, who was returning from Jerusalem in a state of confusion. He had been reading of Judaism and the prophets in the book of Isaiah but was not able to understand. The apostle Philip joined him and explained how God could evolve through the culture of the people, and that Jesus had brought a new message, and the concept of a new culture to the world.

Acts 8:36 And as they went on their way, they came unto a certain water: and the eunuch said, See, here is water; what doth hinder me to be baptized? 37. And Philip said, If thou believest with all thine heart, thou mayest. And he answered and said, I believe that Jesus Christ is the Son of God. 38. And he commanded the chariot to stand still: and they went down into the water, both Philip and the eunuch; and he baptized him.

These stories show the true beauty of culture, which is that anyone can change their nature simply by immersing themselves in truth and understanding that brings wisdom. Your race, creed, color, sexual status, occupation, or background is clearly not even a factor.

The relative unimportance of one's background is demonstrated again by the epiphany of a future apostle called Saul (not king Saul), who we recall began as an avid persecutor of the original apostles. Being sure of his belief that his purpose was to serve the God of Statism, he had persecuted the apostles and their followers at every opportunity. He had been present at, and had condoned, the stoning death of the apostle Stephen. However, a problem presented itself in the fact that he had a conscience, and so he began to doubt his own actions. One day, he suddenly saw the light.

> **Acts 9:3 And as he journeyed, he came near Damascus: and suddenly there shine round about him a light from heaven: 4. And he fell to the earth, and head a voice saying unto him, Saul, Saul, why persecutest thou me? 5. And he said, Who art thou, Lord? And the Lord said, I am Jesus whom thou persecutest: it is hard for thee to kick against the pricks** (I know what you're thinking and no, it's bible talk for pangs of conscience).

Suddenly seeing the light and facing up to his conscience must have been confusing to Saul, because he still could not see clearly enough to have full understanding. Ananias, one of the apostles, received word of his plight. Despite his fears because of Saul's reputation for persecution, he went to visit him anyway to help him to see the whole truth.

> **Act 9:17 And Ananias went his way, and entered in to the house; and putting his hands on him said, Brother Saul, the Lord, even Jesus, that appeared unto thee in the way as thou camest, hath sent me, that thou mightest receive thy sight, and be filled with the Holy Ghost. 18. And immediately there fell from his eyes as**

it had been scales: and he received sight forthwith, and arose, and was baptized.

Ananias had explained to Saul, the former persecutor, what was happening. This is how Saul became the apostle Paul. For those who are wondering, Paul and Saul are the same name but in a different dialect, much as John and Juan. In response to his accepting a new culture, Paul's friends and former coworkers within the State would of course now turn on him and attempt to kill him, as he had become a threat. But the point is, just as we saw with the palace eunuch, a person can change their culture the moment they make the decision to do so. Your past and present is your teacher, but does not necessarily predict your future.

There is yet another story in Acts which offers an opportunity for the writers to include two more major reversals of the executive orders of Moses the Statist. One reversal would be the concept of "unclean" animals which cannot be eaten. Again there is another reversal, which was the requirement of circumcision to gain favor from God. Thanks to Paul, Gentiles not circumcised would now be available for salvation also, and they would no longer be thought of as culturally "unclean" for not making a painful sacrifice to be "chosen".

The story continues with the story of Cornelius, a powerful figure in the Roman military, who would be chosen as an unlikely candidate to call a secret meeting. He requested the attendance of the apostle Simon/Peter. Meanwhile, Peter was on a housetop in Joppa praying, but fell into a trance and had a vision.

Acts 10:10 And he became very hungry, and would have eaten: but while they made ready, he fell into a trance, 11. And saw heaven opened, and a certain vessel descending unto him, as it had been a great sheet knit at the corners, and let down to the earth: 12. Wherein were all manner of fourfooted beasts of the earth, and wild beasts, and creeping things, and fowls of the air. 13. And there came a voice to him, Rise, Peter; kill, and eat. 14. But Peter said, Not so, Lord; for I have never eaten any thing that is common or

unclean. 15. And the voice spake unto him again the second time, What God hath cleansed, that call not thou common.

In his vision he discovers that not only can animals not be declared unclean and unfit to eat, but that the same absurdity also applies to judging the "uncleanness" of people because of other beliefs or other superficial differences, such as circumcision. They decided to have their secret and illegal meeting in Caesarea, where Peter discussed his vision and its meaning.

Acts 10:28 And he said unto them, Ye know how that it is an unlawful thing for a man that is a Jew to keep company, or come unto one of another nation; but God hath shewed me that I should not call any man common or unclean. 29. Therefore came I unto you without gainsaying, as soon as I was sent for: I ask therefore for what intent ye have sent for me?

Cornelius explained that an angel (messenger) had requested he meet with Simon/Peter with other Gentiles selected by himself. The first thing Peter decides to discuss relates to the very basis of the teachings of Jesus, which is that no individual should be worshiped or exalted. This would have been a radical revelation to the Gentiles. Also, he explained the spirit of truth and understanding is available to any who believe Jesus is the Son of Man (We The People), and also the Son of God, (the culture we choose for ourselves).

Acts 10:34 Then Peter opened his mouth, and said, Of a truth I perceive that God *is no respecter* (exalter) *of persons:* 35. But in every nation he that feareth (respected) him, and worketh righteousness, is accepted with him.

Also,

Acts 10:38 How God (our chosen culture) **anointed Jesus of Nazareth** (We the People) **with the Holy Ghost** (spirit of truth) **and with power: who went about doing good, and healing all that were oppressed of the devil**

(cultural adversary); **for God was with him. 39. And we are witnesses of all things which he did both in the land of the Jews, and in Jerusalem; whom they slew and hanged on a tree:**

And also,

Acts 10:43 To him give all the prophets witness, that through his name whosoever believeth in him shall receive remission of sins. 44. While Peter yet spake these words, the Holy Ghost fell on all them which heard the word. 45. And they of circumcision which believed were astonished, as many as came with Peter, because that on the Gentiles also was poured out the gift of the Holy Ghost.

This sounds like the usual rebuttal of division and identity politics as they promote the spirit of truth and understanding, but other lessons learned here are also profound. For one thing, God is "no respecter of persons" who can be exalted but is strictly a cultural concern. The same spirit of truth and understanding, as shown by the repentance of Roman centurion Cornelius, is available to anyone regardless of their background or current cultural situation. There is no mention of worshiping Jesus, but simply to have faith in his teachings and his message, so apparently the purpose of gathering is not to promote a cult of personality but to receive the Holy Spirit of truth and understanding and the salvation offered through a virtuous culture of cooperation and acceptance of the Power of each individual.

There is a major distinction between worshiping an individual figurehead and having faith and belief in the message of that individual. Those who teach the worship of Jesus-as-God, rather than faith and belief in his message, are Statists by definition, and reject the Spirit of truth and understanding of his message. It is small wonder Christianity has proven to be so ineffectual at solving cultural problems. Rather than pursue its given purpose to educate, Christianity has historically been simply a cause for more division, just as other equally Statist ideologies that take Power from the People. We can see this in the thousands of different versions of

Christianity, all with a different vision of what culture should be as they search for truth.

The writers emphasize the fallacy of creating a cult of personality through the story of King Herod, who has worked out a peace agreement with former enemies living in Tyre and Sidon. He then gave a grand speech, whereupon the people are given an opportunity to "exalt" their leader.

Acts 12:21 And upon a set day Herod, arrayed in royal apparel, sat upon his throne, and made an oration unto them. 22. And the people gave a shout, saying, It is the voice of a god, and not of a man. 23. And immediately the angel of the Lord smote him, because he gave not God the glory: and he was eaten by worms, and gave up the ghost. 24. But the word of God grew and multiplied.

The people unfortunately had chosen to exalt yet another leader as a god, but that didn't last because like all men Herod died, which showed the foolishness of the people. The lesson is that unlike a man, a concept cannot die so long as there are those that understand, and so has everlasting life. An individual figurehead or a cult of personality can never replace a concept, and will eventually die.

Act 13:36 For David, after he had served his own generation by the will of God, fell on sleep, and was laid unto his fathers, and saw corruption: 37. But he (Jesus), whom God raised again, saw no corruption. 38. Be it known unto you therefore, men and brethren, *that through this man is preached unto you the forgiveness of sins: 39. And by him all that believe are justified from all things, from which ye could not be justified by the law of Moses.* 40. Beware therefore, lest that come upon you, which is spoken of in the prophets; 41. Behold, ye despisers, and wonder, and perish: for I work a work in your days, a work which ye shall in no wise believe, though a man declare it unto you.

Like all men, king David had died just as king Herod, but the message of Jesus was a concept rather than a man, and therefore has everlasting life through those who believe in the concept. The temptation of wanting to hear from gods that promise to save you, rather than a man that tells you the truth about saving yourself, will always be a threat to freedom. On the other hand, Statists are threatened by a desire of the people for the freedom of self-determination and will always respond predictably to any who question their position of authority.

Acts 13: 45 But when the Jews (Pharisee clergy) **saw the multitudes, they were filled with envy, and spake against those things which were spoken by Paul, contradicting and blaspheming. 46. Then Paul and Barnabas waxed bold, and said, It was necessary that the word of God should first have been spoken to you: but seeing ye put it from you, and judge yourselves unworthy of everlasting life, lo we turn to the Gentiles. 47. For so hath the Lord commanded us, saying, I have set thee to be a light of the Gentiles, that thou shouldest be for salvation unto the ends of the earth.**

The Pharisee clerics enjoyed all the benefits of status, authority, and a dependable income that is the temptation of Statism. Sadly, they had responded with resentment and disbelief because these temptations had been made a priority, while the Gentiles were more receptive to a new way of thinking. As always, the fear of the message being taught by the apostles would lead to persecution.

Acts 13:50 But the Jews stirred up the devout and honourable women, and the chief men of the city, and raised persecution against Paul and Barnabas, and expelled them out of their coasts.

After being purged, Paul ended up in Athens, where he is once again compelled to explain the nature if his message. It is worthy of mentioning again, although we already know by now.

Acts 17:22 Then Paul stood in the midst of Mars' hill, and said, Ye men of Athens, I perceive that in all things ye are too superstitious. 23. For as I passed by, and beheld your devotions, I found an altar with this inscription, TO THE UNKNOWN GOD. Whom therefore ye ignorantly worship, him declare I unto you. 24. God that made the world and all things therein, seeing that he is Lord of heaven and earth, *dwelleth not in temples made with hands; 25. Neither is worshiped with men's hands, as though he needed anything,* **seeing he giveth to all life, and breath, and all things;**

And continued with:

Acts 17:28 *For in him we live, and move, and have our being;* **as certain also of your poets have said,** *For we are also his offspring* **(Sons of God), we ought not to think that the Godhead is like unto gold, or silver, or stone, graven by art and man's device. 30. And the times of this ignorance God winked at; but now commandeth all men everywhere to repent: 31. Because he hath appointed a day, in the which he will judge the world in righteousness by that man whom he hath ordained; whereof he hath given assurance unto all men, in that he hath raised him from the dead.**

He then left, knowing he could not convince those who believed only in unknowable gods and false idols. He believed the priests promoting them were promoting a cultural death. They were teaching the worship of gods rather than teaching the people they are their own god. Again, the people were the fig tree that produced no fruit. After many travails Paul would eventually be taken to Rome as a prisoner but would still be allowed to continue to teach his message. He could continue because, for the most part, they still did not understand his message of non-Statism. Once they did realize, he would promptly be beheaded.

A Jew And a Gentile Walk Into a Bar

For Paul, teaching the message in a place like Rome must have been very scary, even though he was a Roman citizen and a former tax collector. After all, Rome was the seat of the great Roman Empire. Since the defeat of republicanism in their civil war, they had become one of the most oppressive Statist regimes of all time. They were also Gentiles that had little use for some dude passing along the message of some Jewish construction worker murdered in one of their conquered provinces. Fortunately, Paul did not yet have to deal with the whole Christianity thing, because it did not yet exist. He needed only to convince his students of a new and improved way of Judaism, or more specifically, Yahwism as taught by Jesus. To do that, he would need to point out the benefits for all concerned.

He would teach that essentially all folks had common needs, which he believed strongly would be served through the message. In short, he needed to make the case that, culturally speaking, if a Jew and a Gentile walked into a bar, they could both benefit from the same contrarian culture. If he could reconcile their differences then both could be together in christ, (which again means the people themselves are anointed, which is not the same as Christianity, which is another form of Statism that would come later) and share a glass of wine. The Pharisee clergy and the Romans did not realize they were both working for the same monotheistic God of Statism, and that Jesus represented the potential of We The People of both groups. If they were to benefit from the message, they would both need to adopt a new culture based on virtue and wisdom, rather than Statist laws and traditions.

In a sense, through Paul, Jesus was saying, "Ok you people, some day both Jewish clerics and you Gentiles will realize you *are* the gods and should stop listening to the God of Statism that keeps you divided. You *are* the messiah, and you can perform miracles and achieve a heavenly culture that will have everlasting life through virtue and truth and wisdom that can resist Statism and take you to Eden. When you figure that out, I will come back, but until then I will be right over here, sitting at the bar and making wine, waiting for you to come to your senses. Let me know when you're tired of waiting for salvation from gods and bureaucrats instead of from yourselves." I may have participated in a little poetic license here, but then so does the bible.

Thanks to the unfortunate corruption that would follow despite the teachings of Jesus and his apostles, and which incidentally still exists, Jesus would eventually become a God himself. Because of this, he has never had the opportunity to return. He has already made it clear he will not return as a king or a god, and so is still banned in most cultures. At the current rate of awareness from us paltry humans, he will be stuck in that bar forever. This makes the Statists very happy, because they never want to see him return. Jesus was a troublemaker for Statists, until he was made one himself by an emperor warlord and complicit clergy. Meanwhile, Saul/Paul knew the cultural problems he was up against and spelled them out for all to see.

> **Romans 1:28 And even as they did not like to retain God in their knowledge, God gave them over to a reprobate mind, to do those things which are not convenient; 29. Being filled with all unrighteousness, fornication, wickedness, covetousness, maliciousness; full of envy, murder, debate, deceit, malignity; whisperers, 30. Backbiters, haters of God, despiteful, proud, boasters, inventors of evil things, disobedient to parents, 31. Without understanding, covenant breakers, without natural affection, implacable, unmerciful: 32. Who knowing the judgment of God, that they which commit such things are worthy of death, not only do the same, but have pleasure in them that do them.**

Paul knew all these iniquities were greatly magnified and even encouraged under a system of Statism, because if you do not control your own culture then debasement and corruption is inevitable. As we discovered in the Old Testament, Statism depends heavily on cultural degradation which provides cover for even more Statism through the creation of even more laws and more bureaucracy. As debasement grows, the leaders are then quite happy to create even more laws to "save and serve" the people, and then proceed to live above the laws they create. For Paul, the artificial contradictions between Jewish laws and Gentile laws would present a problem. He began by expressing his disdain for the fact the Jewish clergy had books of laws and tried to use them to judge the Gentiles, and vice versa. To make progress, most of the laws would need to be repealed.

> **Romans 2:10 but glory, honour, and peace, to every man that worketh good, to the Jew first, and also to the Gentile: 11.** *For there is no respect of persons with God.* **12. For as many without law shall also perish without law: and as many as have sinned in the law shall be judged by the law; 13. (For not the hearers of the law are just before God, but the doers of the law shall be justified. 14. For when the Gentiles, which have not the law, do by nature the things contained in the law, these, having not the law, are a law unto themselves: 15. Which shew the work of the law written in their hearts, their conscience also bearing witness, and their thoughts the mean while accusing or else excusing one another;)**

It is not the written laws that matter in society, it is the cultural laws "which are written in their hearts". Written laws can never replace culture, which is why a successful culture which allows prosperity should always be protected from threats of unbridled bureaucratic law making. Likewise, permanent newcomers into a land should be respectful not just of superficial written laws, but even more importantly to agree to assimilate and be tolerant of unwritten cultural laws.

These and other cultural problems had to be addressed between the Jews and the Roman Gentiles, because neither had any desire to assimilate. Both were also victims of rampant Statist cultural debasement, as described in the previous passage. Since his purpose was to assimilate them both into a new, non-Statist community he would first have to deal with cultural issues to achieve harmony long enough for him to achieve his goal. Paul had to begin with the basics by addressing the circumcision thing again and continued the process of reversing executive orders from Moses the Statist.

Romans 3:27 And shall not uncircumcision which is by nature, if it fulfill the law, judge thee, who by the letter of the law and circumcision dost transgress the law? 28. For he is not a Jew, which is one outwardly; neither is that circumcision, which is outward in the flesh: 29. But he is a Jew, which is one inwardly; and circumcision is that of the heart, in the spirit, and not in the letter; whose praise is not of men, but of God.

Culture is always in the heart and "in the spirit, and not the letter". Ritual laws, such as circumcision, did not make a better person. He pointed out they all had much in common, and so should work with each other. They all had imperfect cultures and could all benefit from a culture based more on virtue, truth, and understanding, rather than laws and customs and rituals. It's amazing that despite the writers endlessly beating the drums of this message in their books that the message is still mostly lost, and that is because of the perpetuation of Statist narrative control and propaganda that nullifies the teachings.

Romans 3:9 What then? Are we better than they? No, in no wise: for we have before proved both Jews and Gentiles, that they are all under sin: 10. As it is written, There is none righteous, no, not one. 11. There is none that understandeth, there is none that seeketh after God.

Romans 4:28 Therefore we conclude that a man is justified by faith without the deeds of law.

Again, the message is made clear. All the laws in the world that man can think to put in a book will never replace a virtuous culture. Even worse, violation of written laws defines and brands a person,

311

whereas culture is living and flowing so that people can evolve within the society, provided they can learn from their sins.

> **Romans 8:16 The Spirit itself beareth witness with our spirit, that we are the children of God: 17. And if children, then heirs; heirs of God, and joint-heirs with Christ, if so be that we suffer with him, that we may be also glorified together. 18.** *For I reckon that the sufferings of this present time are not worthy to be compared with the glory which shall be revealed in us.*

Paul then lamented how both Judaism and the Roman Empire had become Statist, and how he hoped to help them both escape the trap they had fallen into. He was particularly well suited for this task in Rome because he was a former employee of the State of Rome. In addition, unlike most Jews he was a full-fledged citizen, which gave him more freedom to speak. He was confident his efforts would pay off eventually, when "the glory which shall be revealed in us" can be on full display.

> **Romans 9:30 What shall we say then? That the Gentiles, which followed not after righteousness, have attained righteousness, even the righteousness which is of faith. 31. But Israel, which followed after the law of righteousness, hath not attained to the law of righteousness. 32. Wherefore? Because they sought it not by faith, but as it were by the works of the law. For they stumbled at that stumbling-stone; 33. As it is written, Behold, I lay in Sion a stumbling stone and rock of offence:** (by creating lots of laws, which is a common thing for the God of Statism to do) **and whosoever believeth on him shall not be ashamed. Romans 10:1 Brethren, my hearts' desire and prayer to God for Israel is, that they might be saved. 2. For I bear them record that they have a zeal of God, but not according to knowledge. 3. For they being ignorant of God's righteousness, and going about to establish their own righteousness, have not submitted of God. 4.** *For*

Christ is the end of the law for righteousness to everyone that believeth.

So much for the efforts of Moses to use his written laws to be used as a bureaucratic tool of witness *against* the people. This concept is also now being reversed. Paul finally finishes with the revelation to the people that the mystery of the bible has now been explained to those who understand.

Romans 16:25 Now to him that is of power to stablish you according to my gospel, and the preaching of Jesus Christ, according to the revelation of the mystery, which was kept secret since the world began. 26. But now is made manifest, and by the scriptures of the prophets, according to the commandment of the everlasting God, made known to all nations for the obedience of faith. 27. To God only wise, be glory through Jesus Christ for ever. Amen.

The mystery of who God is has been revealed for those who understand the message, and through that message you can now receive the wisdom and the glory. As one of the best of the apostles, Paul continued to be busy. We have epistles (letters) that he wrote to members of a church he had founded for the people of Corinth called, oddly enough, the Corinthians. This gave him another opportunity to pass along some more of what he had learned. Here are some of the passages.

I Corinthians 3:16 *Know ye not that ye are the temple of God, and that the Spirit of God dwelleth in you?* **17. If any man defileth the temple of God, him shall God destroy;** *for the temple of God is holy, which temples ye are.*

That the People themselves are the gods, and are also the temple, is a consistent message throughout the New Testament.

I Corinthians 4:9 For I think that God hath set forth us the apostles last, as it were appointed to death: for we are made a spectacle unto the world, and to angels, and to men. 10. We are fools for Christ's sake

(Christianity) **but ye are wise in Christ; we are weak, but ye are strong; ye are honourable, but we are despised. 11. Even unto this present hour we both hunger, and thirst, and are naked, and are buffeted, and have no certain dwelling place; 12. And labour, working with our own hands: being reviled, we bless; being persecuted, we suffer it; 13. Being defamed, we entreat: we are made as the filth of the world, and are the offscouring of all things unto this day. 14. I write not these things to shame you, but as my beloved sons I warn you.**

For obvious reasons, those who wish to resurrect the truth and understanding of a virtuous non-Statist culture always end up being the persecuted, even though they are trying to help. No matter how much the common people may agree with the true message, the religious and political Statist elites will always begin the purging and division process to maintain their power, authority, and job security. He expressly warns them again to avoid enabling the Statists through their legal system as much as possible.

I Corinthians 6:1 Dare any of you, having a matter against another, go to law before the unjust, and not before the saints? 2. Do ye not know that the saints shall judge the world? And if the world shall be judged by you, are ye unworthy to judge the smallest matters? 3. Know ye not that we shall judge angels? How much more things that pertain to this life? 4. If then ye have judgments of things pertaining to this life, set them to judge who are least esteemed in the church. 5. I speak to your shame. Is it so, that there is not a wise man among you? No, not one that shall be able to judge between his brethren? 6. But brother goeth to law with brother, and that before the unbelievers.

Yet again, we have explained to us one of the best ways to defeat Statism would be to render their legal system and written laws to be irrelevant among the people by learning to settle matters among ourselves as much as possible. If we are capable of judging angels, then we can judge ourselves. This again shows why we should create a privately-run judicial system made of volunteers, rather than government employees, and who would dispense cultural wisdom instead of fines and indictments. He then addresses another issue that still creates havoc all through modern societies, and that is the abduction of charity by the State, which turns it into welfare both to exalt themselves and to create even more dependency.

> **I Corinthians 13:1 Though I speak with the tongues of men and of angels, and have not charity, I am become as sounding brass, or a tinkling cymbal. 2. And though I have the gift of prophecy, and understand all mysteries, and all knowledge; and though I have all faith, so that I could remove mountains, and have not charity, I am nothing. 3.** *And though I bestow all my goods to feed the poor, and though I give my body to be burned, and have not charity, it profiteth me nothing.* **4. Charity suffereth long, and is kind; charity envieth not; charity vaunteth not itself, is not puffed up, 5. Doth not behave itself unseemly, seeketh not her own, is not easily provoked, thinketh no evil; 6. Rejoiceth not in equity, but rejoiceth in the truth; 7. Beareth all things, believeth all things, hopeth all things, endureth all things. 8. Charity never faileth: but whether there be prophecies, they shall fail; whether there be tongues, they shall cease; whether there be knowledge, it shall vanish away.**

Clearly, charity is not a welfare department. Charity is a willingness to help others to succeed in life, and not to create dependency. It may involve giving to others but is much more than that. It is through understanding and helping others in ways that improve culture and community. On the other hand, welfare from a State bureaucracy helps to divide and destroy both culture and community by creating dependency. The benefits of expressing charity among the people is then lost and gives the State the opportunity to manipulate culture. Also, since a Statist society is run by a bureaucracy that has no money of its own, it becomes a tool of wealth redistribution whereby money is stolen from some and given to others in ways that benefit the State politically.

Welfare is the opposite of charity, the opposite of benevolence, and is a tool of Statism. Welfare always fails, but charity never fails. Sadly, often those who would never accept charity, which is an act of cultural virtue, will gladly accept welfare, which is an anonymous act of bureaucratic control to increase the size and scope of the State.

The Jewish Bill of Rights

The New Testament movement towards furthering the Jewish declaration of independence was promoted mostly by Paul, a former tax collector. He saw the light and came to recognize the fallacies of creating culture through enforcing Statist laws. He too now recognized the letter of the law would never replace cultural virtue.

II Corinthians 3:3 Forasmuch as ye are manifestly declared to be the epistle of Christ ministered by us, written not with ink, but with the Spirit of the living God; not in tables of stone, but in fleshy tables of the heart. 4. And such trust have we through Christ to God-ward: 5. Not that we are sufficient of ourselves to think any thing as of ourselves; but our sufficiency is of God; 6. *Who also hath made us able ministers of the new testament; not of the letter, but of the spirit: for the letter killeth, but the spirit giveth life.* **7. But if the ministration of death, written and engraven in stones, was glorious, so that the children of Israel could not stedfastly behold the face of Moses for the glory of his countenance; which glory was to be done away: 8. How shall not the ministration of the spirit be rather glorious? 9. For if the ministration of condemnation be glory, much more doth the ministration of righteousness exceed in glory.**

He points out "the ministration of condemnation" is not the answer. In the next passage, we have another observation of the true purpose of the bible. First we hear their warnings as presented in the Old Testament and then the solutions offered in the New Testament. Yet again, we have a reversal of the teachings of Moses. The writers of the New Testament appear to be creating the equivalent of a Bill of Rights and are demonstrating their exuberance in opposing the Statists of the Old Testament.

II Corinthians 3:12 Seeing then that we have such hope, we use great plainness of speech: 13. And not as

Moses, which put a veil over his face, that the children of Israel could not stedfastly look to the end of that which is abolished: 14. But their minds were blinded: for until this day remaineth the same veil untaken away in the reading of the old testament; which veil is done away in Christ. 15. But even unto this day, when Moses is read, the veil is upon their heart. 16. Nevertheless, when it shall turn to the Lord, the veil shall be taken away. 17. *Now the Lord is that Spirit: and where the Spirit of the Lord is, there is liberty.* **18. But we all, with open face beholding as in a glass the glory of the Lord, are changed into the same image from glory to glory, even as by the Spirit of the Lord.**

Again, God is our reflection, and we are in his image. The spirit of truth and understanding had been living in the "fleshy tablets of the heart" among the Yahwists of the Jewish people long before the first commandments had been carved into stone. The writers recognized the iniquities of their political and religious leaders that had exalted themselves all through history and were now speaking openly of the issue. No more would they be satisfied in just sending warnings through parables demonstrating corruption, and pointing to the crucifixions of independent thinkers, but would now occupy themselves with presenting a solution. This same stiff-necked independent spirit still lives within the Jewish community who, despite the very high price paid over the centuries, still have faith their own defiant culture (their own God) rather than kings and leaders.

Unfortunately, their movement would eventually be abducted by those who would separate themselves from the Jewish community and begin to call themselves Christians. Over the centuries they would turn Jesus into a God to be exalted and worshiped as just another Statist central authority figure. In the end, the temptations of Statism were too great for them to resist. Ironically, it would be those who retained their Jewish heritage that would retain the message of being in christ as opposed to being Christian, instinctively understanding it would not be a single individual that would be their Messiah, which is exactly what Jesus was also saying. The Jewish people would continue doing what they had been doing all along, which is to declare their independence and their rights—and seek their own Eden.

Despite all the efforts of kings, clerics, popes, dictators, oligarchs, fuehrers, and emperors, the Jews continue to retain their culture of independence. Not for over a thousand years, until the rebellious Protestant movement, would Christians begin their return to Yahwist truth and understanding. In the Protestant movement they would finally begin to shed the costumes and rituals of Statism, as Jesus had originally intended for the Pharisees, and would again begin to work towards becoming simply We The People. Their journey has not been perfect and is not required to be perfect. Having all the answers is not what matters—it is the freedom to continue to ask all the questions. Christianity failed to realize its potential because for over a thousand years Christians did not even have the right to ask questions, and the leaders even encouraged the persecution of their Jewish brethren for not joining the new Statist culture they had created. Once again, the Jewish people had become the deplorables to those who exalted themselves. With the Protestant movement, The People have begun the journey back to Yahwism, and to the contrarian ideas of those radical Jews called Jesus and John the Baptist. Maybe someday they will arrive.

No matter what institution they hail from, once established, Statists always attack those who are perceived as a threat to the Powers That Be. Christians abandoned their new idea as taught by Jesus, and instead declared war on Jews and others they saw as a threat to their new State.

Meanwhile for Paul, there were still many obstacles to overcome. Keep in mind when Paul refers to Jews, he is referring to the clergy and their loyalists that had despised Jesus and the other radicals, and not the Jewish population in general. After all, he is a Jew. But many in the "establishment" posed a threat to them and their "new thing", just as many within the clergy still do today.

319

II Corinthians 11:22 Are they Hebrews? So am I. Are they Israelites? So am I. Are they the seed of Abraham? So am I. Are they ministers of Christ? (I speak as a fool) I am more; in labours more abundant, in stripes above measure, in prisons more frequent, in deaths oft. **24.** Of the Jews five times received I forty stripes save one (forty or more was considered cruel). **25.** Thrice was I beaten with rods, once I was stoned (not the popular kind), thrice I suffered shipwreck, a night and a day I have been in the deep; **26.** In journeying often, in perils by mine own countrymen, in perils by the heathen, in perils in the city, in perils in the wilderness, in perils in the sea, in perils among false brethren; **27.** In weariness and painfulness, in watchings often, in hunger and thirst, in fastings often, in cold and nakedness. **28.** Beside those things that are without, that which cometh upon me daily, the care of all the churches.

Starting a new culture that defies Statism has many challenges, but it can also have its benefits in helping us reexamine our own culture, just as he had. Paul himself had previously been a persecutor of Jews until he saw the light. He had especially despised the original non-Statist Jews that were pushing the radical and threatening message of Jesus, whose crime was ignoring meaningless rituals and religious laws. In his letter he gives a final bit of advice to his Corinthian disciples to remember the value of introspection, by which he had also freed himself.

II Corinthians 13:5. Examine yourselves, whether ye be in the faith; *prove your own selves. Know ye not your own selves, how that Jesus Christ is in you, except ye be reprobates?*

Paul also wrote a letter to the Galatians, and he had more to say of the endless laws of Moses. He also expressed concern that the still weak and wobbly apostle Peter was afraid to openly hang out with the Gentiles because of Jewish laws.

Galatians 2:11 But when Peter was come to Antioch, I withstood him to the face, because he was to be blamed. 12. For before that certain came from James, he did eat with the Gentiles: but when they were come, he withdrew and separated himself, fearing them which were of the circumcision. 13. And the other Jews dissembled likewise with him; insomuch that Barnabas also was carried away with their dissimulation. 14. But when I saw that they walked not uprightly according to the truth of the gospel, I said unto Peter before them all, If thou, being a Jew livest after the manner of Gentiles, and not as do the manner of Jews, why compellest thou the Gentiles to live as do the Jews? 15. We who are Jews by nature, and not sinners of the Gentiles, 16. *Knowing that a man is not justified by the works of the law, but by the faith of Jesus Christ, even we have believed in Jesus Christ, that we might be justified by the faith of Christ, and not by the works of the law: for by the works of the law shall no flesh be justified.*

Also:

Galatians 3:22 But the scripture hath concluded all under sin, that the promise by faith of Jesus Christ might be given to them that believe. 23. *But before faith came, we were kept under the law, shut up into the faith which should afterwards be revealed.* **24. Wherefore the law was our schoolmaster to bring us unto Christ, that we might be justified by faith. 25. But after that faith is come, we are no longer under a schoolmaster. 26. For ye are all the children of God by faith in Christ Jesus.**

Galatians 5:5 Christ is become of no effect unto you, *whosoever of you are justified by the law; ye are fallen from grace.*

The latter quote was the exact same lesson of the story of king David who, although completely enthralled by all the commandments, statutes, and precepts of Moses, had pretty much zero grace or virtue, and acted accordingly. However, Paul also warned of thinking their newly-envisioned freedom was an excuse for debasement of culture.

> **Galatians 5:13** *For, brethren, ye have been called unto liberty; only use not liberty for an occasion to the flesh, but by love serve one another.* **14. For all the law is fulfilled in one word, even in this; Thou shalt love thy neighbor as thyself. 15. But if ye bite and devour one another, take heed that ye be not consumed one of another. 16. This I say then, Walk in the Spirit, and ye shall not fulfill the lust of the flesh. 17. For the flesh lustesth against the Spirit, and the Spirit against the flesh: and these are contrary one to the other: so that ye cannot do the things that ye would.**

The writers make it clear why is it better to follow a culture of virtue, and the Spirit of truth and understanding in our culture, rather than Statist laws. Statist laws always encourage a degradation of culture and a lack of wisdom among the population.

> **Galatians 5:18 But if ye be led of the Spirit, ye are not under the law. 19. Now the works of the flesh are manifest, which are these; Adultery, fornication, uncleaness, lasciviousness, 20. Idolatry, witchcraft, hatred variance, emulations, wrath, strife, seditions, heresies, 21. Envyings, murders, drunkeness, revellings, and such like: of the which I tell you before, as I have also told you time past, that they which do such things shall not inherit the kingdom of God. 22. But the fruit of the Spirit is love, joy, peace, long suffering, gentleness, goodness, faith, 23. Meekness, temperance: against such there is no law.**

In a culture of "love, joy, and peace", there would be little need for written laws because the cultural degradation and dependency of Statism would be greatly diminished. In Ephesians, Paul again provides a reminder of the purpose of the apostles in the various churches that had been created.

322

Ephesians 6:11 Put on the whole armour of God, that ye may be able to stand against the wiles of the devil. *12. For we wrestle not against flesh and blood, but against principalities, against powers, against the rulers of the darkness of this world, against spiritual wickedness in high places.* 13. Wherefore take unto you the whole armour of God, that ye may be able to withstand in the evil day, and having done all, to stand.

Their purpose was to teach the true message of Jesus and his role in wrestling with the God of Statism, with their "powers", "the rulers of the darkness of this world", and "wickedness in high places". Jesus represented the end of the need for We The People to continue to sacrifice ourselves to the God of Statism. If we adopt his message, we now could usher in a new culture of virtue, truth, and understanding that could withstand their temptations. To do so, the people will have to stand together, not in military strength, but in the strength of a common language and culture based on virtue.

Philippians 2:2 Fulfill ye my joy, that ye be likeminded, having the same love, being of one accord, of one mind. 3. Let nothing be done through strife or vainglory; but in lowliness of mind let each esteem other better than themselves. 4. Look not every man on his own things, but every man also on the things of others. 5. Let this mind be in you, which was also in Christ Jesus: 6. Who, being in the form of God, thought it not robbery to be equal with God: 7. *But made himself of no reputation, and took upon him the form of a servant, and was made in the likeness of men: 8. And being found in fashion as a man, he humbled himself, and became obedient unto death, even the death of the cross.*

It is not robbery to think of ourselves as equal to The Powers That Be. Being anointed (christ) as our own leaders does not mean we exalt ourselves any more than Jesus did. It is fortunate that we have copies of letters he wrote to those maintaining the churches

Paul established, because it shows he had the same concerns we have today, and the same fear of the temptations of Statism. Those fears are just as valid today as they were then. Paul knew things would be hard because the purveyors of Statism would be relentless in their attempts to defend themselves against truth and understanding among the people. It would be easy to fall victim to their propaganda.

> **Thessalonians 3:4 For verily, when we were with you, we told you before that we should suffer tribulation; even as it came to pass, and ye know. 5. For this cause, when I could no longer forbear, I sent to know your faith, lest by some means the tempter have tempted you, and our labour be in vain. 6. But now when Timotheus came from you unto us, and brought us good tidings of your faith and charity, and that ye have good remembrance of us always, desiring greatly to see us, as we also to see you: 7. Therefore, brethren, we were comforted over you in all our affliction and distress by your faith: 8. For now we live, if ye stand fast in the Lord.**

Paul informed his disciples of a shift in attitude that would need to take place before there could be a true cultural revolution of peace.

> **Thessalonians 2:1 Now we beseech you, brethren, by the coming of our Lord Jesus Christ, and by our gathering either by spirit, nor by word, nor by letter as from us, as that the day of Christ is at hand. 3. Let no man deceive you by any means: for that day shall not come, except there come a falling away first, and that man of sin be revealed, the son of perdition; 4. Who opposeth and exalteth himself above all that is called God, or that is worshipped; so that he as God sitteth in the temple of God, shewing himself that he is God. 5. Remember ye not, that, when I was yet with you, I told these things?**

Only when the God of Statism is understood sufficiently for all to finally recognize him will the people fully reject Statism and immerse themselves in a new culture. Before the people finally believe, there will be a "falling away first, and that man of sin be revealed, the son of perdition. Who opposeth and exalteth himself above all that is called God". Before there can be an end there will be a falling away from those who exalt themselves above a culture of We The People.

II Thessalonians 2:6 And now ye know what withholdeth that he might be revealed in his time. 7. For the mystery of iniquity doth already work: only he who now letteth will let, until he be taken out of the way. 8. And then shall that Wicked be revealed, whom the Lord shall consume with the spirit of his mouth, and shall destroy with the brightness of his coming: 9. Even him, whose coming is after the working of Satan with all power and signs and lying wonders, 10. And with all deceivableness of unrighteousness in them that perish; because they received not the lobe of the truth, that they might be saved. 11. And for this cause God shall send them strong delusion, that they should believe a lie: 12. That they all might be damned who believed not the truth, but had pleasure in unrighteousness.

Again, a strong culture lies in the ability to reach understanding. "The Lord shall consume with the spirit of his mouth and shall destroy with the brightness of his coming" doesn't exactly sound like a war cry. This isn't a weapon you would use to go into battle with an enemy you want to physically destroy, even if the enemy is Satan. It sounds like Satan can only be defeated through speaking of knowledge and the spirit of truth instead of "strong delusion".

I Timothy 2:1 I exhort therefore, that, first of all, supplications, prayers, intercessions, and giving of thanks, be made for all men; 2. For kings, and for all that are in authority; that we may lead a quiet and

peaceable life in all godliness and honesty. 3. For this is good and acceptable in the sight of God our Saviour; 4. Who will have all men to be saved, and to come unto the knowledge of the truth.

For those who follow the teachings of the apostles and their disciples, there is no animosity, even against kings and other authority figures. They can all be wished well because they are victims, but it is recognized there are many traps that may befall the rich and powerful because they are often closely associated with Statism, and should take special care.

I Timothy 6:7 For we brought nothing into this world, and it is certain we can carry nothing out. 8. And having food and raiment let us be therewith content. 9. But they that will be rich fall into temptation and a snare, and into many foolish and hurtful lusts, which drown men in destruction and perdition 10. *For the love of money is the root of all evil: which while some coveted after, they have erred from the faith, and pierced themselves through with many sorrows.*

As Paul points out, it is not prosperity that is the root of all evil, which we also know from the story of Job. It is the love of money, which is Statist by its very nature, that is the root of all evil. That Statists will produce, and then manipulate money and the people who use it in ways that benefit the State to maintain power and job security for themselves is far too great a temptation. We see this in every economy still today. Without manipulation of Statist money, you can't have depressions, recessions, inflation, fluctuating market and credit cycles, or any of the other maladies that still afflict us in the modern world. All of these are symptoms of the deliberate economic manipulation of Statist money used to control and manipulate.

Statism money doesn't just produce degradation of culture, it also produces poverty. In fact, poverty was only invented when money was invented and provides another division between the people. This is a division between the haves and have nots. Statists and their cronies want to be the haves and when things go wrong, it is always We The People who must sacrifice and become the have nots. Meanwhile, Statists always manage to hold onto their wine and oil.

In the epistle of Hebrews, there is further distancing from the God of Statism and Moses in the description of a new covenant that will work for the people, instead of the failed covenant of the "promised land" from the God of Statism.

> **Hebrews 8:7 For if that first covenant had been faultless, then should no place have been sought for the second. 8. For finding fault with them, he saith, Behold, the days come saith the Lord, when I will make a new covenant with the house of Judah: 9. Not according to the covenant that I made with their fathers in the day when I took them by the hand to lead them out of the land of Egypt; because they continued not in my covenant, and I regarded them not, saith the Lord. 10. For this is the covenant that I will make with the house of Israel after those days, saith the Lord; I will put my laws into their mind, and write them in their hearts: and I will be to them a God, and they shall be to me a people: 11. And they shall not teach every man his neighbor, and every man his brother, saying, Know the Lord: for all shall know me, from the least to the greatest. 12. For I will be merciful to their unrighteousness, and their sins and their iniquities will I remember no more. 13. In that he saith, A new covenant, he hath made the first old. Now that which decayeth and waxeth old is ready to vanish away.**

The writers have begun the process of replacing the old covenant with something more like a Bill of Rights. Success will be when there are no longer laws being written and passed down from the God of Statism without regard to culture, and without input from the people. The goal is for a new culture to be born that comes from the Powers within us to create our own heavenly culture. That is something We The People have been waiting to achieve for a very long time. The admission fee to enter the inner sanctuary of the tabernacle has been paid, and no more sacrifices and tithes are necessary. It is now up to us to create a culture based on virtue and wisdom rather than a fear of God, so that there can be a resurrection of the freedom that was taken from us by the God of Statism which we created. We are reminded the "Original Sin" of man was in the creation of the God of Statism.

> **I John 3:1 Behold, what manner of love the Father hath bestowed upon us, that we should be called the sons of God: therefore the world knoweth us not, because it knew him not. 2. Beloved, now are we the sons of God, and it doth not yet appear what we shall be: but we know that, *when he shall appear, we shall be like him; for we shall see him as he is.***

On other words, we will make God in our new image and "we shall be like him: for we shall see him as he is". There will be a new culture before we can see our way back to Eden. Then, lest there be any confusion because of the various references of the nature of understanding and truth, they include this:

> **I John 5:7 For there are three that bear record in heaven, the Father, the Word, and the Holy Ghost: and these three are one. 8. And there are three that bear witness in earth, the Spirit, and the water, and the blood: and these three agree in one.**

Culture consists of the Father, which is the sum of our history and our teacher; the Word, the message of a living and flowing natural culture; and the Holy Ghost, which is the spirit of truth and understanding. These three ingredients must "agree in one" before we can be cleansed sufficiently of our cultural sins and Eden can exist. The writers must have considered this message to be so important they were willing to address the issue repeatedly and in as many ways as possible. Jesus is way better than any individual person or even a god—he is We The People, and teaches of the within ourselves to create this new culture if we are unimpeded.

Revelation—Revealing The Cycles of Failure

The word "revelation" and the word "apocalypse" {[63]} in the bible have the same meaning, which is to uncover or reveal. What Revelation uncovers are the repetitive cycles of failures of Statism and the effects upon the people. In short, the Revelation is somewhat a summation of the message of the bible, with the characters now being involved in a tragic drama using the politics of the day in which it was written—along with some fantastical imagery. It is still very relevant. If you were to take our current political events and characters and use metaphorical images to describe the players and their actions and their effects on society in general, you would again have something very similar to the Revelation.

Even today right here in the United States, if you were to take New York, Los Angeles, or Chicago, then write of the influence they have over the rest of the entire nation culturally, economically, and politically and refer to them as the "Whore of Babylon" with their many languages and cultures, you would have a very similar story to the Revelation. You would first refer to their centralized power and influence, then include all the palace eunuchs, cherubim, and seraphim that run our country from behind the scenes that mostly originate from these areas. Washington D.C. is less important because it is simply a bedroom community in which to house the palace eunuchs. Pointing out the major cities that so heavily influence the rest of the country because of their large voting blocs and concentration of resources is the same context in which the books of the bible were originally written, but within the politics and geography of the time in which the writers were living.

For John, who presumably wrote the Revelation, we can assume the "Whore of Babylon" {[64]} would have referred to the concentration of power within Rome, but the reference could just as easily be applied at various times to London, Constantinople,

---

[63]https://www.gotquestions.org/apocalypse.html
[64] https://en.wikipedia.org/wiki/Whore_of_Babylon

Beijing, Moscow, Berlin, and any number of other power centers. The Powers That Be is a monotheistic God and stays the same no matter when or where the power is concentrated. There is no point in making references to past cities or wars because the message is just as relevant today, and we have our own revelations playing out before us in our own time.

The word "apocalypse" has become associated with complete destruction. It is nothing of the sort. There is no end times or final destruction of the earth in Revelation. All the disasters in Revelation revisit the same metaphors of cultural dysfunction now familiar in the Old Testament. Rather than predicting the end, Revelation has an optimistic view of how culture could save the day, once the vagaries of cultural dysfunction have been uncovered and the causes revealed and examined. There are images of great destruction and torment, but they are referring to the necessary destruction of cultural attributes with great focus on Statism, and not actual people.

Revelation is not a story of a great judgment that will be brought by a god, it is a story of the destruction caused by a dysfunctional culture, and the battles of Armageddon are something humankind brings upon itself repeatedly and often. This is nothing new. We don't need a god to bring plagues and torment, as we do fine on our own, and that is the whole point. If there was a deity separate from man that wanted to punish us for our iniquities the easiest way to do that would be to leave us to our own devices, because we constantly allow our culture to be manipulated and degraded by those who tell us they will save us from ourselves and take us to a promised land.

As the last book in the New Testament, Revelation is a collection of letters that were written to seven churches in Asia. It isn't clear why the last book would be devoted to Asian churches. We don't know. One thing is apparent, and that is the letters were used to promote even further their message of independence and virtue as a weapon against the plagues of Statism.

The Revelation is a great work of human imagination, which is always a wonderful thing. The way the writers also find in it a way to continue the message of the bible is inspirational. It is basically a montage of references not only to the Old Testament, but also many contemporary books of the time outside the scriptures. Some of it may even have been meant to be poetry or Greek tragedy but didn't translate sufficiently to maintain the original beauty in that form. Fortunately, much of the imagery remains. You could spend a lifetime reading meaning into every sentence and researching every reference to some historical context. For our purposes we still just need to know whether the intent is consistent with the main theme, which is of the need for a virtuous culture based on wisdom and truth built by and for We The People that resists Statism.

Just as the Jesus story, the Revelation has always been controversial. There have even been debates as to whether the Revelation should be a part of the bible at all. To this day there are churches that do not include it in their teachings, which is probably because it can be hard to understand in modern languages and in modern culture. Now that we know the message, the Revelation is very easy to understand, and the prose and metaphors make it even more interesting. Without the Revelation, the previous stories are much less useful because they don't offer a solution.

One ongoing controversy is that no one knows for sure when Revelation was written. Some believe it was written decades after the original apostles had all died off, and some believe it was written much sooner. We don't need to be concerned about those debates. Just as the rest of bible, it sticks to the same subjects which are always politics and culture and the effects they both have on We The People and our interactions. This is a timeless subject. This subject is particularly pertinent for John, because he supposedly wrote them while in exile on an island called Patmos, where he had gone to escape persecution from the Statists. We don't know if he exiled himself or if that decision was made for him.

If the writer was John the apostle, then the exile worked out great for him because he was the only apostle that didn't die a violent death at the hands of the Statists as Jesus and the rest of the

331

gang, which gave him more time to exercise his imagination and, lucky for us, to write The Revelation. The Revelations show how we can use the power of We The People.

The story begins with a spirit from heaven speaking directly to John about the letters he needed to dictate to the seven Asian churches, and also provided him with some visions for inspiration. I think those who wrote some parts of the bible should be considered among the first sci-fi authors and were prophets in the same way that some modern sci-fi writers are sometimes proven to be prophets. A prophet is someone who can take current information and then extrapolate and predict the future with accuracy, especially where it concerns culture or technology. The book provides a description of the talking spirit, who is appropriately referred to as the Son of man, that includes the following...

> **Revelation 1:16 And he had in his right hand seven stars: and out of his mouth went a sharp two-edged sword: and his countenance was as the sun shineth in his strength. 18. I am he that liveth, and was dead; and, behold, I am alive for evermore, Amen; and have the keys of hell and of death. Write the things which thou hast seen, and the things which are, and the things which shall be hereafter; 20. The mystery of the seven stars which thou sawest in my right hand, and the seven golden candlesticks. The seven stars are the angels of the seven churches: and the seven candlesticks which thou sawest are the seven churches.**

As noted before, the number seven had special significance to the ancients, so it could be that including the seven churches just provided another convenient excuse for using that number, which almost always meant the completeness of a cycle. He was speaking "and out of his mouth went a sharp two-edged sword" which refers to teaching a new culture, which can be always be either good or bad, depending on which path we choose. This is consistent with the previous stories.

Also "I am he that liveth, and was dead; and, behold, I am alive for evermore, Amen; and have the keys of hell and of death" fits very well into the bible narrative that our cultural potential has been dead since being tossed from Eden under a system of political and religious Statism. On the other hand, a heavenly culture could be reborn, and be "alive for evermore" for those who "hath an ear". However, we still hold "the keys to hell and death" which refers to the wrong path, one of which could lead to the "second death" or a relapse referred to in the next passages. We also have another of the ongoing reversals of the actions of the God of Statism from Genesis, which refers to that very first book.

> **Revelation 2:7 He that hath an ear, let him hear what the Spirit saith unto the churches; To him that overcometh will I give to eat of the tree of life, which is in the midst of the paradise of God.**

Since the fear of our eating "of the tree of life" was the reason We The People were ejected from paradise by The Powers That Be in the very beginning, this is in fact quite a "revelation" to find there is a way to regain that freedom. It would also indicate that if this were finally achieved, then the cycles of failure would stop and we could create our own paradise. At that point, we could then be included into the completeness of the seventh day of Earth's creation, which is portrayed as a day of restfulness and peace. It turns out the reason it has been necessary to stress the importance of a day of Sabbath, which is the only day of the week named in the bible, is to remind us of our goal to achieve the completeness of a heavenly culture by completing the cycle into the seventh day. Otherwise, the cycles of failure would repeat themselves, and we will never reach the number seven. Towards reaching that goal, there are great rewards to those who "overcometh" the temptations of Statism:

> **Revelation 2:11 He that hath an ear, let him hear what the Spirit saith unto the churches; He that overcometh shall not be hurt of the second death.**

> **Revelation 2:26 And he that overcometh, and keepeth my works unto the end, *to him will I give power over***

the nations: **27.** *And he shall rule over them with a rod of iron; as the vessels of a potter shall they be broken to shivers: even as I received of my Father.* **28. And I will give him the morning star. 29. He that hath an ear, let him hear what the Spirit saith unto the churches.**

Revelation 3:12 Him that overcometh will I make a pillar in the temple of my God, and he shall go no more out: and I will write upon him the name of my God, and the name of the city of my God, which is new Jerusalem, which cometh down out of the heaven from my God: and I will write upon him my new name.

The hope is that We The People that "overcometh" and will someday *rule over all nations,* and as for Statist regimes *"shall they be broken to shivers: even as I received of my Father"*. Just as the God of Statism, which is still the chosen religion for many, eventually forsakes We The People and allows us to be sacrificed, so shall nations ruled by Statists be forsaken and sacrificed instead. They will be "broken to shivers", and there will be a new time and this system will definitely require a new name. The end game, of course, is that there will no longer be Powers that are higher than We The People, and then we can all be together on the throne of power. We know Jerusalem was famous for being populated by those considered stiff-necked and rebellious against the God of Statism, which would have made it a prime candidate to start a new cultural paradigm.

Revelation 3:21 To him that overcometh will I grant to sit with me in my throne, even as I also overcame, and am set down with my Father in his throne.

Cultural Statism will no longer have centralized power over We The People, and the throne must be shared by all.

The Casting of The Crowns

John then has a vision of the Powers That Be (God) on a throne surrounded by beasts much like those used by God earlier to help evict We The People from Eden.

> **Revelation 4:7 And the first beast was like a lion, and the second beast like a calf, and the third beast had a face as a man, and the fourth beast was like a flying eagle. 8. And the four beasts had each of them six wings about him; and they were full of eyes within: and they rest not day and night, saying Holy, holy, holy, Lord God Almighty, which was, and is, and is to come. 9. And when those beasts give glory and honour and thanks to him that sat on the throne who liveth for ever and ever, 10. The four and twenty elders fall down before him that sat on the throne, and worship him that liveth for ever and ever, and cast their crowns before the throne, saying 11. Thou art worthy, O Lord, to receive glory and honour and power: for thou hast created all things, and for thy pleasure they are and were created.**

It may appear at first as if the elders are worshiping the standard issue centralized figure of God, with the ever-present bureaucracies whose purpose is to support and praise the figure on the throne. They remove their crowns and place them before the throne. The figure on the throne also holds a book of many secrets, but the book is sealed. At first, John...

> **Revelation 5:4 ...wept much, because no man was found worthy to open and to read the book, neither to look thereon. 5. And one of the elders saith unto me, Weep not: behold, the Lion** (the people) **of the tribe of Juda, the Root of David, hath prevailed to open the book, and to loose the seven seals thereof.**

Knowing what we have learned from the previous writings of the Judaic tribes now deemed worthy of opening the book, I think it would be a good bet those seven seals will have something to do with the characteristics of The God of Statism and its relationship with We The People.

> **Revelation 5:6 And I beheld, and, lo, in the midst of the throne and of the four beasts, and in the midst of the elders, stood a Lamb as it had been slain, having seven horns and seven eyes, which are the seven Spirits of God sent forth into all the earth. 7. And he came and took the book out of the right hand of him that sat on the throne. 8. And when he had taken the book, the four beasts and four and twenty elders fell down before the Lamb, having everyone of them harps, and golden vials full of odours, which are the prayers of saints.**

The Lamb then took the book "out of the right hand of him that sat on the throne". It's time to sing a new song because thanks to the book, the Lamb previously suitable only for sacrifice and slaughter, will now have equal footing. Suddenly we realize the Lamb, who is now "in the midst of the throne", is actually the focus of the elders who have cast off their crowns...

> **Revelation 5:9 And they sung a new song, saying, Thou art worthy to take the book, and to open the seals thereof: for thou wast slain, and hast redeemed us to God by thy blood out of every kindred, and tongue, and people, and nation; 10. And hast made us unto our God kings and priests: and we shall reign on earth. 11. And I beheld, and I heard the voice of many angels round about the throne and the beasts and the elders: and the number of them was ten thousand times ten thousand, and thousands of thousands; 12. Saying with a loud voice, Worthy is the Lamb that was slain to receive power, and riches, and wisdom, and strength, and honour, and glory, and blessing.**

The prophecy is the sacrificial Lamb (We The People) will now be the one worthy to receive "power, and riches, and wisdom, and strength, and honour, and glory, and blessing". It will now be the multitudes that would benefit instead of always becoming the slain Lamb. Because of the new power of the Lamb, the people of the Judaic tribes can now begin opening the secret seals and witness the lessons they contain, which are no longer any secret to those who understand the message. They are as follows:

> **Revelation 6:1 And I saw when the Lamb opened one of the seals, and I heard, as it were the noise of thunder, one of the four beasts saying, Come and see. 2. And I saw, and behold a white horse: and he that sat on him had a bow; and a crown was given unto him: and he went forth conquering, and to conquer.**

Lesson 1: Statism requires powerful central figures who exalt themselves, usually intent on conquering to achieve power and control by which to gain the crown.

> **Revelation 6:3. And when he had opened the second seal, I heard the second beast say, Come and see. 4. And there went out another horse that was red: and power was given to him that sat thereon to take peace from the earth, and that they should kill one another: and there was given to him a great sword.**

Lesson 2: Wherever there is a "crowned" central authority, there are armies and usually warfare, for which the Lamb (We the People) *is given to sacrifice.*

> **Revelation 6:5. And when he had opened the third seal, I heard the third beast say, Come and see. And I beheld and lo a black horse; and he that sat on him had a pair of balances on his hand. 6. And I heard a voice in the midst of the four beasts say, a measure of wheat for a penny, and three measures of barley for a penny; and see thou hurt not the oil and the wine.**

Lesson 3: Statism requires currency (manna) manipulation to create dependency, introduce poverty, create inflation, induce cultural degradations such as greed and criminality, but which the elitists still find abundant and plentiful for purchasing luxury items such as oil and wine.

Revelation 6:7. And when he had opened the fourth seal, I heard the voice of the fourth beast say, Come and see. 8. And I looked, and behold a pale horse: and his name was Death, and Hell followed with him. And power was given unto him. And power was given unto them over the fourth part of the earth, to kill with sword, and with hunger, and with death, and with the beasts of the earth.

Lesson 4: Statism induces the death of culture, and hell is the result. Warfare, famine, and cultural death are all symptoms of Statist social degradation.

Revelation 6:9. And when he had opened the fifth seal, I saw under the altar the souls of them that were slain for the word of God, and for the testimony which they held: 10. And they cried with a loud voice, saying, How long, O Lord, holy and true, dost thou not judge and avenge our blood on them that dwell on the earth. 11. And white robes were given unto every one of them; and it was said unto them, that they should rest yet a little season, until their fellow-servants also and their brethren, that should be killed as they were, should be fulfilled.

Lesson 5: Persecution becomes State policy to maintain power and authority, and those delivering a message of independence and freedom will be purged, often through violence, once Statism is firmly established. The prophecy is they will eventually be redeemed and learn to avoid the second death.

Revelation 6:12. And I beheld when he had opened the sixth seal, and, lo, there was a great earthquake and the sun became black as sackcloth of hair, and the moon became as blood; 13. And the stars of heaven fell unto the earth, even as a fig tree casteth her untimely figs, when she is shaken of a mighty wind. 14. And the heaven departed as a scroll when it is rolled together; and every mountain and island were moved out of their places. 15. And the kings of the earth, and the great men, and the rich men, and every bondman, and every free man, hid themselves in the dens and in the rocks of the mountains; 16. And said to the mountains and rocks, Fall on us, and hide us from the face of him that sitteth on the throne, and from the wrath of the Lamb: 17. For the great day of his wrath is come; and who shall be able to stand?

Lesson 6: More than anything, those benefiting from Statism fear We The People. We who have been the sacrificial Lamb since the beginning of history can become a force that must be subdued and restricted from Eden by whatever means necessary. We must be kept busy with wars, division, identity politics, economic manipulation, dependency, propaganda, and persecution to prevent those who profit from Statism from experiencing the "wrath of the Lamb".

Only through these extreme methods can the sacrificial Lamb be kept at bay, and so these methods are used each day and have been since time immemorial. But if We The People exercise our power to rise from the cultural death in which we have been living, and "overcometh" so that we can be reborn into the tree of life, then there can be a new day. The sacrificial Lamb of We The People can gain power and share the throne among ourselves.

Huge progress has been made since John wrote these last stories, and in some parts of the world Eden was in sight, but we are now seeing our freedom slip away once again. The God of Statism is once again rearing its ugly Leviathan head, even in the freest of countries, and has creeped up on us quietly as a thief while we have been more concerned with the mundane issues of our daily lives, just as Esau before he lost his birthright.

Satan the beast, who has always been the assistant to the God of Statism, has not yet been confined, and always pulls We The People towards perdition to devour our chances for freedom. Defeating him permanently will not be easy, and we have not yet opened the seventh seal. That will be a story unto itself and predicts all the travails that will befall us before the cycle is completed with the seventh angel.

Unfortunately, rather than reaching completion the cycle will begin again, because as the Lamb opens the seventh seal, the process is stopped by an angel wishing to prevent the coming plagues from affecting everyone, as another angel inoculates a portion of each of the twelve tribes of Israel who have now gotten the message. Of each tribe there are portions of the population that will be protected through receiving the message of a new cultural paradigm.

> **Revelation 7:2 And I saw another angel ascending from the east, having the seal of the living God: and he cried with a loud voice to the four angels, to whom it was given to hurt the earth and the sea, 3. Saying, Hurt not the earth, neither the sea, nor the trees, till we have sealed the servants of our God in their foreheads. 4. And I heard the number of them which were sealed: and they were sealed an hundred and forty and four thousand of all the tribes of the children of Israel.**

There is probably something interesting about the symbolism of the 12,000 for each of the twelve tribes, or the number 144,000 but unfortunately we no longer know what that might be and it must be left to speculation. Suffice it to say, in the bible a symbolic portion each of the tribes of Israel who receive and understand the message will be the first to gain from the revelations, and many of them will now be immune to the temptations of Statism, just as in the original Passover. So far, their immunity is still holding, at least in Israel. One of the elders who had received the seal asks John if he knows who "the sealed" represent.

> **Revelation 7:13 And one of the elders answered, saying unto me, What are these which are arrayed in white robes? And whence came they? 14. And I said unto him, Sir, thou knowest. And he said to me, These are they which came out of great tribulation, and have washed their robes, and made them white in the blood**

of the Lamb. 15. **Therefore are they before the throne of God, and serve him day and might in his temple:** *and he that sitteth on the throne shall dwell among them.* 16. **They shall hunger no more, neither thirst any more; neither shall the sun light on them, nor any heat.** 17. **For the Lamb which is in the midst of the throne shall feed them, and shall lead them unto living fountains of waters: and God shall wipe away all tears from their eyes.**

These portions of the tribes will create a new beginning free from chaos, where those who received the message will have the freedom to pursue a new cultural paradise. However, the seventh seal begins a whole new cycle, with the seven angels now stepping in with a new set of plagues. Rather than achieving the Sabbath, which represents peace and rest, Statism simply begets more Statism and the cycle begins anew. Even though the message may be seen and understood by some, the writers emphasize it will never be universal. Those not understanding will continue to suffer the plagues, and the second death for those will be the result.

Now that some have been inoculated, the seven angels are used once again to demonstrate cultural death to all those do not repent (change their minds) about how they approach life and culture. The angels now standing before God begin a repeat of the plagues placed upon Egypt in the Old Testament. This is the second round of torment, symbolizing a new cycle.

Revelation 8:2 And I saw the seven angels which stood before God; and to them were given seven trumpets.

The first angel attacks nature on land, which provides sustenance, knowledge, and natural wisdom.

Revelation 8:7 The first angel sounded, and there followed hail and fire mingled with blood, and they were cast upon the earth: and the third part of trees was burnt up, and all green grass was burnt up.

They then attack the plants which grow upon the land. Importantly, they make the point that not all is destroyed—only one third. Then the angels attack the sea.

> **Revelation 8:8 And the second angel sounded, and as it were a great mountain burning with fire was cast into the sea: and the third part of the sea became blood; 9. And the third part of the creatures which were in the sea, and had life, died; and the third part of the ships were destroyed.**

Then they attacked the creatures and the people that lived in the rivers and springs.

> **Revelation 8:10 And the third angel sounded, and there fell a great star from heaven, burning as it were a lamp, and it fell upon a third part of the rivers, and upon the fountains of waters; 11. And the name of the star is called Wormwood: and the third part of the waters became wormwood; and many men died of the waters, because they were made bitter.**

Not to leave anything out, the angels then attack the sky.

> **Revelation 8:12 And the fourth angel sounded, and the third part of the sun was smitten, and the third part of the moon, and the third part of the stars; so as the third part of them darkened, and the day shone for for a third part of it, and the night likewise.**

Then the angels opened the bottomless pit which leads to the three woes of the last three angels.

> **Revelation 8:13 And I beheld, and heard an angel flying through the midst of heaven, saying with a loud voice, Woe, woe, woe, to the inhabiters of the earth by reason of the other voices of the trumpet of the three angels, which are yet to sound.**

> **Revelation 9:1 And the fifth angel sounded, and I saw a star fall from heaven unto the earth: and to him was given the key of the bottomless pit.**

For those not receiving the message, the plagues of the second death will continue.

First Woe—Attack of The Fierce Hippy Grasshopper Kings

The fifth angel would open the pit and out would come the first woe.

> **Revelation 9:3 And he opened the bottomless pit; and there arose a smoke out of the pit, as the smoke of a great furnace; and the sun and the air were darkened by reason of the smoke of the pit. 3. And there came out of the smoke locusts upon the earth: and unto to them was given power, as the scorpions of the earth have power.**

We don't know what they were smoking in the pit, but whatever it was it may have limited their effectiveness. (OK, maybe I'm having a little fun with this part, but unlike Statists and the victim groups from which they recruit, the rest of us can have a sense of humor.)

> **Revelation 9:4 And it was commanded them that they should not hurt the grass of the earth, neither any tree; but only those men which have not the seal of God in their foreheads. 5. And to them it was given that they should not kill them, but that they should be tormented five months: and their torment was as the torment of a scorpion, when he striketh a man. 6. And in those days shall men seek death, and shall not find it; and shall desire to die, and death shall flee from them. 7. And the shapes of the locusts were like unto horses prepared unto battle; and on their heads were as it were crowns like gold, and their faces were as the faces of men. 8. And they had hair as the hair of women, and their teeth were as the teeth of lions.**

The hippy grasshopper warriors may have felt as though they were kings with crowns, but apparently their only function was to cause short term torment to those not inoculated, which caused many of their victims to want to die but couldn't. Maybe if this story were written much more recently the smoking pit may have been a hookah lounge.

> **Revelation 9:13 And the sixth angel sounded, and I heard a voice from the four horns of the golden altar which is before God, 14. Saying to the sixth angel which had the trumpet, Loose the four angels which are bound in the great river Euphrates.**

Now for the cycles of the second woe.

Second Woe—Four More Angels That Are Not Angelic

The sixth angel releases four more angels upon mankind with the intention to destroy an additional one third of humanity. The appearance of angels in the bible are usually bad news because they are God's messengers.

> **Revelation 10:15 And the four angels were loosed, which were prepared for an hour, and a day, and a month, and a year, for to slay the third part of men. 16. And the number of the army of the horsemen were two hundred thousand thousand: and I heard the number of them.**

This appears to be a tribute to all those who had ever gone to war and died in battle for the God of Statism. They would now be given a voice to criticize all those who still did not repent and create a different culture, before their lives were also lost.

> **Revelation 9:19 For their power is in their mouth, and in the tails: for their tails were like unto serpents, and had heads, and with them they do hurt. 20. And the rest of the men which were not killed by these plagues yet repented not of the works of their hands, that they should not worship devils, and idols of gold, and silver, and brass, and stone, and of wood: which neither can see, nor hear, nor walk: 21. Neither repented they of their murders, nor of their sorceries, nor of their fornication, nor of their thefts.**

Their power is in their testimony and in their call for a cultural revolution. Otherwise what follows is even worse, as represented by their headed serpent tails. They had lost their lives because of those who preferred to worship false idols such as exalted leaders and gods. They had been guided by a desire for material wealth, security, and a greed for power. Despite the vast numbers of mankind who had fallen to the evils of Statism, many people would remain skeptical rather than repent. The cycle here is once again not complete, but there is an assurance given that once the seventh angel finally speaks, the mystery of God will be revealed again to those who still do not understand.

> **Revelation 10:7 But in the days of the voice of the seventh angel, when he shall begin to sound, the mystery of God should be finished, as he hath declared to his servants the prophets. 8. And the voice which I heard from heaven spake unto me again, and said, Go and take the little book which is open in the hand of the angel which standeth upon the sea and upon the earth.**

Once again, rather than completing the cycle to reach Eden, the seventh angel instead gives John what is clearly now an open book for anyone willing to read it. Just as Jeremiah in days past, he devours the book which is sweet in its knowledge, but now it becomes bitter as he realizes the task before him.

> **Revelation 10:10 And I took the little book out of the angel's hand, and ate it up; and it was in my mouth sweet as honey: and as soon as I had eaten it, my belly was bitter. 11. And he said unto me, Thou must prophecy again before many peoples, and nations, and tongues, and kings.**

John is given the task to spread the message, but unlike Noah and the spread of Statism, it would be "a new thing". Along with the sweetness of understanding, he is now given the bitter task of educating others. Once eaten, the little book must have seemed to John as a very bitter pill, considering the job he was given to continue to recruit both Jews and Gentiles. His task was to make them witnesses to his message, just as Paul had attempted to do. First, he would have to reexamine the Judaic church itself and those who attended. It would have to be redesigned to include the Gentiles.

> **Revelation 11:1 And there was given me a reed like unto a rod: and the angel stood, saying, Rise, and measure the temple of God, and the altar, and them**

that worship therein. 2. But the court which is without the temple leave out, and measure it not; for it is given unto the Gentiles: and the holy city shall they tread under foot forty and two months. 3. And I will give power unto my two witnesses, and they shall prophesy a thousand two hundred and threescore days, clothed in sackcloth. 4. These are the two olive trees, and the two candlesticks standing before the God of the earth.

The two witnesses are both the Jews and Gentiles that would be educated and then recruited in the cause against Statism, and after a time would receive power. Once they were educated to the point they could work together, they would bring peace, as represented by the two olive trees. In response, the beast will rise to make war against them to prevent them from successfully completing the cycle to seven.

Revelation 11:7 And when they shall have finished their testimony, the beast that ascendeth out of the bottomless pit shall make war against them, and shall overcome them, and kill them.

Those who preferred the temporary security and dependence of a culture of political and religious Statism do not want to receive the message, and at first are glad the witnesses among the Jews and Gentiles who have received the message are killed.

Revelation 11:10 And they that dwell upon the earth shall rejoice over them, and make merry, and shall send gifts one to another; because these two prophets tormented them that dwelt on the earth. 11. And after three days and an half the Spirit of life from God entered into them, and they stood upon their feet; and great fear fell upon them which saw them.

Despite being destroyed, the two witnesses are resurrected in three days (and a half, so apparently resurrecting two at once is slightly more difficult) just as was Jesus and was pulled into the safety of heaven. Then the seventh angel makes another proclamation regarding the mystery of God.

Revelation 11:15 And the seventh angel sounded; and there were great voices in heaven, saying, The kingdoms of this world are become the kingdoms of our Lord, and of his Christ; and he shall reign for ever and ever.

The mystery of God, as always, is the message that we should become---not Christians as is often taught---but *"of his Christ"*, which means we must become the anointed and become our own gods and our own kings and create a culture of virtue and wisdom if we are to obtain Eden and lasting peace. For this to happen we must above all resist Statism. Of course, this will always make the remaining Statist nations and their kings and palace eunuchs very angry because of their own cultures of Statism.

Revelation 11:18 And the nations were angry, and thy wrath is come, and the time of the dead, that they should be judged, and that thou shouldest give reward unto thy servants the prophets, and to the saints, and them that fear thy name, small and great; and shouldest destroy them which destroy the earth.

We The People prefer to reward the lowly servants and prophets rather than those who have the power and authority to "destroy the earth" and bring cultural death. Since the next cycle still is not yet complete, there will be more struggles and plagues.

Revelation 12:1 And there appeared a great wonder in heaven; a woman clothed with the sun, and the moon under her feet, and upon her head a crown of twelve stars: 2. And she being with child cried, travailing in birth, and pained to be delivered. 3. And there appeared another wonder in heaven, and behold a great red dragon, having seven heads and ten horns, and seven crowns upon his heads. 4. And his tail drew the third part of the stars of heaven, and did cast them to earth: and the dragon stood before the woman which was ready to be delivered, for to devour her child as soon as it was born. 5. And she brought forth a man child, who was to rule all nations with a rod of

iron: and her child was caught up to God, and to his throne.

This is basically a repeat of Jesus having been introduced to represent an entirely new social construct, and then narrowly escaping death at birth from the dragon (the king's men), who wants to devour the movement "as it is being born". Michael, which you will recall is a spokesman who protects us from Satan, and whose name means "Who is God?" struggles against the dragon again and casts him out of heaven. The dragon is then sent to earth to plague mankind. Michael may cast Satan out of heaven, but it is up to We The People to cast him out of earth.

Revelation 12:17 And the dragon was wroth with the woman, and went to make war with the remnant of her seed, which keep the commandments of God, and have the testimony of Jesus Christ.

The wily dragon has a few tricks up his sleeve and recruits a couple of other beasts to help with the persecution of those who understand the message of Jesus. John has more visions.

Revelation 13:1 And I stood upon the sand of the sea, and saw a beast rise up out of the sea, having seven heads and ten crowns, and upon his heads the name of blasphemy. 2. And the beast which I saw was like unto a leopard, and his feet were as the feet of a bear, and the mouth of a lion: and the dragon gave him his power, and his seat, and great authority.

Unfortunately for many, they would repeatedly be duped by this bureaucratic beast who serves the dragon, and which uses State power and authority to claim control over the people.

Revelation 13:4 And they worshipped the dragon which gave power unto the beast: and they worshipped the beast, saying, Who is like unto the beast? Who is able to make war with him?

Rather than attempt to defeat the beast, many would instead choose to worship him. Then the dragon pulled in yet another bureaucratic beast to help with the effort to subdue mankind.

Revelation 13:11 And I beheld another beast coming up out of the earth; and he had two horns like a lamb, and he spake as a dragon. 12. And he exerciseth all the power of the first beast before him, and causeth the earth and them which dwell therein to worship the first beast, whose deadly wound was healed.

Without resistance, the beast of Statism will grow to have many heads and grow even stronger. The other heads will heal and protect each other if wounded. In this case they are probably referring to a kingdom which regained power with the assistance of Rome, which then installed another corrupt king of their own choosing. Nowadays, it could just as easily represent bureaucrats protecting agencies and modern departmental monarchies to prevent them from being eliminated or reduced in size, even though they no longer serve a useful purpose.

Revelation 13:13 And he doeth great wonders, so that he maketh fire come down from heaven on the earth in the sight of men. 14. And deceiveth them that dwell on the earth by the means of those miracles which he had power to do in the sight of the beast; saying to them that dwell on the earth, that they should make an image of the beast, which had a wound by the sword, and did live. 15. And he had power to give life unto the image of the beast, that the image of the beast should both speak, and cause that as many as would not worship the image of the beast should be killed.

It is sad that so many fall for the temporary miracles and wonders and to worship the enabler beasts. Those who do will now suffer persecution if they refuse to adequately worship the State. We now have three incomplete cycles, which represent the failed cycles of Statism and the effects on culture. Rather than achieving rest and peace on the seventh day of Sabbath, the incomplete cycles of failed States just repeat themselves. This is described in the next passage and is represented by the number 666. We want to be saved by our false idols, and so we are stuck in endless cycles of failure.

Revelation 13:16 And he causeth all, both small and great, rich and poor, free and bond, to receive a mark in their right hand, or in their foreheads: 17. And that no man might buy or sell, save he that had the mark, or the name of the beast, or the number of his name. 18. Here is wisdom, Let him that hath understanding count the number of the beast: for it is the number of a man; and his number is Six hundred threescore and six.

It is the goal of those that wrote the books that as many as possible should escape the repetitive cycles of failure to achieve the freedom, rest, and peace of the Sabbath. Those who worship the beast with his wonders and power will never defeat the repetitive cycles of Statism, and so will forever be marked with 6-6-6. This number represents the equivalent of almost, almost, almost, but never achieving the goal of seven before beginning a new cycle of failure. It is the history of man that we continuously create Statist institutions, both political and religious, believing that through their power and authority they will be our savior. Then there is a process whereby there is increased centralization, more false visions of a promised land, and more oppression and corruption until there is a social and economic collapse and the cycle starts all over again. We should beware these beasts and their markings, and their threats and plagues that control us, so that "no man might buy or sell, save he that had the mark".

We still have not reached the end of the cycle, and there is even a third woe waiting for us. The writers point out we cannot wait for all to understand, as that will never be the case. We shouldn't be like those who accept a number from the beast, which prevents the completion of the cycle by controlling us through a manipulated economy that favors the "chosen" insiders that worship the beasts.

They point out only a limited number can be expected to receive the message, but those who do will sing another new song.

Revelation 14:3 And they sung as it were a new song before the throne, and before the four beasts, and the elders: and no man could learn that song but the

hundred and forty and four thousand, which were redeemed from the earth.

There are warnings posted in the little open book that show it is a cultural operation manual for the redeemed.

Revelation 14:9 And the third angel followed them, saying with a loud voice, If any man worship the beast and his image, and receive his mark in his forehead, or in his hand, 10. The same shall drink of the wine of the wrath of God, which is poured out without mixture into the cup of his indignation; and he shall be tormented with fire and brimstone in the presence of the holy angels, and in the presence of the Lamb:

As predicted by the number 6-6-6, we now begin a whole new cycle, with new wraths from The Powers That Be. Seven angels appear and pour out vials to further plague those not inoculated with the redemption of truth and understanding. They emphasize these repetitive cycles are never a pleasant experience.

Revelation 15:6 And the seven angels came out of the temple, having the seven plagues, clothed in pure and white linen, and having their breasts girded with golden girdles.

Revelation 16:1 And the first went, and poured out his vial upon earth; and there fell a noisome and grievous sore upon the men which had the mark of the beast, and upon them which worshiped his image. 3. And the second angel poured out his vial upon the sea; and it became as the blood of a dead man; and every living soul died in the sea. 4. And the third angel poured out his vial upon the rivers and mountains of waters; and they became blood.

Revelation 16:8 And the fourth angel poured out his vial upon the sun; and power was given unto him to scorch men with fire. 9. And men were scorched with great heat, and blasphemed the name of God, which hath power over these plagues: and they repented not

to give him glory. 10. And the fifth angel poured out his vial upon the seat of the beast; and his kingdom was full of darkness; and they gnawed their tongues for pain, 11. And blasphemed the God of heaven because of their pains and their sores, and repented not of their deeds. 12. And the sixth angel poured out his vial upon the great river Euphrates, and the water thereof was dried up, that the way of the kings of the east might be prepared.

When we continue to turn to the Statist God for salvation we are preparing the way for another wave of Statists to rule over us. Just as we almost reach the Sabbath of completion, three frogs appear from the mouth of our three worst adversaries.

Revelation 16:13 And I saw three unclean spirits like frogs come out of the mouth of the dragon (Statism), **and out of the mouth of the beast** (bureaucracies), **and out of the mouth of the false prophet** (propagandists). **14. For they are the spirits of devils, working miracles, which go forth unto the kings of the earth and of the whole world, to gather them to the battle of that great day of God Almighty. 15. Behold, I come as a thief. Blessed is he that watcheth, and keepeth his garments, lest he walk naked, and they see his shame. 16. And he gathered them together into a place called in the Hebrew tongue Armageddon. 17. And the seventh angel poured out his vial into the air; and there came a great voice out of the temple of heaven, from the throne, saying, It is done.**

Those who "overcometh" will gather themselves in Armageddon and declare their freedom and independence. If they are successful, the cycle may finally be allowed to reach the final goal of seven, and the hoped-for prophecies would come into play...

Revelation 16:19 And the great city was divided into three parts, and the cities of the nations fell: and great Babylon came in remembrance before God, to give

unto her the cup of the wine of the fierceness of his wrath.

This revelation may be another example of being incredibly prophetic. As a "new thing" called a republic created to resist Statism, here in the U.S. our "great city" of government was also divided into three parts. Those three parts are the Executive, Legislative, and Judicial. They were created to resist the God of Statism.

Unfortunately, the beasts are rising once again and have begun a new cycle of warfare against We The People as predicted in revelation to create another cycle of failure. Many of the palace eunuchs in Washington have begun to once again worship the beasts of bureaucracy. It isn't difficult to see how the cities of the nations fall into decadence and failure just as in the Old Testament. To show why there will always be a huge battle between the dragon and the Lamb, one of the angels offers to show John around and to explain the "uncovering" (Revelation) of the enemy that always brings plagues upon the people.

Revelation 17:1 And there came one of the seven angels which had the seven vials, and talked with me, Come hither; I will shew unto thee the judgment of the great whore that sitteth upon many waters: 2. With whom the kings of the earth have committed fornication, and the inhabitants of the earth have been made drunk with the wine of her fornication. 3. So he carried me away in the spirit into the wilderness: and I saw a woman sit upon a scarlet coloured beast, full of names of blasphemy, having seven heads and ten horns. 4. And the woman was arrayed in purple and scarlet colour, and decked with gold and precious stones and pearls, having a golden cup in her hand full of abominations and filthiness of her fornication: 5. And upon her forehead was a name written, MYSTERY, BABYLON THE GREAT, THE MOTHER OF HARLOTS AND ABOMINATIONS OF THE EARTH. 6. And I saw the woman drunken

with the blood of the saints, and with the blood of the martyrs of Jesus: and when I saw her, I wondered with great admiration.

It's impossible to ignore the connection between the images described and their clear references to vast and far reaching powers of the State and their centers of power. They refer to a symbolic Babylon, but as mentioned before there have been many such cities in history. It is inarguable that cities can often be tantalizingly beautiful with large ornate buildings and great shows of opulence derived from wealth stolen from the productivity of We The People. The angel then goes on to explain further, showing the writers had contempt for the Powers of the time.

Revelation 17:7 And the angel said unto me, Wherefore didst thou marvel? I will tell thee the mystery of the woman, and of the beast that carrieth her, which hath the seven heads and ten horns. 8. The beast that thou sawest was, and is not; and shall ascend out of the bottomless pit, and go into perdition: and they that dwell on the earth shall wonder, whose names were not written in the book of life from the foundation of the world, when they behold the beast that was, and is not, and yet is. 9. And here is the wisdom. The seven heads are seven mountains, on which the woman sitteth *(seven hills of Rome)*. **10. And there are seven kings: five are fallen, and one is, and the other is not yet come; and when he cometh, he must continue a short space. 11. And the beast that was, and is not, even he is the eighth, and is of the seven, and goeth into perdition** (a constant state of self-inflicted punishment).

In addition to the power centralized in the city referred to as the Whore of Babylon, there are also those that collude and cooperate with the beast. Whether from self-preservation or for personal reward, these are the kings of the surrounding nations or cities that constantly come and go and rise and fall in power while cooperating with the State, which is a phenomenon that perpetuates the oppression. Collectively, they eventually form one huge power center of collusion that protect each other.

Statists today have an even more ambitious goal, and that is to create one centralized power worldwide. This is called Globalism, which is a brand new "ism" favored by modern Statists. Speaking of these kings, the story continues.

> **Revelation 17:13 These have one mind, and shall give their power and strength unto the beast. 14. These shall make war with the Lamb, and the Lamb shall overcome them: for he is Lord of lords, and King of kings: and they that are with him are called, and chosen, and faithful. 15. And he saith unto me, The waters which thou sawest, where the whore sitteth, are peoples, and multitudes, and nations, and tongues. 16. And the ten horns which thou sawest upon the beast, these shall hate the whore, and shall make her desolate and naked, and shall eat her flesh, and burn her with fire. 17. For God hath put in their hearts to fulfil his will, and to agree, and give their kingdom unto the beast, until the words of God shall be fulfilled. 18. And the woman which thou sawest is that great city, which reigneth over the kings of the earth.**

Those of "one mind" do not think for themselves and they wage war against the Lamb by giving control of their culture to the beast. Not only do the writers resent the corruption of centralized power, but they also have a serious beef with the crony capitalists and colluding kings and bureaucracies that become enablers. These become wealthy themselves from the inevitable excesses of the ruling elites.

> **Revelation 18:11 And the merchants of the earth shall weep and mourn over her; for no man buyeth their merchandise any more: 12. The merchandise of gold, and silver, and precious stones, and of pearls, and fine linen, and purple, and silk, and scarlet, and all thyine wood, and all manner vessels of ivory, and all manner vessels of most precious wood, and of brass, and iron,**

and marble, 13. And cinnamon, and odours, and ointments, and frankincense, and wine, and oil, and fine flour, and wheat, and beasts, and sheep, and horses, and chariots, and slaves, and souls of men. 14. And the fruits that thy soul lusted after departed from thee, and all things which were dainty and goodly are departed from thee, and thou shalt find them no more at all. 15. The merchants of these things, which were made rich by her, shall stand afar off for the fear of her torment, weeping and wailing, 16. And saying, Alas, alas, that great city, that was clothed in fine linen, and purple, and scarlet, and decked with gold, and precious stones, and pearls!

Then there is another lesson about worshiping, as opposed to praising and honoring.

Revelation 19:9 And he saith unto me, Write, Blessed are they which are called unto the marriage supper of the Lamb. And he saith unto me, These are the true sayings of God. 10. And I fell at his feet to worship him. And he saith unto me, See *thou do it not*: I am thy fellow-servant, and of thy brethren that have the testimony of Jesus: worship God: for the testimony of Jesus is the spirit of prophecy. 11. And I saw heaven opened, and behold a white horse; and he that sat upon him was called Faithful and True, and in righteousness he doth judge and make war. 12. His eyes were as a flame of fire, and on his head were many crowns; and he had a name written, that no man knew, but he himself. 13. And he was clothed with a vesture dipped in blood: and his name is called The Word of God.

Again, Jesus clearly represents We The People, and is described as The Word of God (our cultural voice) and not a god himself and he refused to be worshipped. It is also clear that his weapon is not warfare but is through the teaching of virtue in culture called "Faithful and True". It is easy to forget why Jesus was crucified. He was crucified because he was a blasphemous heretic. He was persecuted for being anti-God. He did not buy into the god of the Pharisees and Sadducees. He also did not buy into the gods of the emperors, kings, and pharaohs. Instead, like Job and Daniel, he only obeyed the god within him, which often results in crucifixion in any Statist society. It is still common to be crucified for this type of blasphemy.

If those who teach could help prevent the cycle of Statism from repeating, instead of preaching Statist ideology, then we could rest for a very long time. As anyone who knows history realizes, other than the success of a few fragile republics such as in the U.S., this has not yet happened. Because of those who worship the beasts, this republic may also fail. At the rate at which we are regressing, we may again fall victim to another cycle of failure. Despite setbacks we should never give up, and as demonstrated by those that wrote the books, we should continue to maintain the optimistic goal of achieving the seventh day of Sabbath where there is rest and peace. Our job is to resurrect freedom as often as necessary.

> **Revelation 20:2 And he (an angel) laid hold on the dragon, that old serpent, which is the Devil, and Satan, and bound him a thousand years, 3. And cast him into the bottomless pit, and shut him up, and set a seal upon him, that he should deceive the nations no more, till the thousand years should be fulfilled: and after that he must be loosened a little season. 4. And I saw thrones, and they sat upon, and judgment was given unto them: and I saw the souls of them that were beheaded for the witness of Jesus, and for the word of God, and which had not worshiped the beast, neither his image, neither had received his mark upon their foreheads, or in their hands; and they lived and reigned a thousand years. But the rest of the dead lived not again until the thousand years were finished. This is the first resurrection.**

If we avoid worshiping the beast, and imprison the dragon, we can continue the first true resurrection of freedom since before being exiled from Eden. Another lesson here is that even if we do resurrect freedom, we can never let our guard down or forget. As our adversary, God's assistant Satan will still be among us "as a wild man" to lead us back into Statism. As it stands, we will have to forever be vigilant, and be ready to cast the devil back into the lake of fire and brimstone whenever it rises again.

Revelation 20:7 And when the thousand years are expired, Satan shall be loosed out of his prison, 8. And shall go out to deceive the nations which are in the four quarters of the earth, Gog and Magog, to gather them together to battle: the number of whom is as the sand of the sea. 9. And they went up on the breadth of the earth, and compassed the camp of the saints about, and the beloved: and fire came down from God out of heaven, and devoured them. 10. And the devil that deceived them was cast into the lake of fire and brimstone, where the beast and the false prophet are, and shall be tormented day and night for ever and ever.

Just as in the Old Testament, so long as any republican society exists it will be an everlasting torment to the Statists and will be a threat to be persecuted by the beasts. However, so long as we maintain a culture strong enough to resist, they will be cast back into their own fire.

As we recall, over two thousand years ago Jerusalem had already claimed a very long history of resistance to gods of all sorts and to kings and their taxes. It had been destroyed on several occasions because of their resistance and the inhabitants had on a few occasions even been sold into slavery by God. It was also where the crucifixion of the radical rebel Jesus had taken place, so Jerusalem has always symbolically represented resistance.

Revelation 21:1 And I saw a new heaven and a new earth: for the first heaven and the first earth were passed away; and there was no more sea. 2. And I John saw the holy city, new Jerusalem, coming down from God out of heaven, prepared as a bride (the city

of Jerusalem) adorned for her husband (The Sacrificed Lamb). 3. And I heard a great voice out of heaven saying, Behold, the tabernacle of God is with men, and he will dwell with them, and they shall be his people, and God himself shall be with them, and be their God. 4. And God shall wipe away all tears from their eyes; and there shall be no more death, neither sorrow, nor crying, neither shall there be any more pain: for the former things are passed away.

If this prophecy comes true, we will have created a new culture that serves man, rather than man serving the beasts, but according to the prophets this "new thing" will require a sanctuary that will have big beautiful walls with gates. The adversaries will always be outside the gate, trying to get in to destroy the new culture of freedom, and to reimpose Statism.

Revelation 21:10 And he carried me away in the spirit to a great and high mountain, and shewed me that great city, the holy Jerusalem, descending out of heaven from God, 11. Having the glory of God: and her light was like unto a stone more precious, even like a jasper stone, clear as crystal; 12. And had a wall great and high, and had twelve gates, and at the gates twelve angels, and names written thereon, which are the names of the twelve tribes of the children of Israel: 13. On the east three gates; on the north three gates; on the south three gates; and on the west three gates. 14. And the wall of the city had twelve foundations, and in them the names of the twelve apostles of the Lamb.

The announcement that the writings of the twelve apostles are the foundations for the "wall great and high", built to preserve the new "Foundation of Peace", is another revelation. That the foundation comes from ordinary people like the apostles is a relief to us who recognize our own imperfections and see our own constant learning process from sinning. It would be hard to describe a more imperfect group of people than the apostles, as we

361

have seen in their tribulations. They did, however, give it their best for the most part to spread the message through their testimonies, and through their dedication to the cause deliver the foundation of a wall that would protect a whole new society against the cycles of Statism. Of course, their success is contingent on proving we are as capable of receiving the message as they were and are willing to create a culture that would allow us success in building our own Eden.

No Temples Allowed!

The message of the apostles are again reminiscent of an equally imperfect group of people that created a "new thing" in the Republic of the United States. Although it has become popular to do so, it seems kind of silly to criticize either group when their ideas were literally based on their own imperfections, with the express purpose of improving themselves as well as society in general. That is the power of recognizing our own sins and learning from them, rather than judging and condemning ourselves and others as in the Old Testament. Not surprisingly, considering the nature of the Yahwists that wrote these stories, there will be no Statist temples allowed within the walls.

> **Revelation 21:22 And I saw no temple therein: for the Lord God Almighty and the Lamb are the temple of it.**

However, for this "new thing" to survive, they emphasize this new culture will require a "wall great and high" and not all should be allowed to enter. It should also come as no surprise that Israel recognized the need for a wall to protect their own culture and nation from worshippers of the beast.

> **Revelation: 21:27 And there shall in no wise enter into it any thing that defileth, neither whatsoever worketh abomination, or maketh a lie: but they which are written in the Lamb's book of life.**

You will notice they do not ask for perfect people, which is lucky for most us, but only that those entering do not defile the city with cultural abominations. They must have respect for the current inhabitants, and of course be willing to assimilate. If these rules are followed, and provided no temples are allowed, then finally We The People will become the Powers That Be and we can finally eat of the "tree of life" without fear of again being expelled by the God of Statism. The author becomes our guide in the new culture behind the walls.

> **Revelation 22:1 And he shewed me a pure river of water of life, clear as crystal, proceeding out of the throne of God and of the Lamb. 2. In the midst of the**

street of it, and on either side of the river, was there the tree of life, which bare twelve manner of fruits, and yielded her fruit every month: and the leaves of the tree were for the healing of the nations. 3. And there shall be no more curse: but the throne of God and of the Lamb shall be in it; and his servants shall serve him: 4. And they shall see his face; and his name shall be in their foreheads.

It will finally be acceptable to approach the "tree of life" as you walk the streets. Again, if you want to see the face of God, simply hold your own culture up to the mirror and he will be facing back at you. If you are a Statist, then the God of Statism will be in the reflection. If you believe in freedom, then the god of We The People is the face you will see. Luckily for most of us, the greatest thing about culture is it can be changed at any time, and if found acceptable, you will then be allowed through the gate into the "Foundation of Peace". You are not stuck in the culture you have now. There will be many who will not accept the message, and who do not want to change. It is unrealistic to expect that all will be accepted behind the walls. It will be a live and let live society, but a wall will provide a protective barrier against the destroyers of culture.

Revelation 22:11 He that is unjust, let him be unjust still: and he which is filthy, let him be filthy still: and he that is righteous, let him be righteous still: and he that is holy, let him be holy still. 12. And, behold, I come quickly; and my reward is with me, to give every man according as his work shall be. 13. I am Alpha and Omega, the beginning and the end, the first and last. 14. Blessed are they that do his commandments, that they may have right to the tree of life, and may enter in through the gates into the city. 15. For without are dogs, and sorcerers, and whoremongers, and murderers, and idolaters, and whosoever loveth and maketh a lie.

Those who love lies, such as Statists who worship false idols or the beasts will not be allowed. It is not the intention to prevent entry, but those who enter must be carefully vetted. This is for protection from the God of Statism, who always insists punishment is for the good of the people, which is still a common theme within politics and religion today. It is for their own good that taxes must be raised. It is for their own good that the State is enlarged to offer "better service". It is for their own good that the money supply is controlled, manipulated, and redistributed to increase dependency and then used to purchase loyalty while claiming "compassion". It is for their own good that victim groups are created, and then catered to for the State to act as their savior in return for even more political loyalty. It is for their own good that more laws are added to more laws for the "protection" of the people as did Moses. Only those who recognize these lies, and see the truth, will be allowed into the new paradise.

Revelation 22:17 And the Spirit and the bride say, Come. And let him that heareth say, Come. And let him that is athirst come. And whosoever will, let him take the water of life freely.

Unlike the God of Statism with his taxes and tithes, there will be no charge.

Conclusion

There is great poetic irony in that because of those who recorded their history of resistance in a book called the bible, the nation of their descendants called Israel exists. The reason this is ironic is because the bible was at least partially the source of inspiration for some other rebels who also rejected the "Powers That Be" and chose the God of the People over the "exalted" God of Statism. Because of that inspiration they created a new nation based on a political system based on a republic, which is now the United States. The United States would then become instrumental in the revival of the nation of Israel, where many of the descendants of those who wrote the bible now live. Those two countries now share a great bond based on the same resistance to The God of Statism. Unfortunately, the temptations of the God of Statism are still strong, and both countries continue to be under siege.

So now we see the message of the stories in the bible that show what prevents us from reaching our full potential and achieving Eden. Where does this dragon and the beasts that serve it come from, who are now referred to as Statism? It is a perfectly natural phenomenon that is derived from the entrepreneurial nature of man. Being entrepreneurial is the act of doing those things which are most likely to improve one's odds of survival and is instinctive. Except maybe for those who are suicidal, we all have an entrepreneurial instinct that drives us to do those things most likely to result in survival and prosperity and is expressed in a desire for security. Since the introduction of money into society, this natural instinct most often takes the form of what we now call capitalism. There are three forms of capitalism and they are listed here with the characteristics most common to each.

Free Market Capitalism

This is where you will find those who feel security comes in the form of creativity, self-expression, self-determination, and a sense of community. Their security is felt through mutually beneficial interaction and cooperation with other people who have the same values and interests, and with those who have a need for the products and services they offer. This is where you will find those most active in local community and cultural affairs. This sector makes up the foundation and strength of any free society and if allowed to function freely, results in a prosperous nation for the people. Eighty percent of employment in the U.S. occurs within Free Market Capitalism {[65]}. Determining their needs and serving the people is a source of pride for most free market capitalists.

Although necessarily important, money often does not achieve the highest level of significance. This is the riskiest form of capitalism. Nine out of ten free market capitalists fail because money is not the biggest motivator compared to a desire to express one's skills, to create, and to interact with others. Because of this, financial success is often neglected to their detriment. To make matters worse, they are also susceptible to the many vagaries unique to free market capitalism. Some of these are supply and demand, market fluctuations, credit availability, and overhead. The biggest obstacle, however, is they often fall prey to the social engineers of Statism. Collectively, this makes participants in this sector at high risk of failure but are also the most adaptable and responsive to the people. Despite the hazards, free market capitalism is self-correcting and social interaction is free flowing. These qualities make free market capitalism a source of prosperity for the most people and is where most of us spend our lives.

Crony Capitalism

---

[65] https://en.wikipedia.org/wiki/Free_market

This form of capitalism is much safer and more secure than Free Market Capitalism. This is where you will find mostly large corporations such as those involved with as military weaponry and equipment but includes businesses such as banks. They may also do business with private individuals, but their security depends on government collusion, which often means they will go to extraordinary lengths to obtain contracts and favoritism from the State.

Their lobbying efforts often lead to crony capitalism, which has become a slur as they use money and other favors to influence high level officials willing to become sympathetic to their interests in return for payoffs such as campaign donations. The highest achievement today for crony capitalists is to become "too big to fail", which means they are now considered part of the State and are protected from failure with tax money from the people. The expenditures of most governments are so huge that those successful in this type of capitalism can become very wealthy and secure. Their interests require favoring the State over the population in general and so there is much less social interaction and little sense of community. Their skills and creativity are expended to benefit themselves and the State rather than the people.

Statist Capitalism

Noah's Ark and the Ark of the Covenant are the same Ark. Both represent the elitist collectivism of statist capitalism and the death and destruction they bring to the general public because of their covenant with the State. This is where the God of Statism lives and is the most extreme form of capitalism. It also provides the highest level of security for the participants and is largely self-perpetuating until it reaches the end of another cycle of failure. Here you will find publicans, welfare recipients, organizations and institutions that rely on socialism such as labor unions, organized victim groups, special interest groups, etc. Unlike free market capitalists, less than one in one hundred fail to find security, which is a dramatic reversal of free market capitalism. The temptation to seek security, rather than community, is God's evil tempting spirit.

Financial security is the dominant motivator. Unfortunately, there is little cultural and no economic contribution to society. There is a separation from community interaction, the need to respond to supply and demand, or the need to produce goods and services desirable to others. Rather than producing, Statism capitalism depends on coercing the remaining portion of the population to sacrifice a portion of their productivity to support the God of Statism through sacrifice. This is usually in the form of taxes or dues, which are always mandatory.

You will never find a Statist organization where the costs are voluntary as with Free Markets. Having the power to mandate a paycheck by law, and which today includes a lifetime pension upon retirement at the expense of the economic producers, results in a very secure form of capitalism. Unfortunately, rather than being self-correcting, Statist capitalism is instead self-perpetuating. This type of capitalism becomes more centralized and more powerful over time. This eventually results in a collapse of the system when it can no longer be supported or tolerated by the citizens, which is why the benefits are temporary as demonstrated by Jonah. This results in eventual social chaos following predictable cycles of failure, and results in the repetition of 6-6-6 rather than Eden, which is seven.

Virtually guaranteed wealth, even in the short term of a few generations or less, is a huge temptation and leads to the inevitable growth of Statism at the expense of long-term cultural success. It is also why the God of Statism is so dangerous to most of the population and is such a risk to We The People. Just as in crony capitalism, self-determination and creativity is sacrificed in exchange for security. Statism requires the exploitation and manipulation of culture, which results in a cruel and vengeful god.

However, the understanding that Statist capitalism is a response to an instinct to survive and thrive is what prevents the writers of the bible from condemning those who live and work in a Statist environment. As mentioned before, Jesus was often

369

criticized for a willingness to interact with publicans (government employees) and harlots, publicans and tax collectors, and publicans and sinners. As Jesus pointed out to his gang, it was those groups to whom he needed to be teaching. He wasn't there to preach to the choir. He recognized that publicans are simply victims of the dragon and his beasts, and of their own capitalistic instincts, which are a natural response in seeking security and survival. Through understanding and encouragement, a former publican and tax collector called Paul became an ally to the message and ended up writing about half of the New Testament. We should never underestimate the power of a free and adaptable culture that can evolve and take us closer to Eden if allowed the freedom to do so, as it did for Paul.

The Jewish contention that Jesus is not the Messiah is true in many ways. Of course, he himself said that salvation will not come from any figure that you can point out as a single person, so they are already correct in that sense. However, the Jewish ancestors that wrote the books of the bible are the creators of Jesus, so they must have strongly believed in his message. In their wisdom, the point the authors made repeatedly is the Messiah will arrive when an adequate number within the tribes *become* Jesus the radical. In other words, when they are willing to anoint themselves as their own king.

I believe if it were simply up to Israel or the Jewish people, the messiah would have arrived long before now. As we recall, it must have been a very bitter pill for John when he *"took the little book out of the angel's hand and ate it up; and it was in my mouth very sweet as honey: and as soon as I had eaten it, my belly was bitter. 11. And he said unto me, Thou must prophesy again before many peoples, and nations, and tongues, and kings."* Before the writers of the bible can achieve full success, they must wait for a portion of all the tribes to receive the message. That is going to require a lot of teaching and a lot of work. Unfortunately, many of the republics created because of the "open book" are now regressing back into Statism, so the cycle may end up starting all over again for many nations. Once again, we may fail to reach the Sabbath because of

370

those whose temporary interests are best served by taking us backwards.

However, we are always given another chance at resurrection. There is no "End of Times" in Revelation. The only thing "ending" if we achieve Eden will be Statism, and then only within the walls that contain no temples. Outside the walls, all will remain the same.

The bible begins by having We The People being excommunicated from a state of paradise created by the God of Statism. As they show, We The People were removed because of a search for an understanding of the difference between "good and evil" and to eat of the "tree of life", which was a threat to God. The creation of this god is our "Original Sin". It ends with a manual showing us how to regain a cultural paradise, and that we should begin by taking a stand and building a big beautiful wall against Statism. No temples, religious or political, will be allowed within these walls because as it says, We The People are the temple. To protect this cultural paradise, careful vetting will be required at the gates, "For without are dogs, and whoremongers, and murderers, and idolaters, and whosoever loveth and maketh a lie". Statism is evil because it requires that the State be more powerful than the People. To maintain power, the State must pull on the reins of Free Market Capitalism through oppression of all kinds, including economic oppression. This is why we have "depressions", "recessions" and radical fluctuations of money and credit availability which affect markets and destroy the livelihoods of millions of people. These are quickly dismissed as "business cycles" which is a lie. They are State cycles. They are cycles to prevent this from happening:

Genesis 11:6 And the Lord said, Behold, the people is one, and they have all one language; and this they begin to do: and now nothing will be restrained from them, which they have imagined to do.

Short of beating us over the head with more parables, I don't know how the writers could have made the message of the bible clearer. Do we want to succumb to temporary benefits for the chosen, and be forever stuck in the 6-6-6 of repeating cycles of failed political systems, or do we want to finally reach the seventh day of the Sabbath, where there is peace and rest for all? Do we want to continue to be "restrained" as the sacrificial Lamb, or will we take a stand within the wall and reverse all the executive orders of the God of Statism as Jesus did? The writers concluded long ago that the only solution is to build a culture free of Statism and refuse to build the temples where those live that manipulate us. Regaining paradise is up to We The People and requires nothing more than a virtuous culture that rejects the temptations offered by the evil spirit of The God of Statism. Waiting to be saved by gods or kings who promise to lead us to the "promised land" is simply shirking our responsibility because as the bible says, "ye are gods".

www.ingramcontent.com/pod-product-compliance
Lightning Source LLC
Chambersburg PA
CBHW030002290326
41934CB00005B/195